Ineffective Habits of Financial Advisors (and the Disciplines to Break Them)

A FRAMEWORK FOR AVOIDING THE MISTAKES EVERYONE ELSE MAKES

Steve Moore

with Gary Brooks, CFP®

WILEY

John Wiley & Sons, Inc.

Published by John Wiley & Sons, Inc., Hoboken, New Jersey.
Published simultaneously in Canada.

For general information on our other products and services or for technical support, please contact our Customer Care Department within the United States at (800) 762-2974, outside the United States at (317) 572-3993 or fax (317) 572-4002.

Wiley also publishes its books in a variety of electronic formats. Some content that appears in print may not be available in electronic books. For more information about Wiley products, visit our web site at www.wiley.com.

Library of Congress Cataloging-in-Publication Data:

Moore, Steve, 1947–
  Ineffective Habits of Financial Advisors (and the Disciplines to Break Them) /
Steve Moore, Gary Brooks.
      p. cm.
  Includes bibliographical references and index.
  ISBN 978-0-470-91032-0 (hardback)
  1. Investments.   2. Business consultants.   I. Brooks, Gary, 1971–   II. Title.
III. Title: Ineffective habits of financial advisors (and the disciplines to
  break them).
  HG4515.M66 2010
  332.6–dc22
                                                            2010027089

Printed in the United States of America

10   9   8   7   6   5   4

*This book is dedicated
to the most important person in my life,
Carol,
my wife of 45 years, writing partner, and spell checker.*

Contents

Foreword

You are going to love this book. If you are reading this book, chances are that it is because you want to improve your performance as a financial advisor. *Better still* if that desire is coupled with dissatisfaction with the status quo. And *even better still* if you both recognize the rewards for doing so, and believe those rewards are worth the effort. When that combination is present, transformation is possible. Transformation in your practice, the success and satisfaction of both you and your clients, and positive impact on your practice and your community—all of that can come out of the lessons from this book. There has never been a better time to be an advisor—or a better time to build a great advisory practice. Trust is in precious short supply. If you are just beginning in that profession, this book will help you become a good advisor. If you are a good advisor already, it can help you become a great advisor—really.

Whether your desire to improve is motivated by wanting more revenue and profit from your practice, or wanting to enhance the quality and balance of your work and private lives, or driven by a wish to create excellence inside your firm is irrelevant. All of those are solid reasons. But that list leaves out the most powerful reason of all: to adopt habits that foster excellence in your every client interaction. That is what will build lasting trust with your clients, and ultimately telegraph outward to attract an increasingly affluent and loyal client community. And those are just the positive aspects.

The lessons of this book will also help you avert negative experiences common to advisors that often lead to broken client relationships or damaged trust—the consequences of which are bad for the client and bad for the advisor. Often those damaged relationships lead clients to costly and ill-timed bailing out of the market, a type of investment behavior that more than anything else threatens to deprive them of their future financial security. So reading this book will allow you to do well by doing good at the same time. Good deal!

It is a distinct honor to introduce this book. Steve Moore and I have worked together for over a decade, and I have seen firsthand the transformations in advisors that his coaching brings about. I have benefited from his coaching myself, and I can say with certainty that it works—if you apply yourself to it. This is not just what I think—Steve and I have dozens of clients in common. Of course there are many consultants in the financial advice industry. Some are highly skilled; a few of them are admired, sought after to be quoted in the industry press. But I am aware of none that is equally *beloved* by his clients. This is because Steve's rare combination of business insight and coaching skill helps people not only come to a recognition of what they need to do to improve their business performance—that's good—but bring that together with a recognition of why and how to change their behavior. That is *great*. He helps his clients learn how to win, then to become winners—consistently.

There is a way to read this book. Bring the edginess of your dissatisfaction and an awareness of what you want to be different, coupled with the suppleness of an open mind, what they call the "willing suspension of doubt." Before diving into this book, I strongly encourage you to think about your current practices: Which ones are you proud of that lead to great interactions? Which do you wish that you could change—ones that tend to lead to haphazard or problematic client encounters? If you see that there is sometimes an uncomfortable gap between how you aspire to have clients regard you and how they actually do, here's an opportunity to close the gap.

How can I be so sure? Because I have seen it happen, time and time again. You do not have to be a prodigy to recognize the insights. You do not need to be a paragon of self-discipline to follow the regimen. You do not need magical technology skills to install the processes. Like me, you can be just a regular person. My interactions with the author over more than 10 years taught me two lasting lessons. I earnestly hope you benefit from them as much as I have. The first is the immense value—I would even use the word *power*—that arises from understanding how to convert your dissatisfactions into deliberate behavior that creates advantages for you. Second, I firmly believe that you will discover, as I did, that whatever it is that you think is holding you back from excellence as an investment advisor—gloomy economic climate, dipping markets, punitive regulators, narrow-minded bosses, skeptical or mistrusting clients, complex technological changes, whatever that list includes—it is not true. *It is a falsehood.* What holds you back is yourself. Excellence is there for you, within reach. So reach out and grab it.

Read on . . .

Timothy Noonan
London
April 30, 2010

Introduction: Setting the Stage

On the morning I wrote this, I started with my daily routine. I soaked in the hot tub for 10 minutes, showered, shaved, put on my deodorant, and then got dressed. Including my belt, wallet, iPhone, ChapStick, and pen there are 12 items I deal with. Next, I cooked my oatmeal and added blueberries, walnuts, a scoop of protein powder, and half a cup of yogurt. I gulped my vitamins and a slew of other pills—I love getting older. Finally, I brushed my teeth before heading into my home office to write this section. I booted up my computer, went to Google, and reviewed permutations so that I could give you the number 479,001,600. That is the number of different ways I could have gotten dressed that morning. With the 12 items there are nearly half a billion different combinations. So what do I do? I make the routine a habit.

In this case the habit allowed me to go through my morning routine subconsciously, freeing my mind to think about an interesting approach to explaining the important role habits play in our lives. There are countless habits that we have developed that allow us to perform routines effortlessly. But not all habitual behavior is good. You may have developed a bad habit, one that can have a negative impact on you or those around you.

Business practices are developed and then entrenched in the same way as other habits. You see, the mechanism doesn't stop just because you came to work. You execute a business task (even a complex one), repeat it, and the brain recognizes the pattern. You repeat it again and again and before long you have developed a business habit, one that can be performed unconsciously, allowing your conscious mind to think about other issues or tasks.

Habits wouldn't pose a problem if they were truly optimal and your business never changed. But that is not the case. They operate even if they are suboptimal; or worse, irrelevant; or worse still, damaging to the business. I have found that advisors are prevented from implementing more effective business practices by seven ineffective business habits.

This book was written for experienced financial advisors who want more than the status quo, are open to a new approach, and have a strong belief in their ability to execute.

Over the past 15 years, I have worked with more than 750 financial advisors in High Speed Strategic Planning, a year-long consulting/coaching program. The strategies and disciplines delivered in this program generate impressive business results. A start-up in Seattle went from zero assets under management to over $1 billion in five years. Two advisors, one in San Francisco and one in Milwaukee, went from having over 1,300 clients to fewer than 100 and tripled their revenue. A Vancouver, B.C., team transformed its business in just two years, consistently ranking first or second in PriceMetrix's Business Excellence award. A Chicago team went from managing $17 million to over $170 million in seven years. A well-established registered investment advisor in Long Beach, California, grew from $240 million in assets under management to over $1.4 billion in 10 years.

How did these advisors achieve these results? The simple answer is they implemented more effective strategies than other advisors. But how?

First, they weren't satisfied with the way things were—they wanted more! These advisors wanted more financial security for their families, more work-life balance, more of a sense of doing worthwhile work, more pride in what they were building, and more opportunity for growth for themselves and their teams. You may have seen the classic video clip from *Network* (1976), where newsman Howard Beale rants, "I'm as mad as hell, and I'm not going to take this anymore!" Though this may be a bit overstated, it does convey that people don't change until they are truly dissatisfied with the way things are.

Ralph Waldo Emerson wrote: "There are always two parties—the party of the past and the party of the future, the establishment and the movement." These breakout advisors were fed up with the way it was. They wanted more!

Second, they were willing to consider and then embrace different strategies. In *Competing for the Future*, Gary Hamel and C. K. Prahalad write: "What prevents companies from creating the future is an installed base of thinking—the unquestioned conventions, the my-opic view of opportunities and threats, and the unchallenged prece-dents that comprise the existing managerial frame." Though break-out advisors had success in the past, they were willing to challenge existing practices and consider new and different strategies. After an-alyzing this new approach for acquiring and servicing clients, these advisors developed a strong belief that this new approach would lead them to their desired business success.

Third, they had a strong belief that they could implement this new approach. The importance of this belief cannot be overstated. However hard they imagined it would be, it was harder. However long they thought it would take, it took longer. Worse still, the short-term results they were hoping for just weren't there. But because they believed that they would ultimately be successful and the reward would be worth the effort, they persisted. And because they persisted, the long-term results exceeded what they imagined. Once again, these advisors proved that the number one ingredient in any success is persistence.

This book will provide you with business practices and strategies to bring *more* into reality. You need to bring your dissatisfaction with the status quo, a willingness to consider new ways of doing business, and belief in your ability to execute.

This information is a new perspective on your profession, and here is why.

My wife, Carol, and I were married and had our son when we were in high school—I wasn't quite as rigorous of a planner then as I am now. We were two teenagers on our own, trying to make a life and raise a family. I think it was the extraordinary circumstances of how we started out that made family so very important to us.

With the help of an athletic scholarship, I worked my way through college and then coached football at high schools, colleges, and in the National Football League. When our kids began leaving home to begin their adult lives, I had been in the NFL for 11 years. At that time, I was the offensive coordinator for the Seattle Seahawks.

There is a lot of job security in the NFL—just not with a particular team. Coaching staffs keep getting recycled. At the end of the 1988 season, it was clear that the new Seahawks owner was going to bring in his own people. Because we had just won the division championship, he couldn't do it immediately, but his intentions were clear. Carol and I didn't want to move to Chicago, Kansas City, Tampa, or another

NFL city and have our kids and grandkids still in Seattle, so I set out to begin my consulting career.

It was a painful process and I felt like a fish out of water. I had been going to work in T-shirts and sweatpants for 20 years and I only owned one tie. I had been near the top of my coaching profession, and now it felt like I was performing at the Pop Warner level in the Seattle business community.

In the business world, I knew absolutely nothing. The business language sounded foreign to me. I remember attending a presentation on the global economy. After the talk, the presenter and I were chatting and I asked him, "What would you tell the left tackle and left guard on 29 M if they caught a Buc-I-Change stunt?" He said, "Steve, I don't know what you just said." I replied, "For the last hour and a half I haven't understood anything you said, either." It was the absolute truth, and what a wake-up call.

As a young coach I was a tireless student of the game. When I went to conferences, I sat in the front row taking copious notes. I was an avid reader. While coaching at the college level, our family vacations consisted of attending NFL preseason camps, developing relationships, and studying with the likes of Bill Walsh, Dick Vermeil, Tom Landry, John Ralston, and Chuck Knox.

I decided to study business management the same way I had football theory. I studied Edwards Deming's total quality management, Peter Drucker's worker productivity principles, Gary Hamel's strategic frameworks, Jack Welch's applied management practices, Jim Collins's insights on enduring great companies, Peter Senge's systems thinking, Jeffrey Pfeffer and Robert Sutton's evidence-based management, and many other great business thinkers.

I went back to school and earned my master's degree in education and studied optimal performance psychology from great researchers like Al Bandura, Gary Latham, and Marty Seligman. As I continued to study, it dawned on me that what I had been doing for all of those years—preparing a team to play the Raiders one week and the Broncos or Bears the next—was excellent planning and management. It was just a different language.

So I developed a proprietary business planning process that integrated the best research-based practices with the need for speed and execution that I had learned over my 20 years of coaching football. I had excellent opportunities to engage leadership teams at Microsoft, M&M Mars, NASA Suppliers, Defense Logistics, and Toyota. These consulting relationships provided the feedback necessary for the initial development of my High Speed Strategic Planning program for financial advisors.

In leading this program, I have had a tremendous opportunity to gain insight into issues faced by advisors from every segment of the profession—registered investment advisors (RIAs), brokers, insurance-based advisors, solo practices, ensemble teams, and so forth. I've continuously analyzed the challenges they face and field-tested solutions with them.

This diverse background, in combination with my viewpoint from outside the industry, allows me to work with advisors, unencumbered by emotion or preconceived thinking. An ineffective business habit that an advisor may have difficulty seeing can appear as an elephant in the room to me. While status-quo thinking may prevent an advisor from appreciating a new business discipline, the advantages can be glaringly obvious to me. It is my intent to present this information in such a way that you will benefit from what I have learned over the past 15 years of helping advisors build more profitable businesses.

Business Disciplines

The promise of getting more is realized only through rigorous execution of the disciplines designed to break these ineffective habits. I refer to these proven best practices and field-tested strategies as *disciplines* because they require rigorous implementation.

Though the disciplines are prescriptive, there is ample room for you to apply your creativity. In fact, I strongly encourage you to improve upon these disciplines. As Charles Darwin wrote, "Multiply, vary, let the strongest live, and the weakest die." Use your own creativity to enhance these disciplines as you make them your own. Every one of the disciplines has been enhanced by those who have come before you.

Over the past 15 years I have provided a well-marked path for advisors to take. Because advisors are creative and quite independent, their execution varies. As I continue to enhance my consulting/coaching program, I observe variants in the marketplace, embrace those that enhance the discipline, and let the others die. This book highlights the survivors, the core elements of an efficiently run, profitable advisory business.

Ineffective Habits of Financial Advisors and the Disciplines to Break Them

1. Stop living their dream and start living your dream.

    As advisors begin careers, they tend to view themselves as a financial representative working for a platform, broker-dealer, bank, insurance company, or firm. It doesn't take long for them to develop the ineffective habit of living someone else's dream and playing the role envisioned for them. At a certain point, many feel trapped by the status quo and want more. They want more financial security for their families. They want more work-life balance. They want to feel more like they are doing worthwhile work. They want to have more pride in the businesses they are building. They want more, but they have been living someone else's dream for so long that it is difficult to imagine doing anything other than the status quo. The discipline of creating your dream is a process of envisioning the advisory business you truly desire.

    Creating a compelling vision provides you with the opportunity to design your future. By thinking deeply about what you want, you can determine the worthwhile work you do, the business model that supports your ambitions, the quality of clients you work with, the type of team you build, and the business results you drive. Creating your dream starts by deciding what you truly desire rather than accepting someone else's dream. You determine your future by the vision you create, the decisions you make, and the actions you take.

2. Stop focusing on quantity of clients and start focusing on quality of clients.

    To survive, nearly every financial advisor starts their career focused on the quantity of clients they can acquire. They begin selling to family and friends and then branch out and sell to anyone who can fog a mirror. The low percentage of high-net-worth clients they do acquire is the result of the law of large numbers. Their focus on quantity creates a client base of many unprofitable or marginally profitable clients. Using this ineffective habit will only bring them one to three high-net-worth clients per year. Over time the large number of small clients becomes all-consuming and prevents them from creating a service model that would be attractive to high-net-worth clients.

The discipline of focusing on quality clients allows you to acquire 6 to 12 per year. Quality clients are those who have complex financial needs and an asset base to generate superior revenue results. By building a high-quality client base you will experience the financial and intrinsic rewards as your clients refer their friends and colleagues to you. The first step is to create a strategic focus targeting quality clients.

3. Stop hoarding unprofitable clients and start disengaging unprofitable clients.

The win-lose environment that characterizes this industry promotes scarcity thinking. Hoarding unprofitable clients is a symptom of this thinking. As a result, the bottom 50 percent of an advisor's client base often represents less than 5 percent of the firm's revenue. The bottom 20 percent of the business's client base often generates less than 1 percent of the revenue. The scarcest resource advisors have is their time. Once it is spent it can never be gotten back. The ineffective habit of hoarding unprofitable clients causes advisors to develop a client base that demands too much time and energy while providing little in return. By bending to the discipline of disengaging unprofitable clients, advisors can begin to spend their time where the payback is best—the top 20 percent of their client base.

4. Stop providing only investment advice and start providing wealth management advice.

The commoditization of investment products, the changing needs of baby boomers as they near retirement, the uncertainty in the capital markets, and other industry trends are screaming for advisors to provide more than just investment advice. Today, high-net-worth clients want more from their advisors. They want an advisor who will help them achieve their financial goals—those that require planning, money, time, and the ongoing coordination of their financial ecosystem. They want their advisor to provide wealth management advice.

5. Stop delivering investment reviews and start delivering WOW Wealth Management Reviews.

Many advisors believe their primary value-add is their investment knowledge. To their clients, reviews feel like they are taking a statistics course in a foreign language. Even though the advisor may be aware that clients leave a review confused and embarrassed by their lack of investment acumen, the advisor cannot break the habit of delivering investment reviews. The discipline of delivering WOW Wealth Management Reviews breaks this ineffective habit, allowing the advisor to deliver information within the context of the client's goals and financial ecosystem. The WOW Wealth Management Review also turns the intangible advisory business into a tangible business worthy of referrals.

6. Stop the rainmaker approach and start the team approach.

A high percentage of investment advisory firms are made up of groups organized to maximize a rainmaker's production. By being so dependent on one individual, the business cannot scale and it stops growing when the rainmaker's financial appetite is satisfied or the service capacity is exhausted. The focus on individual rather than team production and the disproportionate amount of the rewards that go to the rainmaker limits the overall quality of the group. The disparity between how the rainmaker is rewarded compared with others in the group can create resentment and passive-aggressive behavior.

This ineffective habit is changed by bending to the discipline of building a wealth management advisory team that scales the organization's service capacity. In *The Wisdom of Teams*, J. R. Katzenbach and Douglas Smith write: "Teams outperform individuals acting alone or in larger organizational groupings, especially when performance requires multiple skills, judgments, and experiences." The team approach is the discipline of organizing to deliver wealth management services as a team and working collaboratively to achieve greater levels of client satisfaction, team rewards, and business success. By developing service teams you can position resources to deliver outstanding, scalable service that will create competitive differentiation. Wealth management requires such a team approach.

7. Stop selling to prospects and start selling through clients.

For the typical advisor, traditional marketing methods acquire one to three affluent clients per year. Though direct marketing initiatives produce little more than chump change, advisors continue the ineffective habit of selling to prospects via seminars, advertising, or cold calls. The discipline of selling through existing clients breaks this habit and allows them to acquire 6 to 12 high-net-worth clients per year.

Engaging clients and arming them with concise, compelling language empowers them to execute an incredibly valuable word-of-mouth viral marketing campaign.

The Framework of the Book

Each chapter is devoted to an ineffective habit and the discipline to break it. The first section of each chapter describes the ineffective habit by telling Jack's story. In Jack you will recognize his ineffective habits and the negative impact they have on his business. The scenarios found in Jack's story are examples derived from advisors I've coached over the years. They are real. These habits show up repeatedly. You will identify with them at some level. My intent is to make you dissatisfied enough to take action and break the habit by implementing the appropriate discipline.

The framework I use to explain the disciplines is called IDA, which is an acronym for insights, decisions, and actions. With better insight you make better strategic decisions, but unless you take action you won't experience the benefits.

Insights

You need to perform fact-based analysis to gain insight into your business. In *The Adventures of Sherlock Homes*, Sir Arthur Conan Doyle writes: "It is a capital mistake to theorize before one has data." To this end, I discuss relevant data and prescribe an analysis that you can perform to gather the facts.

There are two things to keep in mind while gaining insight. The first is that you shouldn't beat yourself up. I work with advisors all the time and know how stupid you can feel when you expose ineffective habits and allow them to continue. Consider yourself normal. Ninety percent of advisors have the same problems. The second important thing is to cut to the core of the issue. Solutions that only address symptoms have little long-term impact. Albert Einstein said, "The significant problems we face cannot be solved at the same level of thinking we were at when we created them." There is an interesting story that supports this principle.

The Jefferson Memorial Parable   The Jefferson Memorial was crumbling. At first, the problem was believed to be acid rain. Further investigation revealed that the combination of detergent and water used for the daily washing was mixing with the cement and creating an acid that was eroding the Memorial. This raised the question, why was it being washed daily? It turned out there was an inordinate number of bird droppings on the Memorial and to keep it presentable it needed daily washings. But why so many bird droppings?

The decision was made to study the problem. After staggering costs and time it was discovered that sparrows found an easy food source and were coming to the Memorial to feast on a plentiful supply of spiders that had taken up residence there. But why were there so many spiders?

It turned out the spiders were eating small insects called midges. The midges were a plentiful and easy food source for the spiders because they were splattering themselves on the Memorial. But why would they splatter themselves on the Memorial?

It was finally discovered that dusk was mating time for midges and they were in an elevated state. This, in combination with the lights that turned on at dusk, put them in a super elevated state, causing them to fly out of control and splatter themselves on the Jefferson Memorial. They provided an easily accessible banquet for the spiders. So the midges provided a food source for the spiders, the spiders for the birds; thus the bird droppings and the washing and eroding of the Memorial.

How did they fix the problem? They left the lights off until one hour after sunset and the problem went away. By asking "why" over and over again, effective advisors are able to understand their competitive world more completely. Rather than treat symptoms, they go to work on curing core problems. You can do the same by shining a light on your habits and understanding your business at a deeper level.

Aristotle lived from 384 to 322 B.C. During this time, he determined that the world is round. That paradigm was not embraced until 1522 A.D. when the Portuguese sailor Juan Sebastián Elcano completed the round-the-world voyage started by Magellan. By understanding that the world was round, people were able to make better navigational choices. Likewise, by gaining insight into specific areas of your business, you will be able to make better decisions. One difference: You can't take hundreds of years to understand the shape of your competitive world.

There will not be complete facts to support every decision you make. Jack Welch provides guidance in his book *Winning* when he writes, "Effective people know when to stop assessing and make a tough call even without total information."

Decisions

Jeff Bezos from Amazon.com states, "Ideas are important but they are relatively easy. What is hard is taking that list of hundreds of ideas, ranking them, and picking the three that you are actually going to do. That's intellectually one of the most challenging things that happens every day in a business that is growing this fast." When you gain insight into your business, you will be better prepared to make well-informed decisions—cornerstone decisions as to how to grow your business.

Each advisor has a unique set of circumstances. They work in different markets, operate on different platforms, have different business models, and serve different clients with varying levels of support from team members. Because of the differences, a specific implementation of a discipline that works for one might damage another. When you begin to evaluate each discipline you should ask yourself:

- Does this discipline address one of my ineffective business habits?
- Can my team execute the discipline?
- What is the downside to implementing the discipline?

It is important to think deeply about any decisions you make regarding the disciplines recommended in this book. They may not fit your practice perfectly. If they don't, they should at least inspire the kind of thinking that will lead to decisions that can transform your business.

> Senior leaders who push for fewer changes and push for them harder are more likely to have success than leaders who introduce so many changes that people become confused about which matters most and least to the company and how to spread their time and money among the initiatives.
> —Jeffrey Pfeffer and Robert Sutton, *Hard Facts,*
> *Dangerous Half-Truths & Total Nonsense*

Actions

Emerson wrote, "Good thoughts are no better than good dreams unless they be executed." When I am working with groups I often pull a $20 bill out of my wallet and hold it up. I then ask the group who would like it. Usually the group looks around at one another and finally someone sheepishly comes up and takes the $20. I then ask the group what that person had to do in order to get the $20. We all agree it only required that they get up off their ass and make it happen.

If you make a decision but don't take action nothing will change. This book provides you guidelines to take action. Results come from decisions that are converted into specific actions. An example comes from a story told me by one of the pioneer rock climbers in the United States, Royal Robbins. He was the first person to climb Half Dome in Yosemite back when serious climbers wore white tennis shoes rather than the rock-climbing gear that is used today.

Royal was solo climbing once and got stuck—he couldn't go up and he couldn't go down. He was tired and his legs were shaking from fatigue. He had to work and work to convince himself that he could climb up just five more feet. Once he made the first five-foot climb, he had to work again to convince himself that he could climb five more feet. He continued this way until he climbed out of this death trap.

I believe this is a useful metaphor for people who are trying to implement the disciplines outlined in this book. If you look at the entire mountain (your business) it can be overwhelming. But if you can break your climb into five-foot increments that you believe you can accomplish, you will persist. The action portion of each chapter is designed to help you make these five-foot climbs.

The regulatory environment, competitive landscape, technological advances, and capital markets are changing faster than at any other time in history. If this rate of change is faster than your ability to embrace new disciplines and acquire new competencies, your business is at risk. Peter Senge captured this point in his book *The Fifth Discipline*, when he wrote, "The only sustainable competitive advantage is the ability to be able to learn faster than your competition."

So . . . let's get started.

Acknowledgments

To the 750-plus financial advisors who have participated in High Speed Strategic Planning: Your camaraderie and friendship are deeply appreciated. Without your willingness to apply the concepts, modify them, and provide feedback I would never have been able to develop the seven disciplines.

To my strategic thinking friends: The discussions, debates, and challenging of my assumptions has not only been enjoyable, it is profoundly important to this project and I thank you!

To the optimal performance and business strategy researchers who provided me with insight and knowledge: Once I became aware of your work, it was like being introduced to someone I knew I was connected to at the deepest level.

To the great football coaches in my life: High Speed Strategic Planning would not be what it is today if you were not willing to share your knowledge about world-class game planning and execution.

To the team at John Wiley & Sons: I appreciate your guidance and willingness to partner with me.

To my wife, Carol, whose patience amazes me: You cover my flat spots and know that this endeavor would not have happened without your help.

1

Stop Living Their Dream and Start Living Your Dream

The First Ineffective Habit: Living Their Dream

Jack was a nice-looking kid from a well-connected family in town. He was confident around money and had developed the ability to meet and greet. He would earn his finance degree from the University of Michigan in a year and was looking for a meaningful internship over the summer break. A family friend and mentor who worked for a respected investment firm spoke with his branch manager and Jack was brought on to learn the business. He worked hard, met his commitments, and was more self-directed than the interns who had come before him. When he headed back to Ann Arbor in the fall, he knew he would have a job waiting for him upon graduation.

There are some advantages for twenty-somethings not having a well-developed sense of future. It makes them fearless, bold, unrealistically optimistic, and their creativity knows no bounds. That combination can lead to breakthroughs in physics, music, athletics, and the creation of new business models like Facebook or Google. Sometimes though, it can lead to unfortunate consequences. You can see this with a young athlete or musician who pursues a professional career at the exclusion of everything else. It can take years to recover from landing on the wrong side of their high-risk, high-reward bet. Sometimes they are never able to recover.

Jack, like most twenty-somethings, ended up somewhere between rock star success and total failure. He had hoped that his academic performance, recommendations, and finance degree would put him on the fast track to investment banking, but reality hit him in the face when he could not get beyond phone interviews with any of the major Wall Street firms. He accepted the opportunity to become a financial rep where he had interned. He would continue to learn the business under the tutelage of his family friend and the branch manager. In the short term it would be okay. Perhaps with real world experience, he would get his big, Wall Street break.

In his new position, Jack spent the first three weeks studying to become a registered investment advisor representative. Though he was a good student, there was a lot to learn and the potential embarrassment of not passing the exam on his first attempt created both stress and focus. He studied in his cubical 10 hours a day, six days a week. It paid off, he easily passed the Financial Industry Regulatory Authority (FINRA) exams, and now he could get on with his orientation.

Having interned in the office less than a year prior allowed him to leapfrog some of the orientation steps, but he still had to sit through HR's "Creating a Friendly Workplace" seminar (a typical cover-your-legal-ass program).

He also had to learn the Kaizen Selling System. His manager explained that *kaizen* is the Japanese word for constant and never-ending improvement. It was presented as a consultative sales methodology, but in reality was a product sales process filled with red-letter language designed to explain the product, overcome objections, and "help" the client make a buying decision.

Goals, compensation, recognition, awards, management attention, best practice sharing, and performance reporting were all designed to help Jack continually improve his execution of the kaizen selling system. And Jack was improving. It looked as though he was going to develop into what they had dreamed for him.

The effort Jack applied to the kaizen selling system paid off. He was among the 15 to 20 percent who actually survived the first five years in this business. He continued to learn the tips and tricks of his trade—how to cross-sell, feed a lead, develop centers of influence, and nest with other young professionals needing insurance and beginning to invest. The more he applied the tried and tested ways of the Kaizen Selling System, the more it paid off. He was definitely living up to the firm's hopes and dreams.

Fast-forward a decade and Jack's exceptional execution of the Kaizen Selling System had brought him an overloaded roster of nondistinguished insurance and investment clients. It may have been the firm's dream but it was a nightmare for Jack.

We talk about a mid-life crisis as though people go through it just once. In reality, we go through the process about every seven years. It can be very healthy to reflect upon how we are spending our life's energy—to evaluate whether it is satisfying and aligned with our vision. But Jack didn't have a vision. For the past 15 years he had been living the firm's vision—their dream.

Jack was deep in thought in his corner office, blankly staring at his e-mail, when the branch manager stuck his head in and said, "Good morning, Jack. How goes the battle?" Jack replied, "Just living the dream." He had said this many times before, but this time it came out a bit cynical. What had once meant, "My life's dreams are coming true" had morphed into, "I'm just grinding away in my role to bring about their dream."

Living their dream wasn't good enough. Jack wanted more.

The First Discipline: Start Living Your Dream

To escape the grind and begin to live with passion, Jack and tens of thousands like him need to create their own dream by designing a compelling vision. Creating a compelling vision provides you with the opportunity to design your future. By thinking deeply about what you want, you can determine the worthwhile work you do, the business model that supports your ambitions, the quality of clients you work with, the type of team you build, and the business results you drive. Creating your dream starts by deciding what you truly desire rather than accepting someone else's dream. You determine your future by the vision you create, the decisions you make, and the actions you take.

Your vision has four component parts:

1. Purpose—the primary reason for the work you do.
2. Business goals—specific objectives that support your purpose.
3. Guiding principles—the fundamental standards that guide daily decisions.

4. Vivid description—a narrative of the business success you intend to create.

The first basic ingredient of leadership is a guiding vision. . . . Unless you know where you're going, and why, you cannot possibly get there.
                                                    —Warren Bennis, *On Becoming a Leader*

Insights

Insights into these four components (purpose, business goals, guiding principles, and vivid description) will better prepare you to develop and then embrace your vision. Each component has its own benefits, which are compounded when combined into a compelling vision.

Purpose: The Primary Reason for the Work You Do

Two insights about teams emerged early, consistently, and emphatically from our interviews. First, high performance teams have both a clear understanding of the goal to be achieved and a belief the goal embodies a worthwhile or important result.
                                    —Carl Larson and Frank LaFasto, *TeamWork: What Must Go Right/What Can Go Wrong*

A purpose is the fundamental reason a team exists. There is a story that articulates the value of a team knowing its purpose. An American drill bit company was confronted with a Japanese competitor that was able to sell high-quality drill bits for what it was costing the American team to manufacture them. A loss in market share prompted this well-established company to take a hard look at itself. At first, discussions focused on efficiency improvements, but after considerable debate and evaluation, it was determined that these improvements would not create the margins they needed to regain their competitive position.

It wasn't until an enlightened member of the team asked, "What is the primary purpose of a drill bit?" that the team members began to think in a way that would secure their future. They realized that they were not in the drill bit business—they were in the business of helping their customers drill holes. Once they recognized the fundamental reason why they existed, they were able to think of alternative ways to satisfy their customer's needs. They developed a laser drilling process that allowed them to regain and even improve their competitive position.

An error made by countless teams is to define their purpose by their activities or the products they deliver, rather than by the fundamental needs that they are satisfying.

Advisors have the need to do worthwhile work. A compelling vision should begin with a definition of that purpose. This provides the compass that gives direction for making all other strategic decisions. In *Built to Last*, Jim Collins and Jerry Porras wrote, "A good purpose statement is broad, fundamental, inspirational and enduring." Your purpose should transcend market life cycles, changes in product development, the regulatory environment, and advances in technology.

Defining the purpose may seem like a simple concept. But defining it in a meaningful way will require thinking deeply about the fundamental reasons your advisory business exists. Your purpose should focus on core client needs and stand as a constant reminder of the value you provide. This is not an exercise to create a marketing tagline. This is an opportunity to internalize the meaningful work you do for clients.

The first step in deciding your purpose is to understand the primary benefit you bring to your clients. When you cut away the layers, what is at the core? What basic client need do you satisfy? The answer to that question is your purpose. This may not be as easy as it sounds, and here is why: Financial service firms are so busy doing daily tasks and implementing strategies that they tend to define themselves by the things they do rather than the value they provide. You can use the why-why-why exercise to drill down and determine your purpose.

Following are some examples of why questions:

- Why does your advisory team exist?
- To help clients invest and keep their financial affairs in order—why?
- To help our clients create and protect their wealth—why?
- To help them reach their financial goals—why?
- Achieving their goals allows them to provide for their family and enjoy retirement—why?

This team's ultimate purpose is "to provide our clients with financial peace of mind."

Sometimes, teams find their final purpose statement to be too abstract to be meaningful. If you find yourself in this situation, you will need to find the balance between making it fundamental yet meaningful to the team. While keeping the intent of the purpose in mind, simply work your way back up the "why-why-why" chain until you get to a level that is tangible enough to be meaningful to your team.

Consider two examples from advisors who found themselves in this situation:

1. Help our clients create and protect their wealth.
2. Help clients reach their financial goals.

Too many advisors are caught in the trap of thinking their purpose is making money. In the 15 years I have helped advisory teams, I have observed that those who are most focused on bringing value to their clients end up doing better financially than those who are focused on "what is in it for me."

This principle is not limited to financial services. I was in a planning session with Bill Gates. He was upset when he heard that something had gone wrong for a Microsoft customer. As he rocked back and forth, deep in thought, he asked, "Why are we doing that to our customers?" The last time I checked, Bill had enough to retire. Like so many others who have done well financially, he is focused on bringing value to his customers as opposed to what's in it for him.

Business Goals: Specific Objectives That Support Your Purpose

> An increasing number of studies of leadership are finding that one of the key functions of leaders is to develop goals for the organization.
>
> —Edwin Locke and Gary Latham, *A Theory of Goal Setting & Task Performance*

I had the great privilege of having a 20-year friendship with Cecil Bell, a former professor of management and organization at the University of Washington. Cecil and I had countless discussions about goal-setting research and how to apply it in a real-world setting. Cecil passed away in the spring of 2009, but I know he would have been pleased that I am sharing our most recent thoughts with you in this section.

Cecil also introduced me to Gary Latham, who co-authored *The Theory of Goal Setting* with Edwin Locke. Together, Latham and Locke have published more on goals research than anyone else in the world. Translating their great work into a practical application for advisors has had a profound impact on those I have worked with.

Effective goals come in three categories—mission, fiscal-year unifying goals, and strategic objectives. These goals must align to provide both long-term and short-term direction.

- Mission: the one or two compelling goals you plan to achieve over the next five years.
- Fiscal-year unifying goals: the one or two most critical goals you plan to achieve over the next fiscal year.
- Strategic objectives: the three to five implementation objectives. If the strategy is correct, achieving these goals will likely lead to achieving your fiscal-year unifying goals and ultimately to "mission accomplished."

The Moon Mission On May 25, 1961, during a joint session of Congress, President John F. Kennedy declared, "I believe this nation should commit itself to achieving the goal, before this decade is out, of landing a man on the moon and returning him safely to earth." These words articulated a goal that was powerful enough to mobilize Congress, suppliers, government agencies, scientists, engineers, the military, education, the news media, and many other resources into a team.

On July 20, 1969, Neil Armstrong told the world, "That's one small step for man, one giant leap for mankind." But it was not "mission accomplished" until the space capsule safety plopped into the Atlantic Ocean on July 24. It was a team win that began with the articulation of the moon mission. This mission was a binary goal. Binary goals are either achieved or they are not. Unlike the moon mission, business goals are expressed in numbers.

The Positive Effect of Goals on Teams

Team goals create alignment. When I facilitate business planning sessions, I ask the participants to close their eyes and point north. Inevitably, they point in all directions. After they open their eyes, I ask

Figure 1.1   Team Goals Create Alignment

what would happen if they were all to walk in the directions they were pointing. It is clear that they would run into one another. And that is what many teams experience. Without goals that are focused on the most vital business imperatives, resources will be squandered by individuals shooting at their own targets, leaving the firm wounded in the crossfire.

You probably think that you and your team know your goals. Consider asking your team to take out a sheet of paper and write down your top three goals. Next, ask each team member to read their answers aloud. At first, the absurdity of the discrepancy in the answers will provoke laughter. Team members quickly see the implications of this lack of alignment and become quite serious. Finally, ask them, "How can we hit a target if we don't agree where it is?" The obvious answer is that you can't!

With goals, such as the target in Figure 1.1, team members can align their efforts to move the business forward.

Goals provide the context to determine mission-critical strategies and make tactical business decisions.   If you had a goal to improve your revenue per client you would probably consider setting a higher minimum, disengaging from your smallest clients, focusing on an affluent target market, and creating a high-net-worth service model. The goal comes first and then the strategies to achieve the goal.

The same holds true for making tactical decisions. Once your goals are in place you can decide whether you should hire that ad-min candidate or purchase that customer relationship management (CRM) software. A common target provides focus to direct the team's resources. A magnifying glass, properly focused, can concentrate the sun's rays, creating enough energy to start a fire. Likewise, focusing a team's time, skills, insight, and technology on a common target can generate enough energy to bring your vision into reality and create the business of your dreams.

Figure 1.2   Course Correction

Goals with feedback provide the information teams need for course correction.   For example, if improvements on your revenue per client stalled, it would cause you to first analyze why, and then make adjustments to the strategy, as depicted in Figure 1.2. I have seen teams work for many years on an ineffective strategy simply because they failed to establish a goal that would trigger a course correction. Goals with feedback provide teams with information that cannot be ignored.

Goals cause teams to spend their time on the best opportunities.   When time is spent, it is gone and can't be reclaimed. When your team has meaningful goals, team members will concentrate their time on those activities that are most likely to bring the goals into reality.

> By making self-satisfaction conditional on certain levels of performance, individuals create self-inducements to persist in their efforts until their performances match internal standards.
> —Albert Bandura and Dale Schunk in the *Journal of Personality and Social Psychology*, 1981

Goals elevate the effort and persistence of team members.   Teams try harder and longer when they have effective goals. It doesn't matter whether it has to do with holding a marriage together during a tough spot, raising teenagers, launching a new product, or migrating your team from investment counseling to providing wealth management advice.

The number one ingredient to success is persistence. Having effective goals can be the difference between providing average and differentiating levels of service; maintaining the status quo or developing a high-net-worth client base.

Another important ingredient to success in any endeavor is effort. Effort plays a large part in performance. It is the difference between an advisory team that exhibits the fire in the belly that is necessary to compete on a world-class level and a group that greets each other with

"Thank God it's Friday" at the end of the week. Moreover, effective, unifying goals cause team members to intensify their efforts at crunch time—the time when the pressure is on and your team must perform at its best.

With goals, team members are more interested in their work.   The team environment is more satisfying and creative when each member is intrinsically interested in his work. When team members have a mission, fiscal-year unifying goals, and, in particular, strategy objectives, they are more interested in their work. Clients benefit immensely from working with an advisor whose team members are engaged in their work. You only need to think about the last time you worked with someone who was not interested in their job to understand the stark difference.

You are more aware of opportunities and threats to your goals.   Goals trigger your reticular activating system. The reticular activating system is a portion of the brain that alerts us to opportunities. Think about the last time you set a goal to buy a car. Remember driving down the street and how that model started jumping out at you? They seemed to be everywhere! They had been there all along, you just were not aware of them. Likewise, you can walk right by opportunity after opportunity unless you have set meaningful team goals. These opportunities will begin to jump out at you just like the automobile did. You will discover that opportunities are everywhere.

The reticular activating system can also alert you to threats that will prevent you from achieving your goals. These could be things like a change in policy, a change in capital markets, a team member's change in attitude, or an early warning signal from a financial product you utilize. When you have a goal, you become much more alert to the threats to that goal.

A team goal activates the team's problem-solving skills.   Our brains are solution-finding machines. Create a problem and our minds go to work to solve it. Setting business goals automatically creates a major problem for us: "How are we going to do that?" Whenever your team members are confronted with problems, their fact-based, intuitive, and creative thinking skills automatically go to work to find solutions. But without the goal, these incredibly powerful problem-solving skills remain dormant.

With goals, teams are better able to access their stored knowledge. Over time, we collect huge amounts of information that can go untapped. Once the team goals are set, the information that is relevant to the accomplishment of those goals is unleashed—not just for you but for the entire team. The collective IQ of the team goes up dramatically.

Teams perform more consistently when they have goals. Over time, the "total quality" movement has had many names, but what has not changed is the agreement that reducing variance is the key to improving quality. This principle is as true for an advisory team as it is for a manufacturing company. The quest to improve consistency day in and day out is what leads advisory teams to improve their quality of service.

Characteristics of Effective Goals In order to experience the benefits of team goals they should have the following characteristics.

Goals should align to your purpose. If your purpose is *to improve financial peace of mind for our clients*, the mission, fiscal-year unifying goals, and strategic objectives should point the team in the direction of serving that purpose well.

Goals should be strategic both in quantity (focused on growth) and quality (focused on high-net-worth clients). Goals should inspire strategies to build the type of firm you desire. For example, if you want to wake up on January 1 and know where 80 percent of your income is going to come from, you should consider a recurring revenue goal. You would develop and implement strategies that would drive recurring revenue. These might include developing a service model, taking on only new fee-based clients, and migrating your best transaction-based clients to fee-based relationships.

In the absence of a recurring revenue goal, advisors tend to default to the status quo of setting an assets-under-management (AUM) goal. In their quest to gather AUM they take on small, unprofitable accounts and discount their fees. You should give a lot of thought to the type of business you are attempting to build and make sure your quantity goal is leading you there.

Having a quantity goal that causes you to grow is an important consideration. Several years ago, I decided to take my grandson, Zach, biking on three legs of the Tour de France. Having not done much cycling, I went down to our local bike shop to purchase a bike and all the accessories.

A couple of days later, I set out on my first training ride. I had decided to ride around Mercer Island, and headed down Bellevue Way, took the I-90 Bridge over Lake Washington, and then made a left turn onto East Mercer Way. It was there that I confronted my first stop signal and realized I needed to put my foot down for balance.

Do you know what clamp-ons are? They are a part of the pedal, and the cleats on the bottom of bike shoes clamp into them. I quickly realized you should practice removing your foot from the clamp-on prior to stopping for the first time. It is a little precarious when you come to a stop and realize you are unable to unclamp your foot. Imagine a grown man lying on the pavement with his feet stuck in his bike pedals!

Later, back on my bike, I was reflecting upon the experience. I realized how difficult it is to balance a bike that is standing still. But I will tell you, it is not nearly as difficult as balancing a business that is standing still. A quantity goal that is focused on growth is vitally important.

> All the good-to-great companies attained piercing insight into how to most effectively generate sustained and robust cash flow and profitability. In particular, they discover the single denominator—profit per x—that has the greatest impact on their economics.
>
> —Jim Collins, *Good to Great*

Quality goals are equally as important as quantity goals. Helping advisors begin to think about profit per client has had a profound impact on their businesses. The problem is that in the advisory space, profit is a funky number. Taking a brother-in-law golfing becomes a business expense. A client visit in Orlando, combined with a family trip to Disneyworld, is also written off.

A quality business has a very high percentage of high-net-worth clients. If you don't focus on quality you risk working hard for 15 years and discovering that 60 percent of your client base is not profitable. Because profit is such a funky number, if you intend to build a high-net-worth wealth management practice, your team should consider setting a goal to increase recurring revenue per client. If I asked you what strategies you would implement to improve your recurring revenue per client in a dramatic way, you might list:

- Disengage small, unprofitable clients.
- Set a higher and more rigorous minimum.
- *Wow* your top clients so they will refer their friends.
- Target a more lucrative segment of the market.

An increase in recurring revenue (quantity goal) and an increase in recurring revenue per client (quality goal) have been effective strategic goals for wealth management advisors.

> Clear, attainable goals produce higher levels of performance than general intentions to do one's best, which usually have little or no effect.
> —Albert Bandura, *Self-Efficacy: The Exercise of Control*

Team goals should be specific numbers (metrics) and should be free of ambiguity. Each team member must understand what the target is. Knowing the target orients them toward goal-relevant activities and produces higher performance levels. If team members are not crystal clear on the target, their activities can be off the mark and resources can be misused. When I was coaching at West Point, I was taught, "Don't give a command that can be understood; give a command that cannot be misunderstood."

A specific and clear goal increases the team's consistency. As Locke and Latham state in *A Theory of Goal Setting and Task Performance*, "The more specific the goal, the lower the performance variance." A team performing consistently well, day in and day out, outperforms inconsistent teams. Dependability is one of the attributes that separates average teams from great ones.

The following are examples of specific metrics:

- Mission—the one or two compelling goals you plan to achieve over the next five years.
  - ◆ Recurring revenue: $1.2 million.
  - ◆ Recurring revenue per client: $7,500.
- Fiscal-year unifying goals—the one or two measurable steps toward your mission over the next fiscal year.

- ◆ Recurring revenue: $750,000.
- ◆ Recurring revenue per client: $5,000.
- • Strategic objectives—the three to five implementation objectives. If the strategy is correct, achieving these goals will likely lead to achieving your fiscal-year unifying goals.
  - ◆ Disengage 85 "D" clients.
  - ◆ Engage 35 "A" clients with wealth management.
  - ◆ Acquire 10 clients, each with at least $7,500 fee-based revenue.

Simply adopting a goal, without knowing how one is doing, or knowing how one is doing in the absence of a goal, has no lasting motivational impact.
  —Albert Bandura, *Self-Efficacy: The Exercise of Control*

Team goals should allow for regular and ongoing feedback.   Feedback is the breakfast of champions. Without feedback, the positive effects of goals are lost. "Simply adopting a goal, without knowing how one is doing, or knowing how one is doing in the absence of a goal, has no lasting motivational impact," says Bandura. Feedback should be frequent enough for team members to make a clear connection between their activities and the results they are getting, but far enough apart so that they can see the measurable results of their work.

Figure 1.3 shows the impact of having business goals with feedback. It is hypothetical only in that it shows two areas of research that have not been combined into one study. First, note that there is an increase in performance only when goals have feedback. Without feedback there is no goal effect—it is like having no goal at all. Second, a mission must be supported with fiscal-year unifying goals and those goals need to be supported by strategic objectives to maximize team performance.

Feedback is essential for making course corrections. A pilot doesn't just take off from the San Francisco International Airport, set a course for Honolulu, and then check five and a half hours later to see if the target is in sight. Based on feedback, the pilot (or the automatic pilot) will make thousands of subtle course corrections along the way. Effective feedback needs to be frequent. The more frequent the feedback and course corrections, the less wasted time and fuel en route from San Francisco to Hawaii.

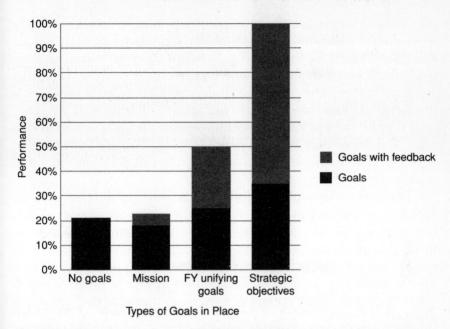

Figure 1.3   Business Goals with Feedback Improve Team Performance (Hypothetical)

Frequent feedback often allows for a more accurate assessment of the current situation and more accurate adjustments. A lecturer at an artificial intelligence seminar I attended provided an excellent example. Her company wanted to improve the accuracy of measuring the volume of gas in a luxury automobile's gas tank. Standard sensing devices did not accommodate changes in incline, acceleration, or deceleration. Although the total volume remained the same, in real-life driving conditions the accuracy of the feedback would vary greatly. They were able to increase the accuracy significantly by adding a number of sensors throughout the tank. But the accuracy was still not at the level they desired. They had two choices: Add more sensors or increase the frequency of the feedback. They found that by doubling the frequency of the feedback they could hit their standard.

Feedback should be positively stated. Throughout elementary and junior high school, my spelling teachers always provided me with negative feedback by marking my paper with a –8, and they would amplify my errors by making certain to use a thick red pencil when they wrote my score in large numbers on my test. We now know that a more effective way to state feedback is in a positive way, such as +17. Feedback should be evaluated to confirm that the team's strategy is on track or to determine where corrections need to be made. Team members have only three choices when corrective feedback is provided: They can reject it; they can accept it and do nothing about it; or they can accept it and make appropriate changes to get back on track. If the feedback is stated positively (e.g., "We are at 90 percent of our goal"), team members are much more likely to accept it and do something about it.

This feedback should also link team activities to the results. Team members must be able to see that it is the work they are doing that is producing the results they are getting. For example, a sales team should be able to make the connection that "because of the quarterly reviews we are delivering, our call-in leads are going up." Taking time to explicitly make these connections in a team meeting is well worth the effort. Team members must know that what they are doing matters.

It would be useless for your team to set a goal and then not look at the results you are getting for an entire year. The commonsense principle must prevail. The only guidelines that research and conventional wisdom can provide are that (1) there needs to be enough space between the action and feedback to be able to see marked changes, and (2) the feedback needs to be close enough for team members to make a clear connection between their activities and the results they are getting.

The following time frames for providing feedback have worked well for many advisors:

- Mission: quarterly.
- Fiscal year unifying goals: monthly.
- Strategic objectives: weekly.

Team goals should have a deadline that creates a sense of urgency. President Kennedy's words "before this decade is out" established a deadline for the moon mission. I have heard it said that the difference between a goal and a dream is a deadline. Far more goals are achieved than dreams. If you want to live your dream it will need to be supported by effective goals that have deadlines.

An effective goal has a deadline that is neither too near nor too far away. A deadline that is placed too far into the future promotes a "we'll get around to it" attitude and diminishes team motivation. It would be like going on a diet and targeting the end of the year to lose 20 pounds. You go out to dinner with friends, order a Caesar salad, fettuccine Alfredo, have a couple of glasses of Chianti and some tiramisu for dessert. The goal is too far away to cause you to sustain a change in your eating behavior today. There is no sense of motivation to lose the 20 pounds; in fact, your motivation goes down. Only when the goal is close enough will it cause goal-relevant behavior.

There are no set standards as to what is too far into the future, so common sense must prevail. The time frame should create a sense of urgency and focus, without causing debilitating stress. A goal that requires the team to produce results in the distant future will always require the support of short-term goals. An NFL team that sets the goal of winning the Super Bowl must still play one game at a time. It is not until the goal is close enough to cause team members to behave differently that the goal becomes effective.

Goals should be developed by the team.   Participatory goal setting will crush assigned goal setting every time. When team members are allowed to participate in establishing the goals, they gain insight into factors influencing the goal and develop more appropriate solution strategies. When team members are allowed to participate in goal setting, they are more likely to establish goals that are:

- Challenging yet realistic.
- Within the team's control.
- Beneficial to team members.

Team goals need to be challenging yet realistic.   Persistence is the number one ingredient to success in taking a team's performance to the next level. Persistence is dependent upon the team members' belief in their ability to accomplish their goals. They must also believe that the reward will be worth their effort. In *Built to Last,* Collins and Porras write, "An effective mission must stretch and challenge the organization, yet be achievable."

These goals must be realistic. It is a common practice in the investment advisory industry to set so-called *stretch goals*, which go beyond your capacity to realistically achieve them. The notion of stretch goals is counter to effective goal setting. Don't walk away from the next presenter you hear talking about stretch goals—run! They don't know what they are talking about.

Bandura provides tremendous insight into the effects of team members' beliefs about their ability to accomplish specific tasks. This body of research clearly demonstrates that team members with strong beliefs in their ability to succeed persist significantly longer than those who don't.

Walk through the hypothetical illustration in Figure 1.4 with me. When confronted with a challenge, a team that believes it will be successful tries harder than one that doesn't believe so. This is significant, but not as significant as what happens after suffering a setback. After a failed attempt, a team that still believes success is imminent tries even harder, while one that does not begins to quit. After a third setback, the team that continues to believe it will be successful

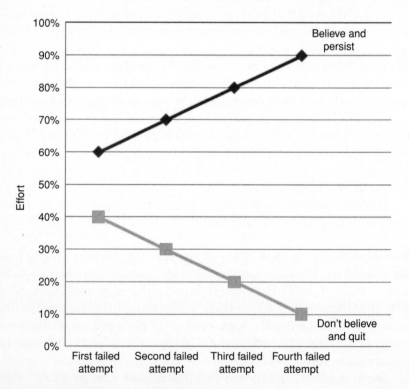

Figure 1.4   Effects of Belief on Effort

Table 1.1   Benchmarking Data

	Current Firm Performance	Top 25% (median)	Difference
Revenue—Investment related	$834,738	$761,882	$72,856
Number of active clients	626	144	482
Full Time Equivalent (FTE)	4	2.8	1.2
Revenue per active client	$1,333	$5,291	($3,957)
AUM per active client	$79,657	$650,972	($571,315)
Active clients per FTE	157	51	105
Revenue per FTE	$208,685	$272,101	($63,416)
AUM per FTE	$12,466,300	$33,478,571	($21,012,272)

Source: Moss Adams/InvestmentNews Research produces two biannual studies; one on compensation and staffing and the other on the financial performance of advisory firms. For more information on the research go to: www.investmentnews.com/section/data.

tries harder still. The other team begins to go through the motions of work. Belief determines persistence. Goals must be believable. Once again, the number one ingredient to success in any endeavor is persistence.

Benchmarking data, as shown in Table 1.1, available from resources that keep up-to-date measures of advisory practices, can be useful in helping a team determine what is realistic. In this table the benchmark is the top 25 percent of other similar firms. By comparing the difference between this benchmark and current firm performance, team members will have a better understanding of realistic standards. They need to know these standards before they can believe that the goal they set is attainable.

Team goals must also be challenging. The excitement, electricity, passion, enthusiasm, and breakthrough creativity associated with a great team win are the result of a goal that is challenging. The initial Microsoft team of Paul Allen and Bill Gates believed they could create the technology that would "put a computer on every desk and in every home." This belief caused them to persist, even in the face of what many would perceive as insurmountable barriers. Their persistence, as it so often does, paid off. Thirty-five years after its inception, Microsoft has become a $58.4 billion company, with no end in sight. And Allen and Gates' challenging goal is becoming a reality.

Locke and Latham believe that hard goals lead to greater effort and persistence than do easy goals. This extra effort can be the difference between winning and losing in the advisory marketplace. Challenging goals do more than increase effort and persistence. They also activate our creativity and problem-solving skills. Putting team members' collective, fact-based, intuitive, and creative thinking skills to work on problems can cause breakthrough performance.

In the 1950s, Moshe Feldenkrais used the following in his Awareness Through Movement exercises. This exercise will allow you to quickly experience the benefit of a challenging goal. Stand and put your right arm out straight in front of you at shoulder level with your thumb pointing up. With your legs and feet straight ahead, look at your thumb and turn your torso to the right as far as you can comfortably twist. Visually mark a spot on the wall that you were able to reach. Return to face front and relax. Now close your eyes. Without moving, imagine raising your right arm out straight again and visualize what your thumb looks like. See your thumb, your thumb nail, its cuticle, the third of a moon at the base of the thumb nail, the wrinkles on the first joint, even the skin color. Now, imagine seeing the wall behind the thumb as you visualize moving smoothly and easily to the spot you previously marked on the wall. Relax your eyes, neck, back, hips, and knees and imagine rotating two feet further. Imagine seeing your thumb even more clearly as you visualize moving another two feet. And another foot, and another, and six more inches. Now, mentally unwind and open your eyes. Then, do the actual exercise again. Most likely you will have turned considerably farther than your initial attempt.

After imagining the possibility of turning so easily and completely, your body was able to organize itself to move further. Using exactly the same resources, you were able to improve your performance. Likewise, a team that stretches what is possible by setting a challenging goal will make subtle adjustments to organize its resources and elevate its performance. As part of the goal-setting process, teams must consider what is possible. Ask, "If we knew we would not fail, what would we do?"

Sometimes you can set a challenging yet realistic goal but over time or because of circumstances it is no longer challenging or realistic. To retain the benefit of having effective goals, teams will need to reassess their goals periodically to make sure they remain challenging and realistic. Effective goals must balance the possible with the believable, the challenging with the realistic.

The goal needs to be within the team's control.   Even though there are few goals that are completely independent of outside influences, team members have to believe that they have enough control over the goal to own it. The team must believe their results are largely dependent upon their activities. They must be able to make the connection that they can cause the goal to come about. Team members will reject any goal they view as beyond their control. This is one reason it is wise to allow team members to participate in the goal-setting process. Through active participation, a team can guide the process toward a goal they feel is within their control. If a team goal is to provide a common target, increase motivation, and activate team members' problem-solving skills, they must own it!

Effective teams demonstrate outstanding persistence. Teams should evaluate their commitment to their unifying goal, their ability to remain innovative, and their capacity to increase effort when things get tough. They should evaluate their ability to recover from setbacks. Above all, teams should assess their willingness to persist until the goal is achieved.

Team goals must be beneficial to team members.   "For workers to do high-quality work, they must be managed in a way that convinces them that the work they are asked to do satisfies their needs. The more it does, the harder they will work," wrote William Glasser in *The Quality School* (New York: Harper & Row, 1990).

Clayton Alderfer's ERG theory suggests that we are all motivated to satisfy our existence, relatedness, and growth needs. Everyone needs food, water, clothing, and shelter in order to exist. In our society, these things cost money. Your team members will work hard if they are able to make the connection that by achieving the team goals they will earn more money to better meet their existence needs.

We all need to relate to others. Everyone has experienced being a member of a winning team of some kind. Think back to one of those experiences. How fast did time go by? Was it a creative environment? Did you kid one another? Were team members accepted for who they really were? These relatedness needs are better met when team members are fully aligned and achieving their goals.

We also have a need to grow, achieve, and be successful—not so much in the eyes of others, but in our own eyes. Team members will be committed to the team's goal if they can see that the task of achieving the goal requires them to acquire new knowledge, skills, and competencies.

Many have been fooled into believing that we can ask team members to "win one for the Gipper." But to remain motivated over the long haul, each team member must be able to answer the unspoken question, "What's in it for me?" The better the team members are able to make the connection that the work they are doing will satisfy their existence, relatedness, and growth needs, the more they will be committed to the team's goal.

Making the assumption that every team member will automatically understand the personal benefits to achieving the team's goal can be a big mistake. Even when they have participated in goal setting it may be difficult for them to make the connection. This is particularly true with abstract goals such as profitability, return on assets, and other financial measures.

It has been my experience that the team members who can see the personal benefits can help make the goal more meaningful by sharing their insights. Initially a team goal of 1.6 return on assets (ROA) was not meaningful to a number of bank tellers who were working in a regional bank. It quickly became meaningful when an insightful team member pointed out that a lesser ROA would make the bank vulnerable to being purchased by a larger bank, thereby putting their jobs in jeopardy.

Anticipating the rewards of achieving goals is what drives people to close the gap. As long as they perceive enough value to warrant the effort required to close the gap, it doesn't seem to matter whether these rewards are extrinsic or intrinsic. This point should not be taken lightly. For years, many researchers stressed that extrinsic rewards (i.e., money) detracted from what really motivated team members—intrinsic rewards. Current research suggests that both extrinsic and intrinsic rewards motivate team members.

Extrinsic rewards are valued outcomes that are provided to team members. Recognition for a significant contribution or receiving a bonus for achieving an objective are both extrinsic rewards that many team members value. The self-satisfaction that comes from achieving an important tactical step or from acquiring a new skill is an intrinsic reward. The anticipation of extrinsic and intrinsic rewards causes team members to persist, as long as they believe that they will be successful.

Guiding Principles: The Rules That Guide Daily Decision Making

> Correct principles are like compasses: they are always pointing
> the way.
>
> —Stephen Covey, *The 7 Habits of Highly Effective People*

Guiding principles are the standards that guide team members as they make day-to-day business decisions. These principles should establish the overall philosophy of the business by determining how team members will treat one another, serve their clients, focus on quality solutions, commit to organizational effectiveness, and provide the cornerstones of empowerment. Guiding principles can lead a team through even the most difficult challenges. They afford team members the guidance to make decisions in a consistent manner.

The Ford Motor Company provides a good example. Ford's motto, "Quality is Job One," began as part of a corporate advertising campaign at a time when their products could barely outlast their payment schedules. Throughout the organization, their teams promoted this principle, and the results have been phenomenal. "Quality is Job One" provided Ford with a compass, allowing the company to successfully navigate the global economy and close the once ominous quality gap between themselves and their Japanese competitors.

The best advisory team guiding principle I've come across in my work comes from the firm that is now Laird Norton Tyee. Kaycee Krysty and Rich Simmons built a truly remarkable wealth management advisory firm with a single guiding principle: "Do great things for our clients and make sure they know about it." Kaycee and Rich based their firm on this fundamental principle and hired people who understood it and could deliver on it. Through the merger of Tyee Asset Strategies and Laird Norton Trust, growing from zero assets under management to well over $3 billion and from a team of 2 to a team of 20, they still do great things for their clients and make sure they know about it. Guiding principles are timeless. They should be highly valued regardless of the changes in your team or your industry.

> We learned that you don't need to create a "soft" or "comfortable" environment to build a visionary company. We found that the visionary companies tend to be more demanding of their

people than other companies, both in terms of performance
and congruence with the ideology (guiding principles).

—Jim Collins and Jerry Porras, *Built to Last*

As a rule, teams must create and then promote their guiding principles until they become part of the team culture. Because principles
are grounded in our beliefs, this is a formidable task. The difficulty
lies in the fact that our present perception of the truth (our beliefs) may be erroneous and may not lead us in the direction of the
team's vision. This dilemma is compounded by other team members
who have their own sets of erroneous beliefs. We all develop our
perception of the truth through our senses, expert opinion, social
persuasion, agreement with others, reason, and science. All of these
methods can be flawed.

Elmer Nordstrom Walked His Talk   The National Football League
college draft is intense. Players are the lifeblood of an NFL franchise,
and too many mistakes in the draft can have dangerous, long-term
consequences. If too many wrong decisions are made, the organization can lose millions of dollars, coaches can lose their jobs, and
players can lose their opportunity for success.

The day of the draft is electric. The importance of the event
creates a level of excitement and tension that smacks you as soon as
you walk in the door. Mock drafts have produced likely scenarios and
the strategies designed to exploit these scenarios are mapped out on
the whiteboards that surround the room. The names of the players
to be drafted are posted under various categories, as are their height,
weight, speed, and overall evaluation grade.

With NFL teams attempting to improve their talent level and satisfy their immediate critical needs, there is plenty of last-minute ma-
neuvering. Some teams, fearful that a coveted player will be drafted
by a team picking ahead of them, attempt to move up in a round
by trading places with a team with different critical needs. This ex-
change will cost the trading team one or more draft picks in the later
rounds. The phones and computers are stretched to their limits to
keep up with the necessary communications.

On a draft day morning, I was making my final preparations by
studying the whiteboards, when the senior member of the Nordstrom
family, Elmer, came into the draft room. The Nordstroms were the
majority owners of the Seattle Seahawks when I coached for them.

Elmer walked over to me, took my arm, and ushered me out of the room and into the hallway.

I was preparing myself to receive some confidential football-related information when he asked, "How's Kim?" Kim is my middle child, and I answered that she was doing just fine. "And how about your other two children, Christy and Steve?" he inquired. At the beginning of one of the most critical days for an NFL franchise, Elmer Nordstrom was asking me about my family!

This was the same Elmer Nordstrom, who, with his two brothers, took a small regional shoe store and developed it into a national apparel chain that stands today as the benchmark for personalized customer service. The Nordstrom leadership emphasized "provide outstanding customer service" and "use your good judgment at all times" strongly enough to permeate to the core of the organization. Team members get the picture right away when their leaders use the principles on an ongoing basis as they make day-to-day decisions. By walking their talk and continually coaching to these principles, Nordstrom leaders were able to knead them into the team culture. Empowered by the guiding principles of "provide outstanding customer service" and "use your good judgment at all times," Nordstrom employees have extended Elmer's genuine concern for people far beyond his lifetime. Unfortunately, situations where leadership's values align precisely with the team's most effective guiding principle are more the exception than the rule.

Characteristics of Effective Guiding Principles   Consider the following:

- *Do they work?* Guiding principles must encompass a broad range of considerations and be useful for making effective day-to-day business decisions. Team members can have responsibilities that require them to make decisions based on many nonstructured situations. Effective guiding principles should function as useful decision-making criteria in these situations.
- *Are they ethical?* Guiding principles should be based on what the team feels is right and good. There will be opportunities for your team to exploit a situation with a strategy that is not morally sound. What would you do? Guiding principles should be ethical both for their own sake and to ensure long-term success. Short-term gains can easily turn into long-term losses

if unethical decisions are being made. The concept of "what goes around comes around" is as predictable as the law of gravity.

• *Are they understood?* The need for teams to clearly define each guiding principle is evidenced by an exercise I have used. After the team members identify their guiding principles, I break the team into groups and ask each group to pick one of the principles. Then I ask each group member to jot down 10 words or bullet statements that define their group's principle. Next, I ask each group to choose a captain and have the captain read his list of 10 definitions aloud. As the captain reads his list, group members say "I don't have it" if they do not have that definition. If the captain hears one or more members say "I don't have it," he strikes it from his list. Finally, I ask the captains how many definitions their entire group shared. Nearly always they will say "*Zero!*"

The challenge becomes clear when the team realizes the potential for each member to be working toward a very different definition of a guiding principle. Therefore, it is important for the team to take time to develop a shared definition of each principle and to have clear examples of how each would be utilized as team members make their daily business decisions. Each guiding principle needs to be defined in a way that encourages team members to act in accordance with the definition.

A good example of this comes from one of Netflix's nine guiding principles—judgment. Netflix management and employees have taken the time to define the "behaviors and skills" that demonstrate each principle, and these are how they define *judgment*:

♦ Make wise decisions despite ambiguity.
♦ Identify root causes and get beyond treating symptoms.
♦ Think strategically, and articulate what you are, and are not, trying to do.
♦ Smartly separate what must be done well now, and what can be improved later.

• *Are they meaningful?* Team members must be able to make the connection that by adhering to guiding principles, not only will the team's unifying goal be achieved, but their own personal needs will be met as well. Making this connection is too often taken for granted. It has been my experience that teams must understand the importance of each principle and its implications before formally embracing them as a group.

- *Do they target the key team functions?* For most organizations, this would include, but not be limited to, customer service, product and service quality, organizational effectiveness, and organizational culture. Too often, I read guiding principles that are feel-good statements rather than principles designed to drive results and create a healthy team culture.

- *Are they ranked?* In 1982, Johnson & Johnson proclaimed, "We have a hierarchy of responsibilities: customers first, employees second, society at large third, and shareholders fourth." There will be times when decision-making criteria will pit one principle against another. In these instances, it is important to know in advance which principle the team values most.

  There are no rules as to the number of guiding principles a team can effectively promote, so common sense must prevail. Advisors have been successful embracing one to three guiding principles. If you have more than three they turn into meaningless "motherhood and apple pie" statements.

The following are four examples of guiding principles that have worked effectively for elite advisors:

1. Do great things for clients and make sure they know about it.
2. Make and keep meaningful commitments.
3. Always put the client first.
4. Make win, win, win decisions: the client, team members, and the business must all win.

Developing Belief in the Guiding Principles   For guiding principles to be more than rhetoric they must be dear to the heart of the team. Too often teams don't walk their talk—they say one thing but do another. If team members are to adhere to the guiding principles, they must first believe in them. This will require more than just participation in their creation. It will require education, coaching, and a system that fosters and promotes the principles.

Often, developing belief in guiding principles requires a process whereby team members can acquire a more complete understanding of those principles. Trust is a good example. When I ask a group what would keep them from trusting another team member, their answers inevitably fall into two categories: "They don't tell the truth," or "They say they are going to do something, but they don't follow through."

For lack of trust, the remedy is tactful honesty. Team members can build trust by developing the skills to effectively present their perception of the truth. For lack of follow-through, the remedy is honoring commitments. Team members can build trust by being realistic about their commitments, by not overcommitting, and by committing only to those things that they have the capacity to deliver.

Gaining insight, making new distinctions, and understanding the implications of embracing each guiding principle are important steps in the process. One of leadership's important roles is to publically recognize team members for making decisions and acting consistently within the framework of the guiding principles. Corrections should be made behind closed doors. It is even more important for leadership to walk their talk.

Developing guiding principles requires coaching. Athletics provide us with this benchmark. When my grandson was five years old he attended a tae kwon do school that had its guiding principles painted in big, bold print on the walls:

RESPECT, PATIENCE, DISCIPLINE, SILENCE, CONCENTRATION, EFFORT

The instructor, Master Lee, regularly defined these principles and pointed out when the students were aligned with them. He also pointed out when they weren't. When Master Lee saw two of the young students misbehaving, he stated, "I'm trying to teach while you two are having your own conversation. Is that showing me respect?" "No, sir" was their reply. If he noticed another youngster flawlessly executing a side kick, he would stop the class and say, "That is what I mean by concentration. Does everyone understand what concentration means and why this is an example of it?" Master Lee used his individual students to help the whole group understand the meaning of each principle throughout each class.

As I continued to observe, I noticed that it wasn't just the instructor coaching the guiding principles; it was the students coaching each other, as well. From warm-up to cooldown, I could hear little voices reminding one another: "Respect, patience, discipline, silence, concentration, effort . . ."

If you want to see athletic teams promoting their guiding principles, read the sports page a day or two before a contest. You will read comments like "We will need to play tougher and smarter"; "We are going to beat them to the punch"; "Mistake-free football wins." When an interviewer attempts to gain insight into the strategy for an event scheduled two or three weeks away, the question is avoided with a simple "We play them one game at a time." Underestimating the benefits of each team member developing a strong belief in the team's guiding principles has caused many teams to avoid this essential discipline of teamwork. Once established, guiding principles provide a framework for successful decisions at the team member level. Considering the speed at which business is moving, the team that has the ability to respond and adapt quickly has a huge competitive advantage. Guiding principles are essential to building the capacity to make swift cornerstone decisions.

Vivid Description: A Narrative of the Business Success You Intend to Create

There is no more powerful engine driving an organization toward excellence and long-range success than an attractive, worthwhile and achievable vision of the future, widely shared.
—Bert Nanus, *Visionary Leadership*

In the advisor game, the vivid description describes the client experience, the team experience, and the business results. Consider this example:

We are a nationally recognized, award-winning wealth management firm, whose competitive advantage is based upon personalized client service, state-of-the-art technology, and delivering peace of mind to our clients. Our consistent, unequaled level of service gives our clients confidence that their financial affairs are handled with the highest level of competency. Our team experience promotes forward thinking, creativity, and open communication. Our office exhibits an atmosphere of enthusiasm and optimism, confirming our position as an integral part of a premier financial services firm. Advisors and staff experience the rewards created by superior team results. By achieving our mission, we have earned the respect and admiration of the financial community.

There is a difference between the way things are and the way you want them to be. It is this discrepancy that creates the drive and energy needed to initiate new and better ideas. This process can break down in two ways: first, if you are not clear on the way you want it to be, and second, if you are not clear on the way things are.

A perfect example of the power of vision can be seen in this story. Midway through my grandson Zach's senior year in high school, his grades were deplorable. After attempting to explain to him for the hundredth time why his grades were important, I walked him into our home office and asked him to Google "girls of Bellevue Community College." He found pictures of a volleyball team, a softball team, girls playing a board game, and several instructors. Then I asked him to Google "girls of Arizona State University." I then asked Zach "where do you want to go to school?" Zach is attending Arizona State University.

The Charle Young Story   At the end of the 1982 season, I moved with my head coach, Chuck Knox, from the Buffalo Bills to the Seattle Seahawks. In their first seven years as an NFL franchise, the Seahawks had just two winning seasons, so it was a big deal when we took the team to the 1983 AFC Championship game. We ended that season losing to the eventual Super Bowl champions, the Los Angeles Raiders. A lot of our success was attributed to Curt Warner, the outstanding rookie running back from Penn State University.

Coming off that magical season, the Seahawks and the Seattle community had high expectations for the 1984 season. In addition to Warner, David Krieg had established himself as an opportunistic quarterback. The future Hall of Fame wide receiver, Steve Largent, was still in his prime, and safety Kenny Easley had become one of the most dominant defensive players in the league. But everyone knew it was Curt Warner who had made the difference.

In spite of the high expectations, we had played three preseason games and the team was still sloppin' around, playing anything but inspired football. The night before our fourth and final preseason game, Chuck Knox was putting the finishing touches on our game plan during a team meeting when Charle Young asked if he could speak to the squad. Charle was winding down an illustrious career in the NFL and had been a major contributor to the San Francisco 49ers' Super Bowl XVI championship season before joining us in Seattle.

Charle said to the team, "I want you to know what it is like to win a Super Bowl championship." He went on to describe his experience of going into the locker room after winning the Super Bowl. He talked about the "hoopin' and hollerin'," the slapping of shoulder pads and helmets, the pounding on lockers, and the ripping sound as the offensive and defensive linemen pulled their jerseys off one another's shoulder pads. In the NFL there is so much holding that linemen put two-way carpet tape on their shoulder pads to keep their jerseys glued to their pads, thereby reducing holding dramatically. At the end of the game, when the jerseys come off, it sounds like carpet being torn off the floor.

Charle went on to tell of players with tears rolling down their cheeks and of a group kneeling in a corner giving thanks. He described the presentation of the trophy to Edward DeBartolo, the 49ers' owner, and Bill Walsh, the head coach. With rich imagery, Charle painted a picture of his team celebrating their dream come true.

Then he reached into his pocket, pulled out his Super Bowl ring, and passed it to a player sitting in the front row. With its inscriptions, mounds of diamonds, and pure mass, it was ridiculous, yet every player wanted one. They began to pass the ring around, some slipping it on, while others just checked it out closely. Everyone was thinking how it would feel to have his own.

While the ring was being passed from player to player, Charle spoke of the Seahawks' success of the previous season and of the high-impact players on the team. He pointed out the similarities between this team and his Super Bowl team. Players began to chime in and voice their support for the goal until it was evident to all that the entire team not only believed they were capable of winning a Super Bowl championship, but were willing to commit themselves fully to this vision and quest.

In spite of losing Curt Warner to a knee injury during the first game of the regular season, this team went on to win a club record of 12 regular season games. Though we came up short of winning a Super Bowl championship, the goal had inspired the team to realize a great deal more of their potential. Goals don't always ensure success—they simply increase the likelihood of it.

Keeping Your Dream Alive

> The teams we investigated that accomplished truly remark-
> able things—or that functioned unusually well in more routine
> activities—were always characterized by genuine dedication to
> the goal and a willingness to expend extraordinary amounts of
> energy to achieve it.
>
> —Carl Larson and Frank LaFasto, *TeamWork:*
> *What Must Go Right/What Can Go Wrong*

Once you have created your vision, it is important to keep it
alive. It can be incorporated in screen savers or made an agenda
item for team meetings. The goals can be put on United Way–type
thermometers and the guiding principles can be posted in the coffee
room. The vivid description can be made into a mock trade journal
article and posted on the bulletin board. All of the vision components
should be revisited at least quarterly. Out of sight, out of mind:
Without leadership paying attention to keeping the dream alive,
it can fade over time.

When I worked in downtown Seattle, to come home in the
evening, I would drive over the I-90 bridge, turn south on I-405,
and exit at Coal Creek Parkway on my way to our home in Newport
Shores. During construction, the floating bridge across Lake Washington filled with water and sank. Did I get home that night? Of
course I did. I just changed my route and went over the 520 bridge.
If my path across the lake had been blocked at both bridges I could
have gone north or south around the lake. The point is that I would
have made it home, no matter what.

Your vision should be this important to your team. It will be your
homing device. You might have to change your course and make
adjustments to your strategies along the way. As long as you keep
the vision alive, you will be able to overcome the challenges that will
inevitably arise.

Decisions

Your insight into creating a compelling vision has prepared you to
make the following critical business decisions.

Determining Your Purpose

Determining your purpose should be a team exercise. Participation
will lead to a greater sense of ownership and commitment. The

insight gained by participating in the process will assist team members in selecting more effective strategies to serve their purpose. When it comes to business planning, people want to dot the I's and cross the T's before they move to the next component of the plan. Good planning doesn't happen that way—it is iterative. As you move downstream, you will discover things that impact your thinking on topics you have already covered. This is normal. Simply iterate and move on.

- *What is the purpose of your advisory team?*

Determining Your Business Goals

Determining your business goals (mission, fiscal-year unifying goals, and strategic objectives) should also be a team exercise. Participation will lead to a greater sense of ownership and commitment. More importantly, the insight gained in the debate as to what the goals should be will help the team discover more effective strategies.

- *What is your five-year mission?*
- *What are your fiscal-year unifying goals?*
- *What are your strategic objectives?*

Reminder: Good planning happens in an iterative way. As you move downstream and into strategies, you will discover things that will impact your team goals. Continue to iterate.

Determining Your Guiding Principles

Determining your guiding principles should be a team exercise. Participation will lead to a greater sense of ownership, commitment, and empowerment. More importantly, the insight gained from a team exercise will help team members discover more effective strategies which will be aligned with your goals and guiding principles.

- *What are your guiding principles?*

Determining Your Vivid Description

Determining a vivid description should be a creative team exercise. The team should write a narrative of the business success you intend to create—the client experience, the team experience, and the business results.

- *What is the narrative of the business success you intend to create?*

Determining How You Plan to Keep the Dream Alive

Figure 1.5 is an example of a one-page vision document that you can adapt as you begin to think about the process of creating one for your business. Being able to synthesize your thinking about your vision and documenting it will force clarity and prioritization. It will give you a tool that can be used to help keep your dream alive.

- *What is your plan to keep your dream alive?*

Purpose Statement: Provide our clients with financial peace of mind.			
2015 Mission			**Fiscal-Year Unifying Goal**
Recurring revenue	$1.2 MM		$750,000
Recurring revenue per client	$7,500		$5,000
Fiscal-Year 2009 Strategic Objectives			
Disengage	85	"D" clients	
Re-engage	35	"A" clients with wealth management	
Add	10	Clients	At least $7,500 annual revenue each
Guiding Principles			
• Do great things for clients and make sure they know about it.			
• Make and keep meaningful commitments			
Vivid Description			
We are a nationally recognized, award-winning wealth management firm, whose competitive advantage is based upon state-of-the-art technology, personalized client service, and delivering peace of mind to our clients. Our consistent, unequalled level of service gives our clients confidence that their financial affairs are handled with the highest level of competency. Our team experience promotes forward thinking, creativity and open communication. Our office exhibits an atmosphere of enthusiasm and optimism, confirming our position as an integral part of a premier financial services firm. Advisors and staff experience the rewards created by superior team results. By achieving our mission, we have earned the respect and admiration of the financial community.			

Figure 1.5   One-Page Vision Document

Actions

> The leader has a clear idea of what he wants to do—professionally
> and personally—and the strength to persist in the face of set-
> backs, even failures.
>
> —Warren Bennis, *On Becoming a Leader*

After gaining insight and making decisions, it is time to take
action. The following provides a framework for you to s*tart living
your dream.*

By taking the time to craft your purpose, mission, fiscal-year unifying goals, supporting strategic objectives, guiding principles, and a
vivid description of your future success, you can begin to align your
team to deliver even more value to your clients. By implementing a
rigorous feedback process, you will experience the benefits of a high-
performance team that is aligned, motivated, and nimble enough to
correct course when appropriate.

Establishing your vision is about clarifying the way you want things
to be in the long term and supporting that image with the steps to
get there. Use the example shown in Figure 1.6 and identify the
necessary steps to create your compelling vision. The steps should
be binary, meaning they can be tracked as having been done or
not done. There should be just one owner for each of the steps.
Others will contribute but there needs to be a single accountability
for the completion of each step. In *Getting Things Done*, author David
Allen writes, "When a culture adopts 'What's the next action?' as a

Milestones	Owner	Date	√
1. Assemble the necessary data for goal setting.			
2. Create your team's purpose.			
3. Develop your five-year mission and one-year unifying goals.			
4. Determine your supporting strategic objectives.			
5. Gain consensus on your guiding principles.			
6. Compose the vivid description of your success.			
7. Create your one-page vision document.			
8. Define process for keeping the dream alive.			
9. Implement processes for keeping the vision alive.			
10. Develop goal feedback process.			

Figure 1.6   Action Plan for Creating a Compelling Vision

standard operating query, there's an automatic increase in energy, productivity, creativity, and focus."

A caution needs to be made regarding time frames. The number one way you build the collective efficacy of a team is to say you are going to do something and do it. The number one way to erode the collective efficacy of a team is to say you are going to do something and not do it. It is vitally important to set realistic time frames so you can be successful and build your team's collective power to produce the desired effect.

By developing your vision, you will create a discrepancy between what you want and what you have. The origin of a team's sustained effort is the need to reduce the discrepancy between the vision and current reality. A compelling vision causes team members to persist and expend effort over time. Persistence can be the factor that determines whether your advisory team experiences the sweet taste of success or the bitter pill of defeat. The tenacity seen in winning advisory teams is partly the result of a compelling vision. Over the next six chapters we will add business disciplines designed to bring your vision into reality and make your dream come true. Figure 1.7 provides a framework for this process.

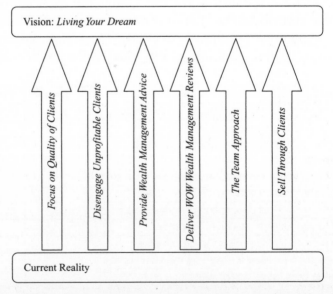

Figure 1.7   Framework to Move from Current Reality to Your Vision

Chapter Summary

Key Points

- As advisors begin careers, they tend to view themselves as financial representatives working for a platform, broker-dealer, bank, insurance company, or firm. It doesn't take long for them to develop the ineffective habit of living someone else's dream and playing the role envisioned for them. At a certain point, many feel trapped by the status quo and want more. They want more financial security for their families. They want more work-life balance. They want to feel more like they are doing worthwhile work. They want to have more pride in the businesses they are building. They want more, but they have been living someone else's dream for so long that it is difficult to imagine doing anything other than the status quo. The discipline of creating your dream is a process of envisioning the advisory business you truly desire.

- Creating a compelling vision provides you with the opportunity to design your future. By thinking deeply about what you want, you can determine the worthwhile work you do, the business model that supports your ambitions, the quality of clients you work with, the type of team you build, and the business results you drive. Creating your dream starts by deciding what you truly desire rather than accepting someone else's dream. You determine your future by the vision you create, the decisions you make, and the actions you take.

- Purpose
    - The primary reason for the work you do.

- Business Goals
    - Objectives that support your purpose.

- Mission
    - One or two compelling goals you plan to achieve over the next five years.

- Fiscal-Year Unifying Goals
    - One or two most critical goals you plan to achieve over the next fiscal year.

Strategic Objectives

- Three to five implementation objectives. If the strategy is correct, achieving these goals will likely lead to achieving your fiscal-year unifying goals and ultimately to "mission accomplished."
- Goals improve team performance because they help team members:
  - Create alignment.
  - Provide the context to determine strategies and tactics.
  - Provide the information needed for course correction.
  - Spend their time on their best opportunities.
  - Elevate team effort and persistence—the most important ingredient for success.
  - Be more interested in their work.
  - Be more aware of opportunities and threats.
  - Activate their problem-solving skills.
  - Access their stored knowledge.
  - Perform more consistently.
- Effective goals:
  - Are aligned to the team's purpose.
  - Are focused on growth and building a higher-quality client base.
  - Are stated as specific numbers (metrics), free of ambiguity.
  - Allow for regular and ongoing feedback.
  - Have a deadline that creates a sense of urgency.
  - Are developed by the team.
  - Are challenging yet realistic: data to make informed decisions.
  - Are within the team's control.
  - Are beneficial to team members.
- Guiding principles—the fundamental standards that guide daily decisions:
  - Provide the cornerstones of empowerment.
  - Provide the guidance for team members to make decisions in a consistent manner.
  - Are timeless. They should be highly valued regardless of the changes in your team or your industry.
  - Must be promoted until they become part of the team culture.
- Characteristics of effective guiding principles:
  - Useful in decision-making criteria in nonstructured situations.
  - Ethical and ensure long-term success.
  - Clearly understood by the team.
  - Meaningful to team members.
  - Ranked.

- Vivid Description
  - A narrative of the business success you intend to create.
  - By implementing a rigorous feedback process, you will experience the benefits of a high-performance team that is aligned, motivated, and nimble enough to correct course when appropriate.

CHAPTER

2

Stop Focusing on Quantity of Clients and Start Focusing on Quality of Clients

The Second Ineffective Habit: Focusing on Quantity of Clients

Jack's parents were incredibly supportive of their son as he began his career as a financial professional. Like most parents, they wanted their son to be successful. They purchased long-term care insurance from Jack, and after making him fight for it, moved the fixed-income portion of their investments to a solution he could provide.

They also directed Jack to family friends they knew would be willing to have conversations with him. Jack couldn't have cared less about the size of these opportunities. He was following his Kaizen Sales System principle of focusing on the quantity of clients. "Six hundred clients will make you bulletproof," his manager said when presenting the principle "Focus on Quantity." Six hundred was the number of clients needed to ensure your long-term success in the firm. That meant selling to anyone who could fog a mirror. Jack had heard it sarcastically described as "spray and pray," but he didn't care. He was going to be one of the few who made it in this business and he was going to stay true to the Kaizen Sales System principle of focus on quantity.

Jack's dad was a senior partner of an engineering firm and found it easy to introduce Jack to the other members of the leadership team. Over the next six months, eight lunches produced three insurance clients and a token investment opportunity. And then something really good happened. Two of the up-and-comers on the leadership team (both Jack's insurance clients) broke away to set up their own firm, taking some staff and clients with them. The growth of the new firm and their referrals to other young professionals created a nice niche for Jack. He was able to sell these young professionals life insurance and help them begin to put their retirement and college funding plans in place. This was the best sales opportunity Jack had going.

Midway through his third year, Jack's peers were dropping like flies. Eight of the 12 who had started around the same time as Jack had already cleaned out their offices. He had heard that just 15 to 20 percent actually survive the first five years, but it hadn't hit home until now. But there was a silver lining in this storm cloud: All of the clients of the dearly departed were being parceled out. Of course, the veterans were given the potential rubies. The other orphaned accounts were given to Jack and the other survivors to cross-sell. This played right into his strategy of focusing on quantity. They all counted in his quest to reach 600 clients and become bulletproof.

Mopping up after the dearly departed did produce some cross-selling opportunities. It was only nickel and dime stuff, but quantity, not quality, was the magic of the Kaizen Sales System. It also connected Jack to a network beyond his own family and friends. By combining these opportunities with an occasional sale from someone he met at Kiwanis or the Chamber of Commerce, or from the start-up engineering firm, he was beginning to have a bigger footprint and his business was growing at a good rate. Jack blew through his fifth year, hardly pausing to celebrate this significant milestone; there were just two out of his class left standing.

By his fifteenth year, the activity level was higher than it had ever been. From an outsider's point of view, Jack was a success. From Jack's point of view, it was just okay. In the Kaizen Sales System training, Jack's manager used the metaphor, "If you cast a broader net, you catch more fish." Asking clients for referrals and then asking the referrals for referrals would create more opportunities. What wasn't made clear was that you would also be catching a lot of snails, slugs, garfish, and sucker clients.

Every January, Jack did a business-planning math exercise. He started with the amount of money he needed to survive. Next, he subtracted the small amount of recurring revenue his existing clients produced. Then he took the average revenue per transaction sale and applied the Kaizen Sales System formula of 10-3-1: Ten leads would produce three appointments, and one appointment would result in a sale of some sort. This year the number of leads he would need was enormous! How could he ever get off of this treadmill?

One of the theories behind focusing on quantity of clients was the law of large numbers. Within a large number of clients you will find a percentage of quality clients. But so far, this principle had produced just one semi-affluent or high-net-worth client per year for Jack.

Focusing on the quantity of clients wasn't good enough. Jack wanted more.

The Second Discipline: Start Focusing on Quality of Clients

The discipline of focusing on quality clients allows you to acquire 6 to 12 per year. Quality clients are those who have complex financial needs and an asset base to generate superior revenue results. By building a high-quality client base you will experience the financial and intrinsic rewards as your clients refer their friends and colleagues to you.

> In the long run, winning companies are ones that are most fo-cused. Losing companies are ones that are the least focused. The guiding principle, the one that should drive your company's every decision is the principle of focus.
>
> —Al Ries, *Focus*

Strategic focus, as demonstrated in Figure 2.1, consists of your target market and the services you intend to bring to that market. Targeting a high-net-worth segment of the marketplace and delivering services that will satisfy their needs is how you begin to build a quality client base. This is your strategic focus and where you should be concentrating your time, money, and other resources.

Insights

The first aspect of strategic focus is your target market. This is the client segment where you intend to deliver your services. It consists

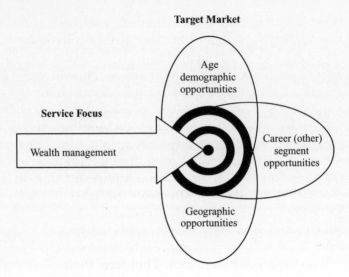

Figure 2.1   Strategic Focus

of the client type (based on career or other groupings), age, and geography. The segment you choose within these opportunities defines your target market.

Target Market

I have consulted for a wide variety of companies. They have varied in size, industry, and location. After a while, I decided to focus solely on best-of-kind companies in the Puget Sound region. This led to consulting work with U.S. Bank's Pacific Northwest leadership team. We worked well together and I was happy to earn a decent consulting fee as I helped guide their strategic and operational planning processes.

A breakthrough opportunity came my way when I got my foot in the door at Microsoft. I went from a decent consulting fee to multiples of that fee while doing similar work. The key is to deliver value to someone who can afford to pay you well. Microsoft understood my value. I rolled up my sleeves and worked on a number of breakthrough projects for the next 10 years. In the beginning I didn't have domain knowledge of the software industry or any inside knowledge of Microsoft. I chuckle when I look back because I went into my first planning session with transparencies, because I didn't know PowerPoint and at the time could barely type.

My first meeting included a Microsoft executive and 10 of his direct reports. Eight of the 10 became vice presidents or held key positions at Microsoft. In their climb up the Microsoft corporate ladder they brought me along with them. I assimilated their language and culture along the way and, by adding value with my insight, was able to build my consulting business around this one relationship. I even learned to type and they taught me how to work pretty darn well with PowerPoint. The people were bright and committed and the business challenges were complex—fun stuff. By focusing on Microsoft I was able to develop domain knowledge that was hard to match. Over time I became a Microsoft specialist and added more and more value to their teams. Microsoft compensated me well and the word-of-mouth viral marketing was spectacular.

There are two ways advisors approach their marketplace. The vast majority tend to be product driven. They have their quiver of arrows (product and service offerings) and they wander out into the marketplace and shoot at any need they can find. It was Abraham Maslow who said, "If the only tool you have is a hammer then the whole world looks like a nail." These advisors just keep hammering at any nail they can find—framing nails, cement nails, drywall nails, decking nails, and many rusty and bent nails. Because their efforts are so scattered, they remain generalists rather than becoming specialists.

A much smaller group of advisors is market driven. They identify a market, develop a deep understanding of the market's needs, and then build the competencies required to address those needs. They become market specialists. Who earns more, a generalist or a specialist? Specialists, of course, and it all begins with defining your target market. By determining the clients who have the greatest needs for your team's services and can afford to pay you a reasonable fee, you will be able to narrow your scope and focus your resources to maximize your market impact. Without this focus, you will run the risk of spreading resources so thin that your efforts have much less impact than desired.

Both quantity and quality matter when you are trying to identify exciting revenue opportunities. Which business would you rather have: a practice with 100 clients generating $1 million, or a practice with 500 clients generating $1 million? You are right again! This is an easy question to answer when you consider the cost to serve a larger client base. But most advisors are trapped by focusing on quantity. They pay little attention to the cost of service and the quality of the client base.

The difference between client fees and the cost of service is your profit. Across a client base, the cost of service is not proportional to the fee. On a percentage basis, there is a significantly higher cost of service for a small client than there is for a high-net-worth client. We will look closely at the cost of service in Chapter 3. But the quest for profit (income beyond a reasonable salary) is why the recurring revenue per client (quality measure) is important.

There are a variety of ways to segment a market. The key is for you to select a segmentation scheme that allows you to effectively target the portion of the market that provides an exciting revenue opportunity and has a service gap that you can satisfy. Advisors have had success targeting a market that is defined by the overlap of three segments: client type, age, and geographic location.

Client Type   When you look at your business, what are the segments you see? What are the client types? The best practice is to segment them by their professions—attorneys, business owners, accountants, or their affiliation with similar others—and/or by their membership in country clubs, churches, or Rotary. There are four questions to ask when evaluating client-type opportunities.

1. *Does the client segment offer an exciting financial opportunity?*

> The Wisdom of the Hive: it sends out scouts in many different directions and trusts that at least one of them will find the best patch, return, and do a good dance so that the hive will know where the food source is.
> —James Surowiecki, *The Wisdom of Crowds*

Begin by taking a fact-based approach. More than likely, your current client base will point the way to attractive opportunities. Create a list of clients and the annual recurring or fee-based revenue that each generates. I use recurring fee-based revenue to analyze a business because it is worth multiples of transaction-based revenue. Throughout this book, when I refer to revenue I am speaking of recurring revenue. Rank your client list (by household) from your highest to lowest revenue generators.

List the number of clients, revenue, and revenue per client for each segment. Also list the segment's rank order

Table 2.1   Client Segment Analysis

Segment	Number	Revenue	Rank	Revenue per Client	Rank
1. Teachers	101	$114,534	5	$1,134	10
2. Swedish Hospital administrators	40	$142,400	3	$3,560	7
3. Construction (employee)	32	$56,712	7	$1,741	9
4. Engineer (employee)	27	$176,580	2	$6,540	2
5. Microsoft Management	25	$201,850	1	$8,074	1
6. Swedish Hospital physicians	21	$122,178	4	$5,818	4
7. Entrepreneur—retail	17	$54,757	8	$3,221	8
8. Entrepreneur—white collar	11	$57,222	6	$5,202	5
9. Entrepreneur—blue collar	8	$34,024	10	$4,253	6
10. Architect (employee)	7	$40,229	9	$5,747	3

in each category. Table 2.1 provides a hypothetical sample based on opportunities near my home in Seattle. Begin to take a fact-based approach to gain insight into your current business and it will highlight your exciting financial opportunities. Then plot each segment based on its rankings—revenue and revenue per client—as shown in Figure 2.2. In this example, the Microsoft Management segment, Engineers, and

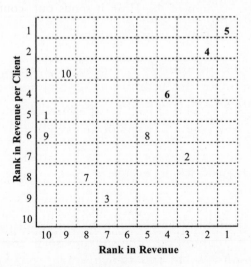

Figure 2.2   Client Revenue Analysis

Swedish Hospital physicians rise above the rest and warrant a closer look.

The Microsoft management segment ranks number one in both revenue and revenue per client. When you consider that the cost of service for firms with revenue between $500,000 and $1 million is $2,100 or more per year (more about this in Chapter 3), this segment's $8,074 per client should produce a reasonable profit margin. With approximately 30,000 employees and 3,000 managers in the Seattle area, the overall revenue opportunity is excellent.

The engineer segment ranks number two in both revenue and revenue per client. The $6,540 revenue per client would produce a good, not great, profit margin. Worldsalaries.org lists physicians, dentists, and engineers at the upper end of the salary scale. A zapdata.com search produced 670 engineering firms in the greater Seattle area with 1 to 49 employees each. This segment would be large enough to keep a wealth management firm fully engaged and provide a good financial opportunity. The Internet offers resources to do helpful market research. You will be much more committed to a market when you know how big it is.

The Swedish Hospital physicians rank fourth in revenue and revenue per client. A phone call to the hospital confirmed that it has more than 1,400 physicians—large enough for 20 wealth managers to build their business around. Their $5,818 revenue per client would produce an above-average profit margin.

2. *Does the client segment offer an exciting viral marketing opportunity?*

Most often the acquisition of high-net-worth clients is the result of referrals from existing clients. This viral marketing requires a community to spread the virus. A company aligned behind "a computer on every desk and in every home, running Microsoft software" assures such a community. Microsoft provides an excellent environment to create viral marketing.

To a slightly lesser degree the Swedish Hospital physicians have a community. The hospital brings the physicians together around a common purpose. As they serve this purpose, they share resources and experience similar risks and challenges. The stronger the community, the stronger the potential for viral marketing. Swedish Hospital physicians would provide a good opportunity.

The engineer segment does not have the same sense of community that Microsoft or the physicians do. Though they are all engineers and do similar work, their businesses are not unified behind a single purpose or mission. They work out of different locations and their own small companies are more important to them than the purpose of engineering. This segment would provide only a modest viral marketing opportunity.

3. *Would this segment be rewarding and enjoyable to work with?*

You can deliver value and make a nice living for a while focused on any particular audience. If you want to sustain a long career, you'd better enjoy the client base and feel well rewarded for your work. You can fake your enjoyment for a while but, in the long run, people know whether you like what you are doing. Working with a segment you do not enjoy is exhausting and not sustainable. When you perform this exercise you will know your clients and will be able to make a subjective evaluation as to whether you would enjoy working with more of them.

4. *Do you have or could you develop the competencies to* WOW *the segment?*

As I mentioned in the Introduction, good planning happens iteratively. You may not be able to answer this question yet. The service model information covered later should provide you the necessary insight.

Age and Geographic Focus

Today's 55+ . . . are just 30 percent of the population, yet control 70 percent of all of the wealth.
> —Ken Dychtwald and Daniel Kadlec, *The Power Years*

Now that you have decided your client segment by type, you can become laser focused by segmenting the client type by age and geography.

The Figure 2.3 shows that the top 20 percent of the 50-plus age group has the assets necessary to provide an exciting financial opportunity. In comparison, only 5 percent of the 30- to 39-year-olds

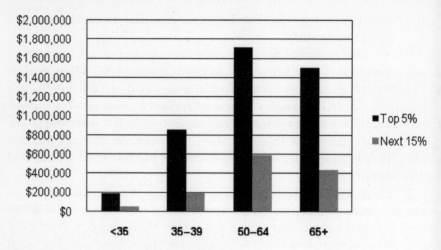

Figure 2.3   Investable Assets by Age
Source: RIA's retirement typology 10/06.

are marginally interesting. If you are truly looking for an exciting revenue opportunity, you should target and optimize for people over 50 years old within your targeted client segment.

An example of creating a subsegment by age goes back to the Swedish Hospital physicians evaluation. There are many younger doctors who are still paying off the cost of their education. Targeting the 50-year-old and older physicians would turn an above-average financial opportunity into an exciting one.

In addition to age, segments should also be evaluated and scoped by geography. Who would get better traction—an advisor focused on business executives age 50 and older in Phoenix or in Old Town Scottsdale? From countless observations, my answer is the advisor who is focused in Old Town Scottsdale. Where would your office be? What Rotary would you join? How would you dress? What periodicals would you read? Do you think you would have face and name recognition in the community? Do you think you could develop viral marketing?

The more concentrated your geographic focus, the more likely you will be to generate awareness within the market. Be mindful of how your geographic reach impacts your service delivery. Many advisors will take on a geographic region that is too large and spend too much time traveling to see prospects when their time would be better spent focusing on local clients. Remember, time is always your most precious resource.

There are some exceptions when considering geographic focus. I know an advisor who was very successful working with airline pilots. They flew all over, but he made his home in one of their hubs to have more physical access to them. Another advisor I know focused his energy on very high-net-worth clients affiliated with a hunting lodge in Canada. These clients lived all over the world but came together at the lodge, and that's where this advisor worked with them.

Service Focus

The second aspect of strategic focus is your service focus. Once you have identified your target market, you need to determine what you will provide in order to satisfy their needs. Client needs and fine-tuning your service model to meet those needs are discussed in detail in Chapters 3 and 4. In the interim, I recommend that you consider providing wealth management advice, and here is why.

Wealth management focuses on financial goals that require planning, money, time, and the ongoing coordination of a client's financial ecosystem. I am not talking about the type of wealth management service provided by a family office. I am talking about wealth management lite, where the advisor coordinates the financial ecosystem, manages the investments, and perhaps the insurance needs. The other services are delivered via a virtual team of suppliers from your community.

In addition to client needs, competitive differentiation, financial rewards, and other industry trends all point to why you should consider wealth management. Let's begin by looking at how you can create competitive differentiation.

Competitive Differentiation

In *The Art of War*, the ancient Chinese general Sun Tzu wrote, "If you know the enemy and know yourself, you need not fear the result of a hundred battles. If you know yourself but not the enemy, for every victory gained you will also suffer a defeat. If you know neither the enemy nor yourself, you will succumb in every battle." And yet it is rare to find an advisor who has gained the necessary insight to build differentiating strategies and organizational competencies to win the market-share war. Because others are not benefiting from studying their competitive environment, you can gain significant competitive advantage by doing so.

A competitive analysis, understanding your strengths and weaknesses relative to your competition, can provide valuable insight into your ability to compete within your target market. Because every competitive environment is unique, I can only provide you with examples to consider and the process for conducting your own competitive analysis.

The first aspect of your competitive analysis needs to begin by thinking about the following two questions:

1. Where are your competitors winning?
2. Which competitor best represents that competitive advantage?

By recognizing the specific advantages of your competition you can identify service strategies that need to be improved. By calling out specific competitors you will identify the key attributes of their service that are differentiators. Table 2.2 gives you examples of these.

After analyzing how each of the competitive advantages is utilized by the competition, wealth managers have had success in employing two tactics.

Me, Too, Plus a Few   The first strategy consists of copying (or, if you prefer, creative swiping) the competitive advantage and adding new components to it. This was a prominent tactic used in the dot-com era. Because the competition is committed to their way of doing it, it could be several years before they realize that you have leapfrogged them.

I asked Bill Walsh, the San Francisco 49ers Hall of Fame coach, if he studied the best teams in the NFL intending to steal best practices.

Table 2.2   Competitor Advantages

Where Are Your Competitors Winning?	Competitor
Financial planning	ABC Wealth Management
Investment management	XYZ Investments
Systems to deliver wealth management	ABC Advisors
In-house network of wealth management suppliers	XYZ Wealth Management

He told me that for years he had studied the game film of the best teams but had gotten away from this practice because, he said, "If there is something to be invented I want to invent it and I don't want to be over influenced by what others are doing." However, until you are performing at a Hall of Fame level, I suggest that creative swiping is an effective strategy.

How can you use the "me, too, plus a few" strategy to leapfrog the competition?

Get Creative   If you do not have the resources or competencies to compete head-to-head with the competition, you can lock onto the goal and get creative about the strategy to get there. A competitor's staff may have the ability to deliver comprehensive wealth management. In addition to financial planning and investment counseling, services might include legacy planning, bill paying, insurance, trust services, and so forth. Your firm may not be able to provide these services directly, but you can leapfrog your competition by leveraging an expert team of suppliers from the community. This virtual team of specialists can provide the same competencies at a higher level of service than the competition.

Where will it be necessary to lock onto the goal and get creative about the strategy? Table 2.3 shows the second aspect of the competitive analysis. Here you will identify the competencies, attributes, or services that are your competitive advantages. You will gain clarity about which aspects you should continue to leverage in your service delivery. Think about the following question: What are your competitive strengths and how can they be better leveraged to service clients and create demand for your services? Many of the winning advisors I have worked with have been exceptionally creative in how they have leveraged their competitive strengths to take their business to the next level of competitive differentiation.

Creating Differentiation   Delivering wealth management will allow you to differentiate yourself from 95 percent of your competitors. You have to be good and different. The Rolling Stones are good and different. *Mamma Mia!* (the play or the movie) is good and different. The best restaurant in your town is good and different.

There are four ways to be good and different in your delivery of wealth management. First, you can create differentiation by taking a consultative approach to help clients clarify their financial vision. A

Table 2.3   Competitive Advantages

What are Your Competitive Advantages?	How Can They be Better Leveraged to Service Clients and Create Demand for Your Services?
Being independent allows you to be more objective.	Do great things for clients and make sure they know about it. Let clients know your objectivity and the solutions available to help the client achieve their goals.
We cross-sell opportunities with our CPA firm (this assumes the advisor is affiliated with a CPA firm).	Use our customer satisfaction survey results to provide the proof point that we are the CPA firm's valued partner.
We use a total wealth management service model and offer a financial planning background of principles.	Communicate that we know what you need because we are baby boomer specialists. This is a foundational service required for the baby boomers that are nearing retirement.
We have 72 high net-worth clients.	Create viral marketing campaign—sell through our existing client base to other high net-worth clients.

2007 survey from *Best Practices of Elite Advisors: Wealth Management Edge* found, after interviewing 2,094 advisors, that fewer than 7 percent used a consultative approach. Imagine separating yourself from 93 percent of your competitors simply by taking a consultative approach as you help your clients create their financial vision.

Second, you can create differentiation by coordinating the client's financial ecosystem to achieve their vision and goals. Figure 2.4 creates a visual representation of a sample financial ecosystem. I use this galaxy to convey that all aspects of a couple's financial ecosystem are interconnected. At the center of the system is the couple's vision, what they hope to accomplish that will require planning, money, and time. The components (asset protection, retirement planning, investment strategy, tax strategies, charitable giving, wealth transfer, life insurance, spending plans, education planning, business succession planning, etc.) must be orchestrated to make the financial vision a reality. In *The Fifth Discipline*, Peter Senge wrote that in a system, "cause and effect are far removed in space and time." This coordination can bring valuable peace of mind to the client.

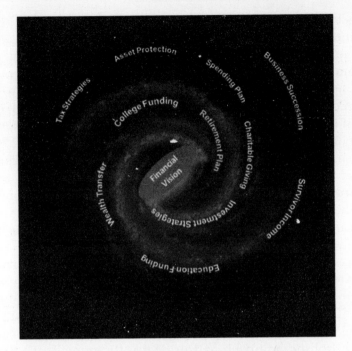

Figure 2.4   Financial Ecosystem

Consider this example of what life is like when professionals whom you rely on do not coordinate their efforts. I woke up after surgery from my first knee replacement and found that my knee was already being mechanically flexed. Shortly after, an internist came in and explained that while I was in surgery I experienced some atrial fibrillation. Apparently it's not a big deal if you're on blood thinners, but if you've never had any issues with your heart and you get that message, you're concerned. A little later, my orthopedic surgeon came in and asked, "How's the knee?" He explained that the surgery went well and there were no problems. I said, "Okay, glad to hear it, but what about the ticker?" He waved me off as he left my room, saying, "I don't have anything to do with that."

I wanted to know about my heart condition and the need for blood thinners. I couldn't reach my primary care physician. I located a cardiologist but he could not see me until the next day. There I was, still a bit foggy from the anesthesia and painkillers, trying to orchestrate all these silos by myself. Later, it dawned on me that this is the experience many people have with their financial professionals—investment guy, tax guy, insurance guy, estate attorney, and so on. People are trying to orchestrate it themselves, and the consequences of not doing it correctly can be severe.

Something you do today, an aspect of your financial ecosystem, could have a ripple effect years later in a different area. Part of my financial vision was to put away enough for my grandson's education. What if I hadn't? What would I do? Perhaps I would have taken a second mortgage on my house. How would that affect my retirement? There are infinite possibilities that can have delayed consequences. Financial peace of mind doesn't come from dealing with issues as if they are disconnected. The most satisfied clients are the ones who trust that the moving parts of their financial life are being orchestrated and cared for in a way that takes into consideration the impact on the whole.

As a wealth manager, you can step into this valuable role and generate confidence for your clients by making sure the components of their system work together to help them achieve their financial vision. These clients will likely have financial ecosystems with many interrelated variables. By becoming a wealth manager you can take a more holistic approach as you deal with your client's financial security, goals, and peace of mind.

The third way to differentiate yourself is to zero in on client needs. Effective teams deliver products and services that satisfy a client's precise needs. Any delivered product or service that does not precisely fit is a waste of resources.

The fourth thing you can do to create differentiation is to provide goals-based progress reports, not benchmark-focused performance reports. The primary purpose of reporting is to provide feedback on progress toward a goal. Whether it is a couple's vision of how they would like to live the next phase of their lives or funding a grandchild's college education, a dollar amount is necessary. The primary focus of wealth management should be on how to fund the vision, not how it competes against benchmarks. Wealth management views money as a means to realizing a vision.

Industry Trends Point to Wealth Management   Effective teams are aware of, and take advantage of, technological advances. Teams should consider the implications of these potentially revolutionary facts and make it their business to track the rapid technological advances that could impact the way they do business in the future.

Effective teams are aware of, and take advantage of, changes in government regulations. Recent changes in telecommunication laws allow long distance and cable companies to challenge local phone companies for service and allow for local phone companies to offer long distance service. What changes in government regulations could impact the way your team does business in the future?

Effective teams are aware of, and take advantage of, changes in their social environment. The aging wave of baby boomers nearing retirement has huge implications for teams in many industries, from clothing manufacturers preparing additional lines of leisure attire to funeral homes increasing their capacity. What changes in the social environment could impact the way your team does business in the future?

The best wealth management teams I have worked with can clearly articulate the four or five industry trends they expect will influence businesses, and they know how to turn each trend into an opportunity.

The wind can blow hard off of Lake Erie. It blows easterly, swooping over the left rim of Buffalo's Ralph Wilson Stadium, down to the field and then back up over the luxury suites on the right. It can swirl and have a modest impact on the outcome of a football game. You can't control the wind, but you can use it to your advantage—make it an opportunity.

I was the special teams coach for the Buffalo Bills in the early 1980s. In our pregame warm-up, as we prepared to play the New England Patriots, the wind was blowing hard. I figured we could create a wind tunnel if we opened the east-side tunnel door of the stadium when New England was kicking against the wind. I worked with our equipment managers and told them, on my signal, to open the doors. Thinking back about it, I do feel a little bad for the New England punter. On his first punt against the wind, the ball came off his foot nicely, but then the wind punted it right back at him. In a game with dozens of consequential plays, sometimes it's just one that can make a big difference. I used the wind to our advantage. We won the game and that's why I only feel a little bad.

> If a management team cannot clearly articulate the five or six fundamental industry trends that most threaten its firm's continued success, it is not in control of the firm's destiny.
> —Gary Hamel and C.K. Prahalad, *Competing for the Future*

The following are the four industry trends I hear about most frequently from advisors, along with how they plan to use them to their advantage.

1. Baby boomers are ideal for wealth management. There are 78 million baby boomers in the United States. In 2010, the oldest of these are turning 64 and on the cusp of retirement. Winning advisors are developing the competencies to address the needs of the wealthiest 20 percent of baby boomers over the age of 50. In *Boom Bust Echo: Profiting from the Demographic Shift in the 21st Century,* David Foot writes, "As they age, people's financial priorities change. They move from debt management to asset management." These folks have complex needs, the maturity to do long-term planning, and the resources to pay to have these needs met. Wealth managers will be compensated well for meeting the needs of these clients.

   Both the financial advisor and the wealth manager work their 40-plus hours per week. One works hard finding and opening new accounts, the other works hard bringing more value to a higher level of client. Wealth managers find that the more value they give, the more they get back. Table 2.4 shows the comparison between the average assets under management (AUM) and income for financial advisors and wealth managers. When you consider the need to create competitive differentiation, the industry trends, and the financial rewards, I hope you will strongly consider wealth management as your service focus.

2. Fees must be justified in a low-return environment. Over the long term, most advisors now anticipate investment returns lower than historical averages. When the returns are dull or down, the fee issue amps up. The solution to low returns and fee justification is the same. Winning advisors need to

Table 2.4   Financial Advisor versus Wealth Manager

	Financial Advisor	Wealth Manager
Average AUM	$308,000,000	$645,000,000
Average income	$279,000	$881,000

Source: 2007 "Best Practices of Elite Advisors: The Wealth Management Edge." A survey of 2,094 advisors with at least $50 million assets under management.

build competencies and service models to deliver wealth management that demonstrates value beyond investment performance. There are many ways to provide valuable insight and recommendations that impact a client's broad financial ecosystem. There are times when spending plans, tax strategies, or modifications to financial goals are more appropriate than an investment solution. Advisors are not casually developing competencies and incrementally migrating to wealth management, they are sprinting to this new service model.

3. Regulatory obligations will continue to grow. Advisors are unanimous in thinking that the regulatory environment is going to become more rigorous. With an increase in investor protection, advisors anticipate more audits, more fiduciary standards, commission reform, and death by disclosure. They also see an increase in the cost of compliance and errors and omission insurance. Winning advisors are quick to assimilate the new rules into their practices and view new requirements as an opportunity to create better processes. They see the changes as a way of distancing themselves from their less attentive competitors.

4. Technological advances are accelerating. The combination of fiber-optic cable, fourth-generation wireless technology, and cloud strategy (the big server in the sky) is very close to delivering on the promise of information and communication anytime, anywhere. Winning advisors embrace these changes and discover new ways to better serve their clients by leveraging technology. The best advisors I have observed stay on the leading edge, not the bleeding edge, of technological advances.

Today, leading advisors are integrating client relationship management (CRM) tools with performance reporting and financial planning to deliver better and more efficient service. They are using Web-based archival and backup capabilities to meet compliance standards in a paperless way. They are providing their clients online vaults and reporting. Unified managed account capability is making a wealth manager's ability to manage his client's ecosystem significantly easier. These advisors also utilize services like GoToMeeing or Live Meeting to stay connected with their out-of-town clients or those averse to coming into office meetings. Any of these could improve client service while reducing costs and preparation time.

Decisions

> Strategy means making clear-cut choices about how to compete.
> You cannot be everything to everybody, no matter what the size
> of your business or how deep its pockets.
>
> —Jack Welch, *Winning*

After gaining insight from the examples, one may conclude that the strategic focus would look like this:

- *Target market:* Physicians 50 and older affiliated with Swedish Hospital.
- *Service focus:* Wealth management.

If I were personally going to be in the advisory business, my target market would be attorneys 45 and older working in the Columbia Tower in Seattle, Washington. Eighty percent of all attorneys reside in North America. At one time there were more attorneys in the Columbia Tower than in all of Japan. Forty-five-year-old attorneys are partners, or very close to being partners, and have complex financial needs, so my service focus would be wealth management.

If this was my strategic focus, where would I office? The Columbia Tower, of course. Where would I have coffee in the morning? At Starbucks in the lobby of the Columbia Tower, of course. Do you think I would have face and name recognition? Do you think I would have access to these attorneys that others might not have? A similar scenario will be your reward by answering and taking action on the following questions:

- What should your strategic focus be?
- What should your target market be?
- What should your service focus be?

The Common Sense Principle

There will be opportunities that fall outside your strategic focus. I used to drag Carol to action movies and am now paying her back by going to see her chick flicks. My favorite so far is *Notting Hill*. In one scene Julia Roberts (playing the part of a movie star) says to Hugh Grant (playing her love interest), "I'm just a girl, standing in front of a boy, asking him to love her."

There are times when things pop up that you should probably jump on. If the opportunity is large enough, be willing to grab it and then get right back to your target market. The more traction you have within your target market, the more tantalizing the low-hanging fruit needs to be before reaching out to grab it.

A very successful advisory firm in Seattle has a target market of business executives within walking distance of their office and on Microsoft's campus. When they started their business there was a $5 million low-hanging-fruit opportunity in Portland. At the time, they traveled to that opportunity. Ask them if they would do it today and the answer would be "absolutely not!" They would say, "Why would I go to Portland when there are so many opportunities right outside my door?" The common sense principle can prevail until you are in the same position.

Actions

> Plans by their very nature are designed to promote inflexibility—
> they are meant to establish clear direction to impose stability on
> an organization.
>
> —Henry Mintzberg, Bruce Ahlstrand,
> Joseph Lampel, *Strategy Safari*

After gaining insight and making decisions, it is time to take action. Figure 2.5 provides a framework for you to begin to *start focusing on the quality of your clients.*

Milestones	Owner	Date	✓
Create a stack-ranked list of clients based on annual recurring revenue.			
Create a table of client segments with revenue and revenue per client.			
Plot segments on scattergram based on revenue and revenue per client.			
Analyze client segment opportunities—the four-question framework.			
Determine strategic focus—target market and service focus.			
Conduct a team competency gap analysis to evaluate service competencies.			
Create a development plan for the team to close the service competency gaps.			

Figure 2.5   Focus on Quality Clients Action Plan

Chapter Summary

Key Points

- Nearly all financial advisors begin their career focused on acquiring a quantity of clients. They begin selling to family and friends and then branch out and sell to anyone who can fog a mirror.
- Their focus on quantity creates a client base of many unprofitable or marginally profitable clients while adding just one to three high-net-worth clients per year.
- The large number of small clients most financial advisors have becomes all consuming and prevents them from creating a service model that would be attractive to high-net-worth clients.
- The discipline of focusing on a quality segment of the market will allow you to acquire 6 to 12 high-net-worth clients per year.
- Strategic focus consists of your target market and the services you intend to bring to that market. Targeting a high-net-worth segment of the market-place and delivering services that will satisfy the complex financial needs of that market is how you begin to build a quality client base.
- Your target market is the client segment where you intend to deliver your services. It consists of the client type (based on career or other groupings), age segment, and geographic location.
- An analysis of your current client base can provide valuable insight into potential target markets. Consider evaluating each client segment's opportunities by asking:
  - Does the client segment offer an exciting financial opportunity?
  - Does the client segment offer an exciting viral marketing opportunity?
  - Would this segment be rewarding and enjoyable to work with?
  - Do you have or could you develop the competencies to *wow* this segment?
- Evaluating the client segment opportunities by age is another important consideration. The wealthiest 20 percent of the 50-plus age group has the complex financial needs to satisfy and the assets necessary to provide an exciting financial opportunity.
- The more geographically concentrated your target market, the more likely you will be to benefit from word-of-mouth marketing.
- Once you have determined your target market, you should apply the common sense principle for opportunities that come your way that are outside of your target market. If an opportunity is large enough, be willing to grab it and then get back to your target market. The more traction you get within your target market, the more tantalizing the low-hanging fruit needs to be before reaching out to grab it.

- Wealth management advice lite focuses on financial goals that require planning, money, time, and the ongoing coordination of a client's financial ecosystem.
- You should strongly consider delivering wealth management advice to a high-net-worth target market because:
  - It will satisfy the complex financial needs of high-net-worth client segments.
  - There is a window of opportunity for you to create competitive differentiation.
  - Your competitors are migrating quickly to provide wealth management advice.
  - It will allow you to deliver more value than just market returns.
  - Technology is increasingly enabling advisors to present a holistic, integrated view of a client's financial ecosystem.
  - Because you will be delivering more value, you will earn more money in return.

CHAPTER 3

Stop Hoarding Unprofitable Clients and Start Disengaging Unprofitable Clients

The Third Ineffective Habit: Hoarding Unprofitable Clients

There were numerous business practices in Jack's firm that perpetuated the belief that there is not enough good stuff to go around. The Kaizen sales system principle of focusing on quantity was based on the belief that there were not enough quality clients in the marketplace to grow the business the way they would like. There were not enough corner or window offices to go around, so they went to the winners. The losers worked from cubicles. There was just one winner of the monthly sales contest. Everyone else lost. There was only so much time for the manager to spend with advisors. It had to go to the winners. At the end of the year, the top three producers would join the chairman on a week-long cruise. The losers would receive digital pictures from their so-called friends.

In such a win/lose environment it is not surprising that Jack developed a scarcity mentality. He felt compelled to make the scarcity decision not to set an asset minimum for clients. He believed, as did the firm, that there were not enough affluent clients in the marketplace for Jack to build a high-net-worth-only practice.

65

He had read about target marketing and had discussed it numerous times with other advisors, but he still made the scarcity decision not to have a target market. He held the fundamental belief that there would not be enough prospects in any one segment to sustain him.

When Jack made hiring decisions he would consider a candidate's experience, competencies, and whether they would work well with the team. But when it came down to making the call, he always made the scarcity decision to hire the candidate he could get for the smallest salary.

The lowest cost was the decision-making criterion that carried the most weight regardless of whether the decision was the purchase of a customer relationship management (CRM) system, training for the staff, or a ream of paper. Jack always made the scarcity decision. That is what you do when you think revenue will be scarce.

Jack's most costly scarcity decision came in his twelfth year as a financial advisor. That was the year his mentor decided to retire. Over the mentor's 38-year career he had acquired 737 clients and wanted to get a reasonable return for his efforts. He was realistic about how much he could get for a mostly transaction-based book of business and it would make things easy if Jack was interested.

He knew Jack didn't have the cash to buy his business outright and that the firm had stopped financing internal sales years ago. But the deal could come together if Jack would be willing to purchase it via a fee- and commission-sharing agreement. It would work if Jack would split the fees 50/50 with him for three years. That would give him a little retirement cushion and Jack would become bulletproof. It would be a real win-win!

Hoarding comes hand-in-glove with scarcity thinking. When you don't think there is enough to go around, you grab whatever you can and you hoard it. Jack made the scarcity decision to purchase his mentor's book of business—even thought it was not the quality he wanted. It took just a month to pull the deal together and Jack's mentor was gone two months after the agreement was signed.

To begin to get a handle on his expanded book of business, Jack asked for a stack-ranked list of his client households by revenue. This would be the first time he actually looked at the facts about his book of business. He knew it was going to be ugly, he just didn't know *how* ugly.

The report listed his 911 households from largest revenue producer to smallest. The bottom 20 percent of his book (182 households) produced a little less than 1 percent of his revenue. The bottom 50 percent of his book (456 households), produced just 5.5 percent of his revenue. Then he looked at the top portion of his book. The top 20 percent of clients (182 households) produced 78 percent of his revenue.

The strategy to become bulletproof had backfired. He and his team were swamped with time-consuming, unprofitable clients. He was not deriving the satisfaction that comes from having deep, meaningful client relationships. Nor was he experiencing the high-net-worth client referrals he longed for. He felt the stress of working with clients in a reactive rather than proactive way. Jack realized that the only thing he had to give to clients was his time, and once spent, it was gone. For the first time Jack questioned the ethics of taking time from a client who has paid for it (someone in the top 20 percent) and giving it to someone who has not. He also began to question the ethics of having his team work at a frantic pace, often after hours.

Making scarcity decisions to hoard unprofitable clients wasn't good enough. Jack wanted more.

The Third Discipline: Start Disengaging Unprofitable Clients

I have not found a best practice that has a more positive impact on business results than disengaging from unprofitable clients and investing the service time saved on quality clients. The win-lose environment that characterizes this industry promotes scarcity thinking. Hoarding unprofitable clients is a symptom of this thinking. As a result, the bottom 50 percent of an advisor's client base often represents less than 5 percent of his revenue. The bottom 20 percent of the business often generates less than 1 percent of the revenue. The scarcest resource that advisors have is their time. Once it is spent it can never be gotten back. The ineffective habit of hoarding unprofitable clients causes advisors to develop a client base that demands too much time and energy while providing little in return. By bending to the discipline of disengaging unprofitable clients, advisors can begin to spend their time where the payback is best—the top 20 percent of their client base.

In the United States, independent advisory firms sell for between 1.5 and 3.5 times revenue. If I were to ask you the reason for such a range, you probably would say differences in profitability, the amount and percent of recurring revenue, the quality of the staff, the quality of the systems, a differentiated service model, brand recognition, and/or the quality of the client base. All of these are explicitly linked to the last one—the quality of the client base. An advisory firm cannot generate profit, recruit and train quality staff, invest time and money in building quality systems, and deliver distinguished service consistently enough to build a brand without the client-generated revenue to do so.

Insights

Vilfredo Pareto was an eighteenth-century Italian economist who determined that 20 percent of the Italian population owned 80 percent of the land. Later, Edwards Deming, the father of the quality movement, applied the 80/20 rule to identify the biggest constraints to a system. When the constraints are removed the system improves. Since Deming's time, people have made broad use of the 80/20 rule. Here, we are going to use it to create a contrast between the top and bottom portions of your client base as a way to better understand the magnitude of your unprofitable client problem—your biggest constraint.

> The key lies not in better information, but in turning information into information that cannot be ignored.
> —Jim Collins, *Good to Great*

Begin by creating a list of your client households with their recurring revenue. Based on their recurring revenue, stack-rank this list in order of highest to lowest. Once you have organized this data, segment it into deciles, as shown in Table 3.1.

Table 3.1 shows you how to take a fact-based approach to gain insight into your business. You probably know that you have an unprofitable account problem, but this 80/20 rule analysis will allow you to confirm or reject some of the assumptions you have made about the makeup of your client base.

Notice that the top 20 percent of the clients are responsible for 80.71 percent of revenue while the bottom 20 percent of clients account for just .08 percent of the revenue. The bottom 40 percent of clients account for .86 percent of revenue, and the bottom 50 percent

Table 3.1   Revenue Analysis Example

Clients Sorted by Revenue	Clients	Revenue	Revenue per Client	Percent Revenue	Percent Revenue
First decile (top 10%)	36	$618,140	$17,171	57.86%	
Second decile (11–20%)	36	$244,139	$6,782	22.85%	**80.71%**
Third decile (21–30%)	36	$105,525	$2,931	9.88%	
Fourth decile (31–40%)	37	$53,840	$1,455	5.04%	
Fifth decile (41–50%)	37	$24,652	$666	2.31%	
Sixth decile (51–60%)	37	$12,902	$349	1.21%	
Seventh decile (61–70%)	37	$5,943	$161	0.56%	
Eighth decile (71–80%)	37	$2,315	$63	0.22%	
Nineth decile (81–90%)	37	$764	$21	0.07%	
Tenth decile (bottom 10%)	37	$123	$3	0.01%	**.08%**
Total	367	$1,068,343	$2,911	100%	

a mere 2.07 percent. You might be thinking I had to dig hard to find such a skewed example. Not at all—in fact, this real-life example is quite typical, as you may soon discover.

People move more aggressively away from pain than they do toward pleasure. They are more motivated to change when they are dissatisfied with the way it is, and I will admit that part of my intent here is to engender enough dissatisfaction so that you will be willing to disengage your unprofitable clients.

What percentage of your revenue comes from:

- Your top 20 percent?
- Your bottom 20 percent?
- Your bottom 50 percent?

The next step in confronting the magnitude of your problem is to gain insight into how many and which clients are unprofitable. The difference between client fees and the cost of service is profit. To identify your unprofitable clients you will first want to know how much it costs to service them. You will then need to determine which clients cost more to service than they are paying. Because few advisors have a rigorous enough accounting system to track their cost of service, having a benchmark is a useful way to begin. According to Moss Adams research, as demonstrated in Table 3.2, a firm with $500,000

Table 3.2   Benchmarking Data

Firm Size	$500K to $1M	$1M to $2M	$2M to $3M
Number of firms	200	150	58
Total nonowner expenses	$68,590	$156,020	$379,045
Nonowner professionals salary/ commission	$64,031	$135,813	$323,014
Nonowner bonus/incentive comp	$4,559	$20,207	$56,031
Referral fees to other professionals	$6,068	$13,059	$23,935
Overhead expenses	$257,284	$498,807	$865,048
Expenses (excluding owner comp)	$331,942	$667,886	$1,268,028
Active clients	156	191	308
Cost per active client	$2,127	$3,496	$4,117

Active client is defined as a household or institution the firm served during the last year. A client may have multiple accounts in the firm. *Professional* means an owner or nonowner employee directly responsible for managing client relationships, formulating and implementing client advice, or business development.
Source: Moss Adams/InvestmentNews Research produces two biannual studies—one on compensation and staffing and the other on the financial performance of advisory firms. For more information on the research go to: www.investmentnews.com/section/data.

to $1 million in revenue had an average cost per client of $2,127. If you can determine your cost per client you will have a guideline for minimum revenue necessary per client. Because advisory firms operate on many different platforms, with different expense structures, you will need to apply the common sense principle and adjust these costs appropriately.

> Time is the scarcest resource and unless it can be managed nothing else can be managed.
> — Peter Drucker, *On the Profession of Management*

Advisors will acknowledge that many of their unprofitable clients can take as much time to service as their high-revenue clients, especially when the markets are volatile. Nonetheless, the habit of hoarding clients is so ingrained that it is painful for them to consider disengaging. It is totally outside their comfort zone. In my coaching sessions, as soon as we begin to discuss disengaging these smaller clients, advisors flip-flop and rationalize keeping them, saying they really are not taking that much time.

A team in Colorado Springs was so adamant about this point, they set out to prove that their smaller clients were not time intensive.

They segmented their client base into A, B, C, and D clients. For a month they tallied the number of proactive or reactive contacts they had with these clients. To their surprise, they found that their D clients had more contacts than their C and B clients and slightly fewer than their A clients. After I shared this story with an advisory firm in New England, they, too, decided to test the hypothesis and came to the same conclusion: Overall, smaller clients take a lot of service time. I believe you will find it very insightful to confront the brutal facts and determine your average cost of service per client.

Many advisors struggle with these issues because they are not clear on the economics of their client base. Directionally they know there is a problem but have not looked at the numbers. By analyzing your client base from a profitability point of view, you can better understand the value of each client relationship. And the data gives you the confidence to make a decision and take action to fix the problem.

Disengaging can be emotional. It helps to identify potential disengagement targets with a fact-based approach measuring the value of each relationship. I've built a model for advisors to use, but my experience in this sort of evaluation goes back to my early days consulting at Microsoft.

We used a similar method to determine the features to include in a software product. Microsoft has a rigorous product development process. The first spec in the process is called a layman's spec—written in a way that a nontechnical person can understand what is to be built. It describes the market opportunity, specific target market, revenue model, dependencies, go-to-market and partner strategies, the optimal date to launch, and potential features. At first these features were put into two categories: must-have or nice-to-have. At this stage, we would get stuck in seemingly endless debates over which features were in and which ones were out. We needed a better decision-making model. As represented in Figure 3.1, we began to plot features against two criteria: market impact (anticipated revenue or customer satisfaction) and the effort to build it.

The features with the greatest market impact and the lowest effort to build would be included in Version 1. Version 2 would include features with the next highest market impact and lowest effort scores. This process cut the debate dramatically and sped up getting the products into the marketplace. If this process was effective in helping Microsoft employees determine what they should be doing, I began

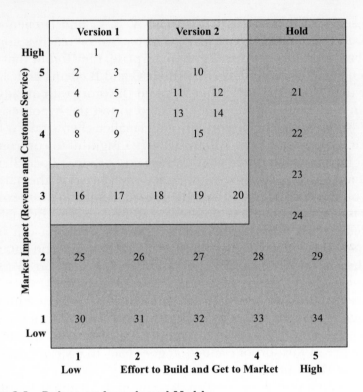

Figure 3.1   Return on Investment Matrix

to wonder if it would be just as effective in helping advisors determine what not to do. Since adopting a similar framework to segment their client base and make actionable decisions, hundreds of advisors have reached new levels of satisfaction with their business.

Who should you disengage and when? Follow Figure 3.2 as a guide. Begin by plotting client households against two criteria: recurring revenue and service effort. Your staff should be included in this evaluation because you may not be aware of the day-to-day service requirements of each client.

Plot your cost-of-service line—this will serve to remind you that you are gaining insight into unprofitable clients. In this example I used $2,100 as the cost of service. Unless you are running a not-for-profit company, every household below this line should be considered a candidate for disengagement.

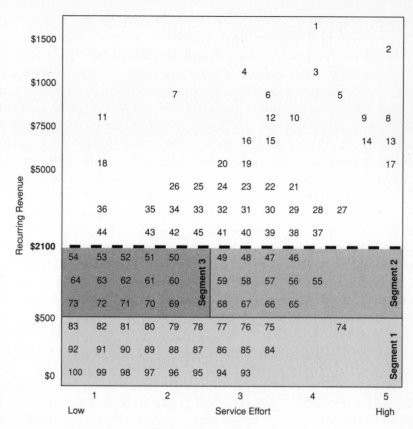

Figure 3.2   Segmenting Unprofitable Clients

Segment the unprofitable clients into three or four groups. I have put them into three groups, attempting to take into account both their revenue and the service effort they require. All of these clients are unprofitable and you should consider disengaging in the following order.

Segment 1: The 20 to 40 Percent That Represents 1 Percent of Revenue

There are times when a blunt instrument is appropriate, and this is one of them. Unless there is a compelling reason not to, these clients should be disengaged immediately. There are few advisors who can't live without this 1 percent. What an opportunity to free up time! By reinvesting the time savings in your quality clients you will recoup this 1 percent and more in a heartbeat.

What is a compelling reason not to disengage? The common sense principle must prevail here. If one of these clients regularly referred you high-net-worth clients, that would be compelling. If one of these clients was a good friend, that would be compelling. If the client were a child of your very best client, that may be compelling. If you knew the client was going to accumulate significant assets in the very near future, that would be compelling. But don't kid yourself. Advisors have a tendency to make excuses for hoarding unprofitable clients. Don't make that mistake. Make good business decisions.

One seasoned advisor was very reluctant to move a child of one of his better clients to someone else in his office. He argued that he needed to continue serving the children of his best clients because eventually they would inherit their parent's assets. I asked him how many of his clients who were producing $7,500 or more of revenue came to him in that manner. He was amazed to find out none of them were children of his best clients. Since that time I have asked other advisors about this strategy and found that it does work once every 75 to 150 years! Don't make this mistake. Make good business decisions.

Where do you send them? You are limited only by your imagination when it comes to how you are going to disengage from these unprofitable clients. Not identifying a solution is almost always creative avoidance to protect your hoarding habit. The way you choose to disengage segment 1 could be different from what you do with the other segments. The following examples describe ways advisors have disengaged clients. Your options will vary depending on your business model.

- *Transition clients to the broker/dealer or firm's small account desk.* More and more broker/dealers recognize that if they can take the burden of small clients off their advisor's plates, the advisors will generate even more revenue. Many broker/dealers have made transitioning clients to the small account desk a turnkey operation. You give them the list; they take your number off the account; the small account desk sends out a transition letter and follows up with a phone call explaining how their accounts are going to be serviced going forward. This tactic is an appropriate solution for your smallest clients—the 20 to 40 percent responsible for just 1 percent of your revenue. Advisors report this to be an effective solution for all of their unprofitable clients.

- *Transition clients to a junior advisor affiliated with the broker/dealer.* With a simple letter from you and a quick follow-up phone call from the junior advisor the relationship can be transitioned. There is a tendency for advisors to want to make that phone call rather than push the call to the junior advisor. Don't let your ego stand in the way of using your time more effectively. Don't let this hurt your feelings, but the client doesn't care. This solution is a win-win-win: The client will now be working with someone who can give them their mind-share; the junior advisor will have more than just a cold-call marketing list; and you will have more time for your profitable clients. A slight variation of this tactic is to identify a more senior advisor who is so locked onto the ineffective habit of hoarding that he becomes an option for your disengaged clients. And a final solution would be to direct these unprofitable clients to your biggest competitor!

- *Send a letter or phone your disengagement prospects and explain that you are now delivering comprehensive wealth management and your minimum fee is $5,000 per year.* Let them know that you would love to retain their business but do not believe they need the level of service you provide. Then point them to another advisor with a service model designed for smaller clients. This has been an effective tactic to address smaller clients who have additional assets that are not invested with you. It provides them one last "get on board" opportunity. In some cases, you may find that people value the relationship with you and are willing to accept higher fees. It's not common, but it does happen. The problem with this tactic is that clients are slow to respond and it often requires the advisor to reach out multiple times.

- *Package these clients and sell them.* Depending on your business environment, this could be an inside sale. If you are an independent advisor, there are a number of services designed to facilitate these sales. This method has been surprisingly effective in terms of both the ease of the sale and the revenue for the segment sold.

- *Many fund companies will service these clients directly.* This tactic will require coordination with the fund company and a simple letter to the clients, communicating the service and cost benefits they will receive. Because this tactic does require coordination with a third party, and because it is likely that your clients are in multiple products, this tactic is a bit more complex and limited.

What needs to be communicated and how? It is important to have a communication plan in place, outlining who, what, how, and when. Who is going to communicate what to whom? What method of communication will be delivered and when? It needs to be put on paper with actionable steps that can be tracked. You may have an approach in mind that fits your communication style. If you're struggling to decide how to introduce the topic to clients, consider the sample disengagement letter shown in Figure 3.3.

This communication is the most important, but not the only one that needs to be considered. While taking confidentiality into account, think through who needs to be informed about the clients you are disengaging—people inside your broker/dealer, key referral sources, other third-party service providers, and so forth.

Dear client,

I am writing to inform you of changes I am making to my business. After careful consideration of our clients' goals and our desire to be more engaged with helping them achieve these goals, we have decided to deliver comprehensive wealth management. This service model requires that we focus on fewer clients in a more comprehensive way. As a result, I believe your needs will be better served by another advisor.

I have formed an alliance with (name), another financial representative in our office. (name) has experience and can service your account going forward. In order to provide you with advice tailored to your needs, (name) will call you over the next week to discuss your situation and answer any questions you may have.

Please don't hesitate to contact me if you have questions or would like to discuss other options.

Sincerely,

Figure 3.3 Sample Disengagement Letter

Creative Avoidance Don't make excuses for hoarding unprofitable clients. Advisors often tell me they feel a commitment to long-held accounts or are afraid they might hurt a client's feelings. Often, when I'm working through this concept in live sessions, there's significant reluctance to disengage from small, unprofitable clients. Some reasons are:

- These people helped me get to where I am.
- They are connected to some of my best clients.
- It will give me a bad reputation in my community.

You sculpt your future with the decisions you make and the actions you take. Have the discipline to make good business decisions. Advisors who have been through High Speed Strategic Planning tell me the one thing that made the biggest difference in their business was disengagement from unprofitable clients. This strategy allowed them to reallocate their time to their profitable clients where payback was greatest. Additionally, those who have done this successfully call it a great feat for operational efficiency. It has a positive impact on the working environment in their office, leading to relieved staff and more productivity.

The most dramatic examples I have worked with occurred when two advisors disengaged more than 1,300 clients each—some of whom they hadn't seen in 10 years. They both moved forward with fewer than 100 quality clients. They both more than tripled their revenue in the process. And now, they have the time to go as deep as they had always desired with their quality clients.

Segments 2 and 3: Others You Are Considering for Disengagement

A blunt instrument may be appropriate when disengaging segment 1, but you will need to be a bit more surgical as you disengage segments 2 and 3. Advisors tend to grow their staffs as their client base grows. So, even though these clients are unprofitable, you may have grown dependent upon the revenue they produce. You have payroll to make, rent to pay, licensing fees, training, insurance, phones, and so forth. The decision to disengage from these client segments must be made in a way that is not disruptive.

The disengagement process may take several years to complete. As you disengage segments 2 and 3 you should think about using a 1:5 ratio or disengage on a revenue-natural basis. In the 1:5 ratio method you will disengage five unprofitable clients for every profitable client acquired. A bit more aggressive method is to work at a revenue-neutral basis: If you bring in a $10,000 recurring revenue client, then disengage $10,000 worth of unprofitable clients.

After disengaging from clients in segment 1, how many unprofitable clients remain? If there are fewer than 15, you may choose to continue working with them the way you have in the past. But if there are more than 15, you should consider using the one-to-many service model to reduce the amount of time and effort used to provide service to these unprofitable clients.

The One-to-Many Service Model

> Complicated, difficult-to-explain strategies may or may not confuse your competitors, but they will almost certainly confuse your organization.
>
> — Jeffrey Pfeffer and Robert Sutton, *Hard Facts, Dangerous Half-Truths & Total Nonsense*

The one-to-many service model has been used effectively by many advisory firms to provide a service level for clients who will be disengaged over time or who are marginally profitable. This model is a staging area for those clients you are going to disengage. In Figure 3.2, clients in segments 2 and 3 are disengagement targets. When implemented effectively, the one-to-many service model has the potential to provide these clients with more proactive service than they have previously experienced. Keep this strategy implementation as simple as you can by standardizing and reducing the number of available options.

One-to-many service allows you to increase efficiency with leveraged resources in three ways:

1. *It provides a dedicated relationship manager.* The best advisors put their best resources on the biggest opportunities and not on their biggest problems. Clients you will disengage are not big opportunities. The principals of the firm and senior advisors should focus on high-net-worth clients. A less credentialed member of the team who is technically savvy can build systems to serve the one-to-many clients. As the single point of contact,

this person should manage all of the day-to-day communications and services delivered to these clients.

2. *It simplifies the product offering.* You can leverage a variety of product features delivered by mutual fund firms or other third-party providers. Outsourcing specific services (manager selection, monitoring, rebalancing, and performance reporting) creates leverage in areas where an advisor may not add unique value. There are a number of suitable active and passive investment products. With due diligence, you can find options that allow you to deliver an institutional type solution to these clients. Pick just one! However, if you migrate clients to a new product solution, you need to make sure that the client will not experience additional fees or tax consequences.

3. *It scales your most expensive resource.* Staff time is your most expensive resource. By delivering services to clients in a group meeting you will be able to leverage this time. Invite all of your one-to-many clients to attend a "market update." In this meeting you will be able to provide:

   ♦ *High-level performance reporting.* Because you have migrated these clients to just one financial solution, you will find it fairly easy to leverage that fund company's wholesaler to present high-level performance reporting. You may have clients who have a 60/40 allocation and others who have a 40/60 allocation, but the fund company's representative can present high-level performance to all. Additionally, the wholesaler can make the audience aware of any manager changes or other tactical product modifications the fund company anticipates making in the future.

   ♦ *Insight into capital markets.* Clients want to know that those looking after their money are thinking deeply about the economic environment. Providing them with a rational explanation for why markets are behaving the way they are is an important part of providing your clients' financial peace of mind. Your team does not have to prepare this presentation. This topic can be outsourced to the fund company's representative or you can utilize a printed report from an investment strategist or economist that you prefer.

   ♦ *One wealth management topic per meeting.* These topics can include education about life insurance, retirement planning, college funding, budgeting, legacy planning, and so forth. This is an important aspect of treating clients fairly, and these topics can easily be outsourced. Invite an expert from the community or another resource to provide insight on these topics, and have the presenter prepared to follow up with clients as necessary.

Marginally Profitable Clients   In addition to using the one-to-many service model as a staging area for disengagement, it has proven to be very effective for those clients deemed marginally profitable. In Figure 3.4, I have classified clients who are producing between $2,100 (the cost of service) and $5,000 as marginally profitable. Clients who fall within this category are profitable but are not delivering

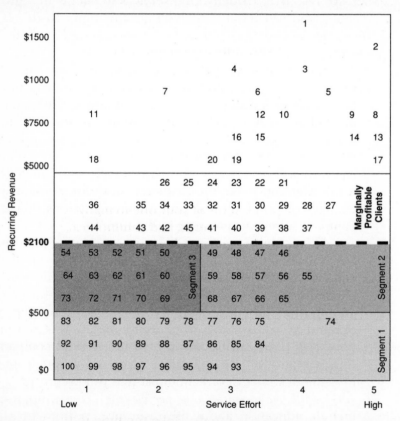

Figure 3.4   Identifying Marginally Profitable Clients

enough revenue to justify servicing them with comprehensive wealth management.

The best advisors I have worked with have just one service model—comprehensive wealth management. Over time they continue to disengage even marginally profitable clients. A word of caution is necessary: Don't kid yourself. Only a small percentage of advisors are able to have a purely high-net-worth practice. The vast majority depend upon these marginally profitable clients.

Decisions

> Winning leaders invest where the payback is the highest. They cut their losses everywhere else.
>
> —Jack Welch, *Winning*

Your insight into disengaging unprofitable clients has prepared you to make the following critical business decisions.

- Who do you disengage and when?
- Where do you send them?
- When you disengage, how should it be communicated and to whom?
- Which clients will you migrate to the one-to-many service model?
- Who is your one-to-many dedicated relationship manager?
- What are the components of your one-to-many service model?
- What are the features, benefits, and communication plan used to migrate clients to your one-to-many service model?

Actions

> Even if you're on the right track, you'll get run over if you just sit there.
>
> —Will Rogers

I regularly hear from advisors who have thought about disengaging clients, but have failed to take action. Often, not taking action is a result of not knowing what to do. Take the time to think through how you would disengage. It will increase your likelihood of doing so.

Milestones	Owner	Date	✓
Identify the clients to be disengaged.			
Ensure no negative financial impact on clients.			
Determine where they are going.			
Create communication plan.			
Align expectations with new service provider.			
Disengage segment 1.			
Conduct a postmortem on the strategy and action plan.			
Plan disengagement for segments 2 & 3.			

Figure 3.5   Disengage Unprofitable Clients Action Plan

In *Leading the Revolution,* Gary Hamel writes, "In this new age, a company that is evolving slowly is already on its way to extinction." I encourage you to move quickly to disengage unprofitable clients and free up capacity to execute new, more effective strategies. After gaining insight and making decisions, it is time to take action. Figure 3.5 provides a framework for you to begin to focus on disengaging unprofitable clients.

Figure 3.6 provides an action plan to implement the one-to-many service model with segments 2 and 3 and your marginally profitable clients.

Milestones	Owner	Date	✓
Identify clients to migrate to one-to-many service model—segments 2 and 3 and the marginally profitable.			
Determine the one-to-many relationship manager.			
Determine the one investment solution.			
Ensure no negative financial impact on clients.			
Determine one-to-many features.			
Execute features, benefits, and communication plan.			
Migrate clients to the one investment solution.			
Determine venue and agenda for one-to-many meetings.			
Prepare third-party resource for one-to-many meeting.			
Invite clients to one-to-many meeting.			
Execute one-to-many meeting.			
Catalog follow-up action items.			
Close on action items.			

Figure 3.6   Implementing the One-to-Many Service Model

Chapter Summary

Key Points

- Disengaging unprofitable clients has had a profound positive impact on hundreds of advisory firms.
- The win-lose environment that characterizes this industry promotes scarcity thinking. Hoarding unprofitable clients is a symptom of this thinking.
- The bottom 50 percent of an advisor's client base often represents less than 5 percent of his revenue. The bottom 20 percent of the business often generates less than 1 percent of the revenue.
- Your most scarce resource is your time. Hoarding unprofitable clients causes advisors to spend too much of their time on unprofitable clients.
- By bending to the discipline of disengaging unprofitable clients, advisors can begin to spend time where their payback is best—with the clients in the top 20 percent of their client base.
- Conducting the 80/20 rule analysis on your client base can provide information that can no longer be ignored.
- Most advisors have not taken the time to calculate their cost of service and therefore do not know the minimum amount of revenue a client must generate to be profitable.
- Small, unprofitable clients take up more time than most advisors are willing to acknowledge.
- Advisors are typically defensive and rationalize their habit of hoarding unprofitable clients.
- Segment 1 is the bottom 20 percent of your client base and represents 1 percent of your revenue. Unless there is a compelling reason not to, these clients should be disengaged very quickly.
- Segments 2 and 3 are unprofitable clients and have been grouped based on the revenue they generate and the effort it takes to service them. While considering cash flow needs, these clients should be disengaged on a 1:5 ratio or a revenue-neutral basis. Disengaging these segments can take two years or more.
- Advisors have disengaged clients in a variety of ways:
  - Transition clients to the broker/dealer or firm's small account desk.
  - Transition clients to a junior advisor affiliated with the broker/dealer.
  - Send a letter or phone your disengagement prospects and explain that you are now delivering comprehensive wealth management and your minimum fee is $5,000 per year.
  - Package these clients and sell them.
  - Many fund companies will service these clients directly.

- A well-thought-through communication plan needs to be in place prior to disengaging clients. Determine who, what, when, and how it should be communicated.
- The one-to-many service model is a staging area for clients who will be disengaged over time or who are marginally profitable.
- Instead of delivering services on a one-to-one basis, advisors can deliver services on a one-to-many basis. Advisors have increased efficiency by:
  - Limiting their product offering.
  - Utilizing outside resources to deliver one-to-many meetings that include (1) high-level performance reporting, (2) insight into capital markets, and (3) one wealth management topic presentation per meeting.
- The best advisors I have worked with have just one service model—comprehensive wealth management. However, the vast majority depend upon their marginally profitable clients.

CHAPTER 4

Stop Providing Only Investment Advice and Start Providing Wealth Management Advice

The Fourth Ineffective Habit: Providing Only Investment Advice

Confronting the brutal facts of hoarding unprofitable clients opened Jack's eyes. How many other ineffective habits had he developed? He began to look at his entire business model with a curiosity that bordered on skepticism. In his fifth year he had decided to become a fee-based advisor and provide purely investment advice. He reflected back upon how he had made that decision.

His manager was big on shadowing. He felt it was one of the best ways to keep investment advisors focused on the tried and true Kaizen sales system. He asked Jack to shadow Eric Greene, one of the better producers in the office. Eric was a Kaizen master and his entire book of business was transaction-based. Jack was asked to keep a diary on his shadowing experience and would later review his key takeaways with his manager—just to make sure the tips and tricks sunk in. Jack pulled out his old diary to read why he had opted for a fee-based rather than a transaction-based model.

From his diary Jack learned that like other senior advisors in the office, Eric started out his practice selling to family and friends; he was tough enough or fortunate enough to outlast 85 percent of his peers and had been living off a mix of orphaned accounts and the

Kaizen Sales System principle of focusing on quantity. He was big on Morningstar and claimed unique insight into the capital markets and stocks. In those days the entire branch was set up to drive transactions. In the lobby, CNBC was on the television, *Money* magazine and the *Wall Street Journal* were on the coffee table. There was a buzz in the air—a level of excitement that was catching. Clients needed to know they must act now!

With Jack in tow, Eric walked out to greet his clients, making immediate eye contact. Jack recalled Eric's sense of anticipation as he walked his clients into his office. Jack could still feel the vibe. Once in his comfort zone and sitting across the desk from his clients, Eric was able to switch to his red-letter language and get the transaction done—just that quick and easy. As his investors departed, Eric looked over to Jack and winked and then mouthed, "Ka-ching."

This experience turned Jack's stomach and he vowed never to make a living like that. That is when Jack decided to build a fee-based investment advisory practice. Though the fee-based approach had been discussed in branch meetings, none of the veteran reps had made the move. Jack would be going against the status quo and his manager's wishes. He made the move anyway and it turned out to be the right decision—at the time. Jack was on the leading edge of this movement, and over the years many advisors followed.

But now, 10 years later, Jack is questioning whether this fee-based investment advice provides enough value to justify his fees. In the early stages of a fee-based relationship, clients felt the value and objectivity that Jack brought to the table. They experienced the risk tolerance tools, setting financial goals, and participation in the asset allocation tactics. The pie charts, product brochures, and web site demos were tangible. The clients felt like they were getting value from Jack providing purely investment advice. His clients received educational pieces and a monthly newsletter that made them feel more informed. He even offered client appreciation events that were a blend of education and entertainment. It was all part of delivering purely investment advice.

By the time a client had worked with Jack for five or six quarters the newness had worn off. Providing purely investment advice didn't seem to be enough to keep his clients satisfied. The benchmark reporting had convinced them that he was providing little more than market returns. His monthly e-mail newsletters were beginning to read like old CNBC financial news. Jack was sure they were beginning to wonder why their quarterly fees had not gone down.

Jack felt he was missing something—something big. He reviewed the meeting and phone notes from 10 high-net-worth clients and discovered that every investment decision made impacted another aspect of the clients' financial lives. It hadn't dawned on him before, but he observed that his clients' financial lives were operating as a system while he had been treating the components of the system as individual parts. Perhaps his clients wouldn't even be able to articulate what was missing, but they could feel that pure investment advice wasn't enough—it was too simplistic. No wonder he was having difficulty getting clients in for investment reviews.

Providing only investment advice wasn't good enough. Jack and his clients wanted more.

The Fourth Discipline: Start Providing Wealth Management Advice

Wealth management focuses on goals that require planning, money, time, and the ongoing coordination of the client's financial ecosystem. The 78 million North American baby boomers born between 1946 and 1964 are the wealthiest population to ever pass through society. They control much of the world's investable assets, have complex financial needs, and are mature enough to plan for the future. The wealthiest 20 percent of the baby boomer population are prime candidates for wealth management. They have the need and can afford to pay for it.

> What I want you to see is that just having satisfied customers isn't good enough anymore. You don't own these customers. They're just parked on your doorstep and will be glad to move along when they find something better.
> —Ken Blanchard and Sheldon Bowles, *Raving Fans*

Insights

> The first step in answering any hard business question is to take an objective, fact-based approach.
> —Bill Gates, *Business @ the Speed of Thought*

Table 4.1   Revenue Analysis

Clients Sorted by Revenue	Clients	Revenue	Revenue per Client	% Revenue	% Revenue
First decile (top 10%)	36	$618,140	$17,171	57.86%	
Second decile (11–20%)	36	$244,139	$6,782	22.85%	80.71%
Third decile (21–30%)	36	$105,525	$2,931	9.88%	
Fourth decile (31–40%)	37	$53,840	$1,455	5.04%	
Fifth decile (41–50%)	37	$24,652	$666	2.31%	
Sixth decile (51–60%)	37	$12,902	$349	1.21%	
Seventh decile (61–70%)	37	$5,943	$161	0.56%	
Eighth decile (71–80%)	37	$2,315	$63	0.22%	
Nineth decile (81–90%)	37	$764	$21	0.07%	
Tenth decile (bottom 10%)	37	$123	$3	0.01%	.08%
Total	367	$1,068,343	$2,911	100%	

Too often, business decisions are based on opinions or assertions. A better way to reduce debate, allow for consensus, and generate more commitment to execution is to present the facts in support of recommendations. So, in the spirit of making fact-based decisions, let's go back to our 80/20 rule and make a fact-based decision about where this advisor should be spending his time, as shown in Table 4.1.

In the example in Table 4.1, the top 20 percent of the client base represents 80.71 percent of the revenue. The top 20 percent averages $11,976 in revenue. This means that a 10-year client relationship will generate almost $120,000 assuming no change in assets under management. This means, further, that a 10-year relationship with the top 72 clients is worth approximately $8,600,000 in revenue. This advisor would be wise to find a strategy to retain these 72 clients. And that is not all these clients bring to the table. When you consider that engaged clients tend to refer their friends and associates, you most certainly should factor in their lifetime referral value.

In 2007, the *Best Practices of Elite Advisors: Wealth Management Edge* study surveyed 2,094 advisors with at least $50 million in assets under management. This study stated that "87.7 percent cite client referrals as the major source for new clients."

This supports insight I gained in 1996 when I first began to work with a group of 15 registered investment advisors. As part of the prep work for a High Speed Strategic Planning session, I asked each

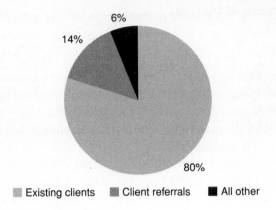

14%

6%

80%

Existing clients ■ Client referrals ■ All other

Figure 4.1   Source of Revenue

firm to calculate the source of their revenue over the past fiscal year. As represented in Figure 4.1, it turned out that 80 percent of their revenue came from clients they had at the beginning of the year, 14 percent came from referrals from those same clients, and the remaining 6 percent from all other sources. With 94 percent of their revenue coming directly or indirectly from their existing client base, where should they be spending their time?

Start Providing Your Top 20 Percent with Wealth Management Advice

When you consider the long-term revenue and referral value of the top 20 percent of your clients, you should strongly consider providing them with wealth management advice. Reengaging clients with wealth management is the process of moving your best fee-based clients from an investment advisory relationship to a wealth management relationship.

There are four major steps to reengage your clients and start providing wealth management advice. The process, outlined in Figure 4.2, allows you to revisit their needs and financial goals at a much deeper level.

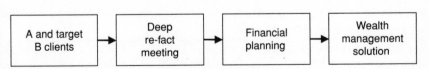

Figure 4.2   The Reengagement Process

Step 1: Determine the Clients to Reengage with Wealth Management

The first step is to identify your wealth management clients. This is the framework I used in the last chapter to identify which clients to disengage and which clients to move to the one-to-many service model. Now I am using this framework to explain which clients should be reengaged with wealth management, as emphasized in Figure 4.3. All of your A clients and the B clients who are in your target market are candidates.

In this example I have classified clients who bring in annual revenue greater than $5,000 as A clients. I have also decided to reengage clients 30 and 43 with wealth management advice. These are B clients who are within the target market. In this marginally profitable area where there are no hard rules, I have decided to disengage clients 37 and 38 because they require too much effort for what they are paying.

The highest return on your time is reengaging these clients with wealth management (Figure 4.4). Reengaging two clients per month

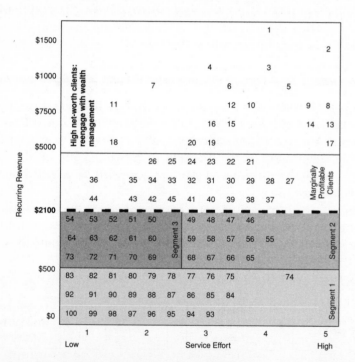

Figure 4.3   Identify Wealth Management Clients

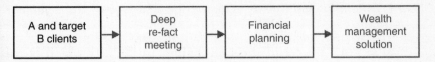

Figure 4.4   Identify A and Target B Clients

is a reasonable pace for the first few months. Once you get the routine down, you can accelerate the pace. Managing this process with a simple pipeline report is an effective way to maintain momentum. The objective of this process is to get the critical mass of your target clients reengaged as quickly as possible.

Once you have fine-tuned the process and have the reengagement system in place, you will want to accelerate the number of clients you migrate to wealth management. Table 4.2 is a simple yet effective way to monitor your progress and stay on track. In the first column, list your reengagement targets and then simply fill in the date that the specific reengagement step was completed. A weekly 10- to 15-minute meeting dedicated to reviewing the progress of your reengagement execution should be sufficient to keep you and your team on track.

Table 4.2   Tracking the Reengagement Progress

Client	Set Re-fact Meeting	Re-fact Meeting	Plan	Solution	Present
Adams	4/7	4/14	4/21	4/28	5/5
Bazley	4/16	4/19	4/26	5/3	
Cunningham	4/16	4/23	4/30	5/7	
Davis	4/23	4/30	5/7		
Everest	4/30	5/7	5/14		
Farmer	5/3	5/10	5/17		
Gross	5/7	5/14			
Hill	5/10	5/17			

Step 2: Have a Deep Re-fact Meeting with Your Clients

The objective of the deep re-fact meeting (Figure 4.5) is to gather the information necessary to help the clients develop their financial vision and the strategies to realize this vision. Most clients are not particularly clear about their vision. Using a consultative approach to create clarity and alignment will bring value to them. Some advisors

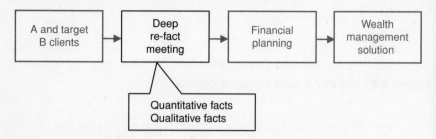

Figure 4.5   Fact Finding

have found it effective to have this meeting in the client's home, rather than in their office. Meeting in their home is an effective way to keep them in their comfort zone and allows for more frank and open conversations.

You've gathered information about your clients over time, but chances are you don't know all of the details that drive their decision making or goals. Reengaging your clients gives you the opportunity to gain deep insight into the things they would like to accomplish and their financial situation.

You should make the call to schedule this meeting. It conveys the importance of the new engagement process. If you reach the client it is a positive touch. If you miss the client it is still a positive touch. You can prevent phone tag by leaving a message asking the client to return the call to your administrative assistant to schedule the meeting.

If the idea of setting this meeting makes you feel uncomfortable, consider yourself normal. Most advisors believe they already know the important details about their clients and are reluctant to set up this re-fact meeting. In my experience, clients aren't put off at all by this request, and the advisor always finds out a great deal more about his clients.

Consider positioning the meeting like this: "We are hearing more and more from our clients that they want to get crystal clear on the things they would like to accomplish and have a roadmap to get there. Would you meet with me in your home for an hour to discuss your plan?" They will say yes.

It is important that you thoroughly diagnose the financial situation, life goals and thought process that drives your clients. Think of yourself as a doctor who needs to know all the details before responding.

When I go in to see my family practitioner, Eric Suh, I sit in the lobby for a short time before his assistant comes out to greet me and walk me back to an examining room. Her name is Sunshine so I'm pretty sure that her parents were hippies. She listens to my heart, takes my blood pressure, and finishes her work by updating my medications. Shortly after Sunshine leaves, Eric walks in. Imagine a situation where, when Eric entered the room, he said: "Steve, I'm going to schedule a gall bladder surgery for you in the morning." Of course, I'd be startled and ask why. His reply? "A patient of mine had one last week and it worked out great!" Eric is a fine young physician so he would never do anything like this. He knows that making a prescription without a diagnosis is malpractice. The re-fact meeting makes sure that you are applying an accurate diagnosis to your clients' financial lives, lives that constantly change.

The re-fact meeting consists of collecting both quantitative and qualitative information from the clients. Quantitative data is the information you need to be able to update their financial plan. Qualitative information provides insight into what the client wants to accomplish in the future, why it's important to them, and how they make critical financial decisions. You will want to spend the vast majority of your re-fact meeting on gathering qualitative information.

Quantitative Fact-Finding   Quantitative facts are the data you need to update your financial planning tool. Items like account balances, insurance amounts, and retirement savings contributions all fall into this category. You want to collect this data in the most unobtrusive way possible because you want to spend 90 percent of your face-to-face time on your qualitative questions. The best place to collect the documents is where they are kept—usually in the client's home. By sending a checklist in advance you can quickly deal with this data so you can get down to your real value-add: listening to the answers to your qualitative questions. The best way to generate your checklist is to go to the planning tool and identify the required inputs. Your document checklist may look as simple as the following:

- Bank statements.
- Tax return.
- Pension estimates.
- Payroll check stubs.
- Insurance policies.

- Estate documents—wills and trusts.
- Employer retirement plan holdings and contribution/distribution level.
- Social Security statements.
- Liabilities.
- Mortgage info, property info.
- Power of attorney.
- Attorney, CPA contact information.

Some advisors use a data input sheet that the client fills out to gather this information. Most experienced wealth managers will tell you the information that they get back is not always accurate because there are too many estimates. Gathering the right documents is the only tried-and-true method of gathering the quantitative facts.

Above all else, do not waste the client's time by gathering quantitative facts that you already have or those that are not necessary to update your planning tool. The following story is how *not* to do it.

My advisor told me I needed more life insurance. He had a well-respected insurance agent he wanted me to see. I setup an appointment to meet him at his office. Why did I have to go to his office? To make it convenient for him. Forget about me and my time—let's just make sure we think about saving his time.

I hate to go downtown—the traffic, the parking; it annoys me, but I went anyway. I parked in a lot where I had to have money to put in the slot in the box. All I had was a $20. There wasn't a place within eyesight to get change, so I put my $20 in the slot and felt a bit more irritated.

The receptionist directed me to the conference room, and the agent came in with his fact-finding sheet. After a cordial greeting, he brought out his fact-finder and asked for my full name. I said, "Please don't tell me I came all the way down here just to give you my name." He shook his head and said, "Oh, no, no, no" and proceeded to ask, "What is your address?" With that I got up and left. He should have gotten my name and address in another way. It was part of the fact-finding process for him, but for me it was a waste of time.

Now, I know I am a bit odd. You don't get to be 63 years old, wired the way I am, and not know that you are a bit different. Though they may not walk out, I bet most people feel the same way as I did.

Now that you have collected this quantitative data in the most unobtrusive way possible, it is time to redirect your attention and ask your qualitative questions.

Table 4.3   Closed-End and Open-Ended Questions

Closed-End Questions	Open-Ended Questions
When do you want to retire?	What does retirement look like to you?
Do you have a budget?	Tell me about your savings and spending plans.
Do you have a will?	When you created your will, what difficult decisions did you make?
Do you have long-term care insurance?	What is your philosophy about long-term care?
When do you plan to sell your business?	Tell me about your transition plan.

Qualitative Fact-Finding   Using a consultative approach allows you to engage clients with qualitative fact-finding. Research from Dow Jones and CEG Worldwide indicates that fewer than 7 percent of advisors use a consultative approach. Just asking good questions puts you ahead of 93 percent of your competition. Qualitative fact-finding provides you with an understanding of what your clients want, why they want it, and how they make their decisions. When you move beyond numbers on a page, you have the chance to gain insight into what is really important to a client. Ninety percent of your face-to-face re-fact meeting time should be focused on listening to the answers to your qualitative questions. Taking a consultative approach is about asking better questions and letting the client talk.

Winning advisors ask open-ended questions. The broader the question, the more talking room it provides for the client. Consider the contrast in Table 4.3 between closed-end and open-ended questions.

The Ultimate Open-Ended Question   Jack Yena is the former president of Johnson & Wales University, the largest culinary arts school in North America. He shared a practice I found very helpful in the qualitative fact-finding process. Jack had been on a panel with Jack Welch and Ava Youngblood of Youngblood Associates, a high-end headhunting firm. Jack asked Ava, "What is the single best question you can ask to learn about someone?" The answer was really simple: "Ask them to tell you their story."

I started to experiment with this question with people I knew well. It turned out I didn't really know them as well as I thought. Then I took the question to advisors I'd been working with. At first, they were reluctant to use it in their fact-finding conversations because it was so darn simple. But those who tried it were shocked to find out things they didn't know about their best clients.

Approaching clients with this question can be as simple as saying, "I know a lot about you, but not everything. Would you please tell me your story? I'd like to know where the two of you grew up, how you met, where you went to school, your careers, and your family—the whole thing." If you try using this question with two of your best clients, you will be sold. If the clients ask, "Where should I begin?" just say "It's your story!"

John Naisbitt taught us a lot about content analysis when he published *Megatrends* in 1984, and the methodology is still valid today. Listen to what the client is saying. How much time are they spending on specific topics? Where do they show their emotion—when are they proud, embarrassed, fearful, enthusiastic, sad, disgusted, angry, or joyful? Your job is to listen, take notes, and more notes, and nod your head. If the client leaves an area too quickly, simply say, "Tell me more about that." Or if they get into an area and there is an obvious omission, ask an open-ended follow-up question. For example, if clients talk about family members but do not mention their parents, simply ask, "What about your parents?"

People love to tell their story. Peter Rekstad, an advisor I've worked with in Minnesota, told me about an experience he had shortly after he started this reengagement process. He prompted a client to tell her story, and an hour and 15 minutes later she concluded by saying, "Now you know me better than anybody else in the world." This has become a regular experience for lots of advisors.

The Wealth Management Question When clients have finished telling you their story, ask, "What would you like to accomplish that will require planning, money, and time?" They will tell you their financial goals as best they can. Don't be surprised to learn that most clients are not very clear about their financial goals. Stephen Covey, in *The 7 Habits of Highly Effective People*, counseled us to "Begin with the end in mind." Unfortunately, few baby boomers actually practice this principle as they near retirement. They may share a random thought like, "Wouldn't it be fun to spend three months a year on the Italian Riviera!" But most baby boomers do not have a well-conceived vision of their future. This is great! It provides you with an opportunity to help them gain clarity over time.

Once again, your job is to listen, take notes and nod your head. When they articulate what they want, ask open-ended follow-up questions to find out why they want it and how they made the decision.

When you are done gathering your qualitative facts, simply thank the clients for the opportunity to hear their story and their vision of their future. Tell them you have some thoughts but don't want to answer off the cuff. Inform them that you would like to go back to your office and think about their goals and how they can be accomplished. Tell them you will use their quantitative information to update their financial plan. Set up the next meeting so that there is a deadline or forcing function for collecting any outstanding quantitative data.

When you schedule fact-finding meetings, leave enough time after the meeting to review your notes. Too much information will be lost by waiting to transcribe your notes. Some advisors have subscribed to Copytalk Mobile Scribe or Dragon Naturally Speaking to translate their bullet-point notes into more comprehensive meeting notes.

Step 3: Financial Planning

The primary purpose of financial planning (Figure 4.6) is to translate vision into realistic, quantifiable goals. There needs to be a specific financial goal attached to each component of their vision. Examples might be funding a grandson's education or experiencing more European travel while living at a level they have grown accustomed to, without needing to work for income.

Wealth managers tell me the most difficult and most important part of the planning process is to help a client develop a realistic financial vision—one that can actually be achieved. An unrealistic plan only creates anxiety and frustration for both the client and the advisor. The best planning is done iteratively over time. This iterative process does not have an end date—it is a constant, never-ending improvement process.

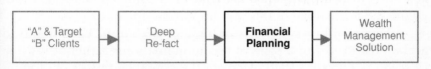

Figure 4.6   Financial Planning

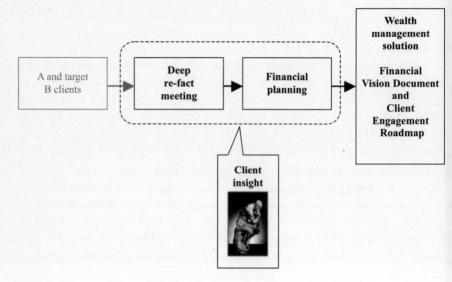

Figure 4.7   The Wealth Management Solution

Step 4: The Wealth Management Solution

In Figure 4.7 I inserted an image of Rodin's *The Thinker* to convey the need to think deeply about what you learn in the re-fact process and the analysis of the client's financial plan. Advisors tend to just blow past this very important step. Taking the time to think deeply about the client and gain the necessary insight to create a realistic wealth management solution is the most valuable and differentiating service an advisor can provide. I've found that the wealth management solution is best delivered via two components—a Financial Vision Document and a Client Engagement Roadmap.

The Financial Vision Document   The Financial Vision Document articulates what the client would like to accomplish that will require planning, money, time, and the ongoing coordination of their financial ecosystem. This articulation of what a client wants to achieve provides a compass to navigate their complex financial world. Figure 4.8 is a sample of this very important document.

A Financial Vision Document highlights what the client wants to accomplish. It is not a page of recommendations; rather, it is three to seven paragraphs that articulate their financial goals. As I mentioned earlier, most clients are not aligned nor have they thought

You said you would like to be financially independent by the time Ed turns 62. To you, financial independence means you would be able to live at the level you have grown accustomed to without needing to work for income.

You believe the college education your children received provided them with tremendous opportunities. You now want to ensure your grandchildren, Stacy and Max, also have an opportunity to receive a college education. You both take great pride in having put yourselves through college and want to give your grandchildren the sense that they have to work hard for this opportunity. To this end, you feel that they should participate in the funding of their own education.

You are planning to move into a condo here in Cleveland because your children are spread throughout the country and you love to travel. You love London and Paris and want the freedom to travel without the concerns of home upkeep.

You feel blessed by the opportunities you have been given throughout life—in particular you are grateful for the opportunities that have come to you by way of your Stanford University degrees. You have passion for providing this same opportunity for success to other young people and want to continue to contribute to Stanford University scholarship funds.

Ed has turned green. In this next phase of life he plans to do part-time management consulting work in the alternative fuel space. Sally plans to continue her volunteer work as a CASA (Court Appointed Special Advocate).

Figure 4.8   Ed and Sally Smith's Financial Vision Document

deeply about what they would like to accomplish in the future. Don't be concerned. There will be ample opportunity to help clients gain additional clarity about their future and the things they would like to accomplish as you continue to reengage them with wealth management advice.

The Client Engagement Roadmap   The Client Engagement Roadmap is your high-level plan designed to help the clients achieve their financial vision. The roadmap has clear application to a wealth management relationship but its roots were actually set during a consulting engagement I had with Microsoft.

When Microsoft was preparing to launch its first smartphone, there were three groups that needed to coordinate their product roadmaps. The mobility group, the pocket PC group, and the embedded group needed to work together closely on this project. Though each group had its product roadmap, it was the job of a cross-sectional group of people and myself to create a joint product roadmap that would address the dependencies between the groups and create an overall product roadmap.

After this all-day planning meeting, I conducted a casual focus group meeting with high-net-worth individuals. It allowed me to gain insight into some of their issues. They told me that they trusted their advisor, they liked their advisor, but they didn't have a clue what the advisor was going to do for them on an ongoing basis. They said their service was random. There was no service plan to tell them what was going to happen, when, and why.

These were all fee-based clients and all had been with their advisors for more than a year. They told me that in the beginning of the relationship with their advisor, they recognized the value they were receiving. The risk tolerance tools, pie charts, Monte Carlo simulations, investment strategies, and investment policy statements made what they were receiving tangible. But over time the value of this service seemed to fade and they were all wondering why the fees were coming out every quarter.

I put two and two together and thought, if a roadmap was tangible enough to keep the wildly independent developers at Microsoft aligned for a product launch, why couldn't it be used as a tool to align expectations between wealth management advisors and their clients?

A roadmap for wealth management advisors and their clients became a reality when I collaborated with Russ Hill, of Halbert Hargrove Investment Management, and Kirk Greene, of Greene Wealth Management. Russ was thinking about providing his clients with a "track to run on." The roadmap concept was just what he was looking for.

We worked with Kirk to populate a generic version of the roadmap. Since that time, hundreds of advisors have found the Client Engagement Roadmap to be invaluable in serving their high-net-worth clients. And with most things it continues to evolve. Figure 4.9 shows the most current form.

However, Figure 4.9 is a generic version of the roadmap. Clients should never see a generic version; they should only see their own customized roadmap. The first quarter reflects tasks or deliverables associated with reengaging the client with wealth management. As part of the re-fact meeting, data is updated, risk tolerance is recalculated, the Financial Vision Document and the Client Engagement

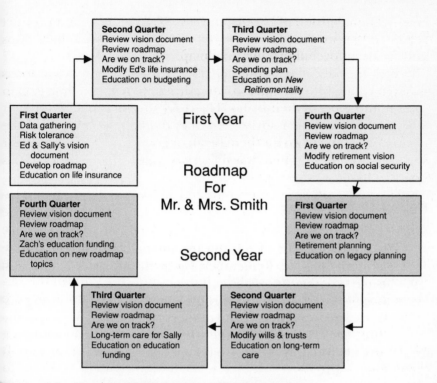

Figure 4.9   Sample Client Engagement Roadmap

Roadmap are created, and education on life insurance is delivered.

After the first quarter, the remaining seven are very similar in structure. The first three items of each quarter are designed to give the clients the information necessary for financial peace of mind.

- *Review the Financial Vision Document.* Looking at the Financial Vision Document every quarter ensures alignment on the only job you have—to help the client achieve their financial vision. Everything you do for the client should be in support of their financial vision. A quick review also gives you the opportunity to modify it along the way—it is a working document.
- *Review the Client Engagement Roadmap.* Reviewing the Client Engagement Roadmap every quarter will remind the client what you have done for them in the past, what is on the agenda for the quarter, and that they have a track to run on in the future.

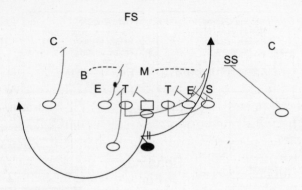

Figure 4.10   The 37 Trap

It is a major part of making the intangible business you are in more tangible. Remember: Do great things for clients and make sure they know about it!

- *Goals-based reporting.* In my High Speed Strategic Planning sessions, I go to a flipchart and draw a play we called 37 Trap—the three back runs through the seven hole with trap blocking . . . Already you don't know what I am talking about. Take look at Figure 4.10.

    I then ask the group, "How many of you have seen a football game in the past year?" It doesn't matter if I am in Canada, the United States, or the United Kingdom, virtually every hand goes up. Then I ask why no one knew the blocking scheme, and inevitably the answer is "We don't care. We just want to see the ball move toward the goal line." And that is the way it is with clients and performance reporting. They just want to see the ball move toward their goal. That is the purpose of goals-based reporting. It is the most important part of delivering financial peace of mind.

- *Prioritize wealth management topics.* In addition to the informational items designed to provide the clients with financial peace of mind, one wealth management topic per quarter is added. Having thought deeply about the clients, what they would like to achieve, the best course to get them there, and where they might be at risk, you should prioritize the wealth management topics with the important and urgent topics coming before the important less urgent topics. The spirit of intent of your prioritization needs to be, "Sally, if you were my sister,

and Ed, you were my brother-in-law, this is what I would recommend you do." In our example I have listed "modify Ed's
life insurance" in the second quarter. Hypothetically the family would be at risk if Ed were to die and not have enough
life insurance to bridge the gap. In the third quarter I've listed
"spending plan." Hypothetically, if spending is a bit out of control, it puts the client's vision of being financially independent
at risk.

Consider adding an educational piece each quarter. This can be
as simple as providing clients with a white paper or guiding them
to a web site. The educational piece that you provide in the current
quarter should better prepare them to make decisions on the wealth
management topic scheduled for the next quarter. In the example
roadmap you'll notice that I have listed life insurance as the educational piece for the first quarter. That is because "modify Ed's life
insurance" is the wealth management topic for the second quarter.
The educational piece for the second quarter, budgeting, should
prepare the couple to make better decisions on their third-quarter
wealth management topic, spending plan.

Perhaps this baby-boomer couple does not have clarity about the
next phase of their life. At the end of your third-quarter meeting you
might hand the couple Mitch Anthony's book, *The New Retirementality*,
and suggest that they read it over the next quarter. Remind them that
the fourth quarter's wealth management topic is retirement planning
and you would like to begin that session by updating that portion of
the Financial Vision Document.

Personalize the Client Engagement Roadmap.   In addition to being prioritized, topics should also be personalized—this brings the roadmap
to life for the client. Life insurance for Ed, modifying the will and
trust for Courtney, and Zach's education funding will all serve to
bring the roadmap to life. Adding locations is also an effective way to
personalize the roadmap. A second-home discussion is interesting; a
Lake Tahoe home discussion would be much more interesting. The
more you can personalize each roadmap, the more the client will
take ownership of the process.

Despite your best efforts, clients can struggle to remember
your valuable guidance. No matter how strong the message, clients
can be easily distracted and diverted. They are inclined to make

emotional, sometimes rash, decisions based upon what is happening at the moment, losing sight of where they have been or where it is they desire to go. The Client Engagement Roadmap can help you solve this problem. Clients need guidance in orchestrating their complex financial affairs. The Client Engagement Roadmap positions you as the coordinator. The roadmap serves a valuable function of letting your clients know what has been accomplished and what priorities will be addressed in the coming quarters. It is tangible elements like these that make your value more clear and prime the pump for word-of-mouth marketing.

A word of caution: The most critical part of implementation and tracking is to make sure that each item on the Client Engagement Roadmap is completed or addressed. The roadmap will become part of your permanent client file so you need to make sure items are completed. If items are not completed they must be advanced to the next quarter in order to address all of the client's needs. Avoid the temptation to overcommit yourself. With rigorous implementation and follow-up, you will demonstrate to your clients tangible evidence of the value you provide.

Effective implementation of the Client Engagement Roadmap will:

- Visibly illustrate the value you provide to clients.
- Provide structure for ongoing communication with your clients.
- Transform client reviews into a wider examination of their total financial picture.
- Spur ongoing discussion about client financial goals and set expectations about ongoing interaction between you and your clients.
- Pinpoint planning areas that require additional resources, such as estate and tax planning.

Key Benefits.   Advisors who have successfully integrated the Client Engagement Roadmap into their client service model report these key benefits:

- The roadmap moves the conversation beyond performance. Returns are important but the Client Engagement Roadmap, in combination with the Financial Vision Document, crystallizes the purpose for the client's saving, investing, and spending plans.

- Clients and advisors are on the same page. It is clear to advisors that the use of the roadmap has caused them to dig deeper into their client's situation and gain better insight into the issues and how best to approach them. The advisor and the client are in tune as to what needs to be addressed and in what priority.
- There are additional sales opportunities. Advisors who use the roadmap say that they capture a larger share of their client's assets and find additional sales opportunities. In many cases, the advisors thought they were already managing all of their client's assets.
- It jump-starts your marketing efforts. The feedback regarding the roadmap creating referrals has been tremendous. Advisors who have utilized the roadmap are getting referred to additional opportunities that fit within their target market.
- The roadmap provides you and your team with a clear plan of record and work agenda. The roadmap serves as a guide not only for your clients, but for your staff as well. With minimal effort, they will be in tune with current planning issues and items that need follow-up. As each quarter progresses, you can file the roadmap, so that at all times you have a documented history of your client's goals and planning issues.

I'm often asked, "What do we do the third year?" In our High Speed Strategic Planning seminars I answer it by asking the attendees, "Over the past two years, have any of you made a major purchase like a home, changed your marital status, had a major educational expense, changed jobs, experienced a major medical incident, or had major losses or gains in the market?" Virtually every hand goes up. There will always be new topics, or modifications to current topics on the roadmap to allow the process to be relevant. This is a constant, never-ending improvement process. Once you have your initial roadmap completed for a client, you can then update it as your client's circumstances change. As you near the eighth quarter, create a new eight-quarter roadmap.

The Client Engagement Roadmap is an overview of the services your client will receive over the next two years. Having a wealth management topic on the roadmap does not necessarily mean you will deliver that service. An effective way to deliver services beyond your competencies is to team with other leading professionals with expertise in the areas such as insurance or estate or tax planning. By referring clients to other experts, you are creating a vital network of specialists who can address all of your client's wealth management needs. This is discussed in detail in Chapter 7.

The Client Engagement Roadmap is as relevant for a new client as it is for an existing client. A roadmap for a new client will focus initially on all the tasks associated with initial discovery, account opening, and one-time events to establish the relationship.

Step 5: Present the Wealth Management Solution—The Financial Vision Document and Client Engagement Roadmap

Once the Financial Vision Document has been completed, the financial planning updated, and the Client Engagement Roadmap prepared, it is time to present the wealth management solution. This meeting should be in person. For whatever reason, advisors have a tendency to send the Financial Vision Document and the Client Engagement Roadmap off to the client and explain it over the phone. Don't do that! Clients need to feel your spirit of intent.

Start the meeting by presenting the Financial Vision Document. You might say something like, "The last time we were together, this is what I heard you say." Hand the client a copy of the Financial Vision Document and read it aloud. At the end of each paragraph or bullet ask, "Did I hear that correctly?" There will be some modifications based on their feedback. That is a good thing. The more they participate, the more committed they will be to execute their plan. After finishing the Financial Vision Document, ask one more time, "Did I hear all of this correctly?" You will probably get a head nod and you can respond, "Good—I want to be the best listener that has ever been in front of you."

The next step is to discuss the Client Engagement Roadmap. Begin by saying to your clients, "We updated your financial plan (pat the plan) and thought deeply about your situation. We created a roadmap I believe will move you toward your vision." Patting the financial plan conveys the fact that it is a tool you use to provide advice to them. This is a very important point. I'm pounding this point because so much effort goes into creating a financial plan that advisors feel compelled to give it to the client. All that does is position you as a planner and confuse the client. The lowest-paid people in the industry are financial planners. The highest-paid people in the industry are wealth managers. Let me see—highest paid, lowest paid . . . highest paid, lowest paid. Pat the plan!

Hand the client a copy of the Client Engagement Roadmap. Go through the Client Engagement Roadmap quarter by quarter, explaining the rationale for presenting the Financial Vision Document, roadmap, and goals-based reporting as a means to provide them financial peace of mind. Then explain the wealth management topics to be covered quarter by quarter and your rationale for choosing each topic. Finally, explain the process of providing them the education to be able to make more informed decisions on each wealth management topic. Once again, there will be some modifications to the roadmap based on the client's preferences and sense of urgency to get specific wealth management tasks completed.

After presenting the wealth management solution (Financial Vision Document and Client Engagement Roadmap), help the client internalize the value of this reengagement process by asking them, "How would you benefit from sticking with this roadmap?" Then ask, "How would that feel?" Close the meeting by scheduling the client's first WOW Wealth Management Review—the topic of Chapter 5.

Decisions

> No worthwhile strategy can be planned without taking into account the organization's ability to execute it.
> —Larry Bossidy and Ram Charan, *Execution*

Your insight into providing wealth management advice has prepared you to make the following critical business decisions:

- Who is the first client to reengage with wealth management advice?
- How do you plan to set the re-fact meeting?
- What language do you plan to use to set the re-fact meeting?

- How do you plan to update the quantitative facts?
- How do you plan to prepare the Financial Vision Document?
- How do you plan to prepare the Client Engagement Roadmap?
- How do you plan to present the solution?

Actions

> No strategy delivers results unless it is converted into specific actions.
>
> —Larry Bossidy and Ram Charan, *Execution*

Advisors who realize the value in the reengagement process tend to want to dig in immediately and address as many of their target market clients as possible. A word of caution: Starting to provide wealth management advice by reengaging A and target B clients may be significantly different from how you have been managing client relationships. It will take time to refine the process and adopt it effectively. It can be overwhelming if you try to apply this approach to all of your targeted clients at once.

The advisors who have been the most effective in reengaging clients with wealth management advice turn it into a system. They create an implementation plan for just one client, execute, and then debrief. What worked well? What didn't? Modify your action plan sheet and do it again. It will take two or three times going through this process, but you will have built your system for reengaging your clients with wealth management advice.

After gaining insight and making decisions, it is time to take action. Figure 4.11 provides a framework for you to process your plan to start providing wealth management advice. Figure 4.12 is your action plan to help you reengage clients with wealth management advice.

A successful reengagement process will enable you to retain your best clients by providing them with service that they truly value. At the same time, it will empower them to become your primary marketing force. Reengaging with wealth management advice is the first half of this very important initiative. Once you have positioned wealth management with the client, you now have to actually deliver it. That is the topic of our next chapter—the WOW Wealth Management Review.

Action Plan	
Check the A and target B clients to reengage with wealth management.	✓
Determine the first client to reengage: Ed and Sally Smith.	
How do you plan to set the re-fact meeting? The principal will set the meetings—callbacks scheduled by administrative assistant.	
What language do you plan to use to set up the re-fact meetings? We are hearing more and more from our clients that they want to get crystal clear on the things they would like to accomplish and have a roadmap to get them there. Would you meet with me for an hour or so to help do a better job of that for you?	
How do you plan to update the quantitative facts? Create a document checklist and send it to the clients prior to the re-fact meeting. Let them know we would like to collect the documents at that time. The relationship manager will follow-up and collect any missing documents.	
How do you plan to prepare the Financial Vision Document? The principal and the relationship manager will collaborate to write the draft Financial Vision Document based on the re-fact notes. They will create the second version after an analysis of the financial plan.	
How do you plan to prepare the Client Engagement Roadmap? Ask, what would I recommend to my sister and brother-in-law? The principal and relationship manager will work in the same manner as above to create the Excel version that is prioritized to the client's needs and personalized with names and locations.	
How do you plan to present your solution? Financial Vision Document: Principal will lead this discussion. "The last time we were together, this is what I heard you say." Hand the client a copy of their Financial Vision Document and read it aloud. At the end of each paragraph or bullet ask, "Did I hear that correctly?" Client Engagement Roadmap: The principal and relationship manager will tag-team the presentation of the roadmap. The principal will kick it off by patting the plan and handing the client their roadmap. Present the financial peace of mind topics and the wealth management topics, followed by how you intend to provide the education to help the client make better-informed decisions. Help the client internalize the value by asking, "How would you benefit from sticking with this roadmap?" and "How would that feel?" Conclude by scheduling their first WOW Wealth Management Review.	

Figure 4.11 Reengage Clients with Wealth Management Advice

Milestones	Owner	Date	√
Determine client: Ed and Sally Smith.			√
Call to set up deep re-fact meeting with Smiths.			
Send thank you/reminder note.			
Review client file.			
Create customized data input sheet.			
Make reminder call.			
Hold re-fact meeting—qualitative and quantitative facts.			
Schedule meeting to present solution.			
Download meeting notes.			
Follow up on quantitative data.			
Update financial plan.			
Create Financial Vision Document.			
Create Client Engagement Roadmap.			
Make reminder call.			
Present/modify solution.			
Schedule first WOW Wealth Management Review.			
Set up pipeline report.			

Figure 4.12   Action Plan to Reengage Clients with Wealth Management Advice

Chapter Summary

Key Points

- Investment advisors have developed the ineffective habit of making investment advice the center of every client conversation. The commoditization of investment products, the changing needs as clients near retirement, the uncertainty in the capital markets, and other industry trends are screaming for advisors to provide more than just investment advice. Today, high-net-worth clients want more from their advisors. They want an advisor who will help them achieve their financial goals—those that require planning, money, time, and the ongoing coordination of their financial ecosystem. They want their advisor to provide wealth management advice.

- When you consider the long-term revenue and referral value of the top 20 percent of your clients, you should strongly consider providing them with wealth management advice.

- The wealthiest 20 percent of the baby boomer population are prime candidates for wealth management. They have the need and can afford to pay for it.

- Step 1: Determine the clients to reengage with wealth management. You should consider reengaging all of your A clients and the B clients who are in your target market.
- Step 2: Have a deep re-fact meeting with your clients to gather the information necessary to help them develop their financial vision and the strategies to realize this vision.
- Quantitative facts: The best place to collect the documents is in the client's home. By sending a checklist in advance you can quickly deal with this data. Do not waste the client's time by gathering quantitative facts that you already have or those that are not necessary to update your planning tool.
- Qualitative fact-finding: The ultimate open-ended question: Would you please tell me your story? The wealth management question: What would you like to accomplish that will require planning, money, and time?
- To insure retention of the information, complete and review the meeting notes right after the meeting.
- Step 3: Do the financial planning.
- The primary purpose of financial planning is to translate vision into realistic, quantifiable goals. An unrealistic plan only creates anxiety and frustration for both the client and the advisor.
- Step 4: Create a wealth management solution.
- Taking the time to think deeply about the client and gain the necessary insight to create a realistic wealth management solution is the most valuable and differentiating service you can provide.
- The Financial Vision Document articulates what the client would like to accomplish that will require planning, money, time, and the ongoing coordination of their financial ecosystem.
- The Client Engagement Roadmap is your high-level plan designed to help clients achieve their financial vision. Consider including the following topics each quarter, for eight quarters:
  - Review the Financial Vision Document.
  - Review the Client Engagement Roadmap.
  - Offer goals-based reporting.
  - Prioritize wealth management topics.
  - Consider adding an educational piece each quarter.
- Personalizing the roadmap with names and locations makes it more meaningful.
- Effective implementation of the Client Engagement Roadmap will:
  - Position you as the coordinator.
  - Illustrate the value you provide to clients.
  - Transition investment reviews into wealth management reviews.
  - Move the conversation beyond performance.

- Keep you and your client on the same page.
- Identify additional sales opportunities.
- Jump-start your viral marketing.
- Provide you and your team with a clear plan of record and work agenda.

- Step 5: Present the wealth management solution—the Financial Vision Document and Client Engagement Roadmap.
- Start out the meeting by presenting the Financial Vision Document. At the end of each paragraph ask, "Did I hear that correctly?" There will be some modifications based on their feedback.
- Next, present the Client Engagement Roadmap. Pat the financial plan to convey that it is a tool you use to provide advice to them. Go through the roadmap quarter by quarter, providing your rationale for the topics.
- Conclude by asking, "How would you benefit from sticking with this roadmap and how it would feel?" Then close the meeting by scheduling the client's first WOW Wealth Management Review.

CHAPTER

5

Stop Delivering Only Investment Reviews and Start Delivering WOW Wealth Management Reviews

The Fifth Ineffective Habit: Delivering Only Investment Reviews

Jack's new attitude of facing the brutal facts caused him to think deeply about all aspects of his service model. An analysis of his investment reviews helped Jack understand that his clients wanted more in-depth financial reviews; not just the investment reviews he had been giving them. Surprisingly this discovery was not a downer. Jack was getting energized by gaining insight, making decisions, and taking action.

Jack was pumped by the possibility of making changes. He decided to disengage from the bottom 50 percent of his clients and reinvest his time on his top 20 percent. He felt, for the first time, he was beginning to make good business decisions. He was managing his business rather than the business managing him. It felt good to Jack and had a very a positive effect on his team.

Jack began to think about the type of business he really wanted to create and the impact he wanted to have on clients. Instead of viewing himself as a rep for the firm, he began to see himself as a businessman, creating his own business. The analysis of his business told him that those clients who produced 78 percent of his revenue didn't receive the level of service they deserved. If this practice continued, the team's livelihood was at risk.

Jack decided he would conduct a postmortem on the investment review he was going to deliver to the Harrisons, who were one of his first clients. Because of their close relationship, Jack knew they would give him candid feedback if he asked for it.

The preparation for reviews was hectic. Though Jack had culled his book down to 519 households, it was still more than a three-person team could effectively handle. Though they prioritized the review preparation, they were constantly randomized by the service requests from the other 518 households.

The Harrisons left the elevator and walked into the reception area just a couple minutes late. The receptionist had seen them before but didn't know who they were. She looked up from the shopping site she was viewing, said a quick good-bye to a friend, and asked the clients, "May I help you?" Telling her of their appointment, she said, "I will let Jack know you are here."

The Harrisons' review appeared to go well. Jack got a lot of head nods, smiles and hums. Jack was very capable of going deep with the benchmark performance reporting and capital market outlook—and he did! An hour and 15 minutes later, with the formal review completed, he told the Harrisons he was intent on improving his review process and asked if they would provide candid feedback on what they had experienced.

Jack asked, "What are we doing for you that you value?" They answered, "We trust you and believe the diversified and long-term investment approach you have guided us to. In dealing with our acquired assets, we are much more interested in keeping what we have rather than making a killing in the market."

Jack was a little uncomfortable when he asked, "What do we do for you that you do not value?" It became clear that the Harrisons had almost no idea what Jack was saying when he reviewed their investment strategies and provided his insight into capital markets. They said it was like taking a statistics course in a foreign language. This disappointed Jack because he took pride in his investment management and assumed that his insight delivered real value. The Harrisons also shared that the reams of paper they received were shredded almost immediately.

Jack was learning a lot and wanted more, so he asked, "What should we be doing for you that we are not?"

The Harrisons circled right back to the fact that the performance reporting was not presented within the context of their financial goals. Though Jack made sure the Harrisons had an investment policy statement, that wasn't what they were looking for. He realized he had never asked them about their vision of the future or helped them develop financial goals that would enable that vision. Jack realized there was a huge gap between the way he and the Harrisons thought about investments. He was all about beating benchmarks. They saw their investments as a means to an end.

The Harrisons told Jack that they needed a plan that would guide them to their financial goals. They went on to explain that they wanted to know who was doing what and when. They wanted to know if, should they reach their milestones, they would have a reasonable chance of bringing their financial vision into reality. As a construction engineer, Mr. Harrison talked about how he viewed the world as a system. He believed you could generate efficiencies and improve performance if you optimize across the entire system rather than merely optimizing each component part. He was looking for the same type of systems thinking from Jack.

As Jack listened, he focused his attention on their stated needs of having a financial vision, financial goals, and a plan made up of milestones to get there, with a reporting process to let them know if they were on or off track and coordination of the components across the system.

After the Harrisons left, the staff approached the postmortem meeting in a nonemotional way—they were just after the facts. What they learned from the Harrisons was eye-opening. But what they learned about their own capacity was staggering. They determined that they did not have enough lead time to properly prepare and the result was that the reviews were assembled in an ad hoc way. They also learned that they did not have control over the client experience and they had too many clients for their team to handle. It was amazing to realize that the Harrisons did not know anything about the behind-the-scenes work. They based their evaluation solely on the review. It was like a Las Vegas show: People don't care about how long it took to prepare, they just evaluate the show.

Scheduling and keeping investment review appointments had become very difficult. Jack realized that delivering investment reviews was not enough. Jack wanted more.

The Fifth Discipline: Start Delivering WOW Wealth Management Reviews

When I was a coach, I worked 85 to 100 hours per week during the season. It took time to study the opponent, strategize, game-plan, and prepare players for the situations that would come up during Sunday's game. And you know what? The fans didn't care. All they cared about was how well we executed and whether we won the game. The same can be said about a Las Vegas show. People don't care about the time and effort it takes to produce the show. They just care about their experience when the curtain goes up—it's show time!

The Wealth Management Review is your show time. Clients really don't care about the amount of work you've done and they rarely comprehend how much time it takes to monitor and rebalance accounts, do continuing education, keep informed on product developments, analyze market trends, or prepare for reviews. What they care about is the experience they have at show time—their review.

Some of what you do for a client is tangible—the return on their assets. Most of what you do is intangible—your intellectual capital and the advice you provide. The wealth management advisory business is primarily intangible. So how do you take this intangible business and make it tangible?

I was reading *The Only Thing That Matters* by Karl Albrecht just as I began consulting with financial advisors. I pulled the WOW concept from his book and modified it for your industry by creating the WOW Wealth Management Review. Over the past 15 years it has had a huge impact for advisors and their clients.

A WOW review is created by outlining all of the client touch points associated with a review and inserting a WOW into each one of them. A WOW is something that touches the senses (hearing, sight, touch, smell, taste) and is designed to make giving advice more tangible. A touch point is a phone call, an e-mail, a handwritten note, or face-to-face contact. WOW Wealth Management Reviews are your greatest opportunity to demonstrate the value you bring to clients—it's your show time!

When you consider the lifetime revenue value and the lifetime referral value of your best clients, the WOW Wealth Management Review is where you should be spending your time. Peter Drucker suggests that "Concentration is the key to economic results. Economic results require that managers concentrate their efforts on the smallest number of activities that will produce the largest amount of revenue." In the long run, putting your effort on delivering WOW Wealth Management Reviews will produce the largest amount of revenue for your firm.

WOW Wealth Management Reviews are the forum for providing advice and coordinating your client's financial ecosystem. Done well, they will engender loyalty and empower your clients to become your lead-generation engine. In order to achieve your vivid description of the future, you need to leverage your most important asset—your existing client base. Quarterly engagement with your A and target B clients provides the framework to deliver value and exceed their expectations.

Many advisors are hesitant to ask clients to meet quarterly for fear that they cannot provide enough value to warrant the frequency of contact. I often hear, "My clients don't want to meet every quarter." I usually respond with, "Having spent some time with you, I can understand why." I'm just kidding, but I'm kidding on the square. If clients have hesitated to have quarterly reviews it is because of past experiences. You can change that perception by finding new ways to bring value to the relationship through WOW Wealth Management Reviews.

Keep in mind that a quarterly review has advantages for you as well as your client. Satisfied, informed clients will help build your business. And the more often you see them, the more you are going to be on their mind when referral opportunities arise.

When approaching the concept of WOW, most advisors think of client appreciation events or sending a greeting card. The value you need to bring them is not found by taking them to dinner, taking them golfing, or sending a card. The value needs to come from your expertise in managing their wealth—that is why they are paying you. You are in an intangible business. Dazzling your clients during quarterly reviews makes the intangible tangible. Client-focused WOW impressions don't require extraordinary effort—just a bit of strategic thinking.

Insights

Let's review some of the important facts in support of delivering wealth management advice.

- The 80/20 rule: The top 20 percent of an advisor's business often generates 80 percent of its revenue.

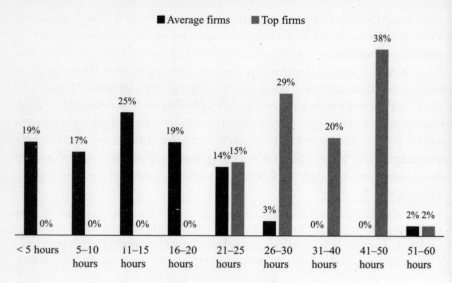

Figure 5.1   Hours per Week Working Directly with Clients.
Source: RYDEX SGI Advisor Benchmarking RIA survey, May 2009; top 26 of 561 firms.

- A survey of a group of high-end, fee-based registered investment advisors (RIAs) revealed that 94 percent of their revenue came from existing clients and their referrals.
- Industry trends suggest a need for advisors to be concerned with more than returns.
- There is a need for competitive differentiation.
- Figure 5.1 shows the hours per week advisors spend working with clients. The difference between average firms and top firms is dramatic. This is further evidence that the best use of your time is direct interaction with your existing clients.

Client Needs Analysis

The organization that is intent on shaping strategic success will not only learn to react to the demand of the marketplace, but will actively aspire to base its shape on the needs of its customers.
—William Pfeiffer, Leonard Goodstein, and
Timothy Nolan, *Shaping Strategic Planning*

A client needs analysis will provide the information you need to design your WOW Wealth Management Reviews. The client satisfaction window framework suggested in Albrecht's *The Only Thing That Matters* is an effective way for advisors to determine what they should provide their clients. The following is an effective way to evaluate your entire service model, but I have scoped this discussion to focus on the review process.

There are things clients want and get from you. There are things clients don't want but get from you anyway. In this area you are wasting resources that should be spent on the things clients want but don't get from you. This is an area of concern because the client is susceptible to leaving you if they find another advisor who will meet this need.

Client Satisfaction Window

Any delivered product or service that does not precisely fit is a waste of resources.

Resources are finite and teams have a limited capacity to deliver products and services. Teams that do not deliver what their clients need will be replaced by another team. Teams that provide products and services their clients do not need or want are wasting their resources. Only teams that focus their strategies and resources to meet the precise, known needs of their clients are maximizing their focus.

Effective teams have their fingers on the pulse of the client. Teams must turn to their clients for direction. A *client* is any person or group whose needs are met by the team. This client can be internal or external to the organization. One of the biggest mistakes I see teams make is their inability to recognize their internal customers. With organizations able to outsource to quality vendors, entire departments can disappear overnight if they are not meeting the needs of their internal customers.

In order to develop appropriate improvement strategies, a team must evaluate its client base to ensure that it is well targeted. The goal is to know how precise the fit is between client needs and team competencies, as outlined in Figure 5.2. Teams need to evaluate client segmentation in terms of present and future needs, market opportunity, price points, the value each market segment places on the team's efforts, and how secure the client base is.

As part of its client audit, the team should evaluate its own level of client knowledge and the capacity of its database to provide required information in a timely, meaningful, user-friendly manner.

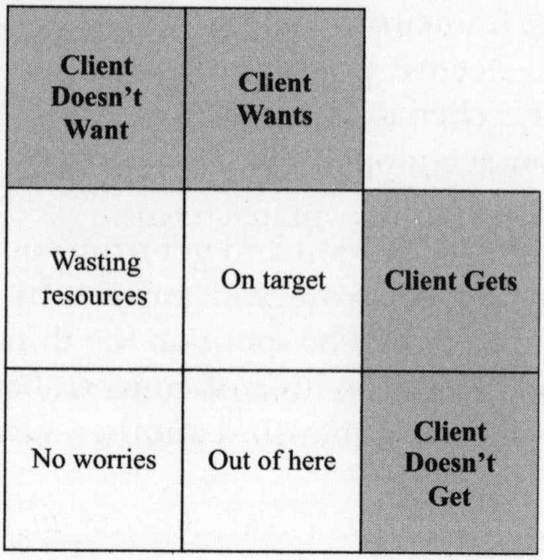

Client Doesn't Want	**Client Wants**	
Wasting resources	On target	**Client Gets**
No worries	Out of here	**Client Doesn't Get**

Figure 5.2   Client Satisfaction Window

Additionally, the team should assess its ability to use this information to target its strategies more effectively and to discover new ways to improve its value to clients.

This framework is an effective way to gain client insight. Invite four to six of your target market clients to an informal focus group. You will need to have the kind of relationship with them that will allow for direct and honest feedback. Simply ask these clients three questions:

1. What do you want that you are getting from us?
2. What don't you want but are getting from us?
3. What do you want but are not getting from us?

The following answers have been collected by advisors:

1. What do you want that you are getting from us?
   * Financial planning.
   * Investment advice.
   * Performance reporting.
   * Financial products.
2. What don't you want but you are getting from us?
   * Too many investment options and product pitches.
   * Too much detail in performance reporting.
   * Industry jargon that we cannot understand.
   * Too much paper.

3. What do you want but are not getting from us?
   - A clear financial vision of our future.
   - Feedback on financial goals.
   - A plan of how we will work together over time.
   - Communication in layman's terms.

Blue Ocean Strategy Exercise

Blue oceans are defined by untapped market space, demand creation . . . most are created by expanding existing industry boundaries.
—Chan Kim and Renee Mauborgne, *Blue Ocean Strategy*

The input from this focus group is critically important but there is a second step. This information, in combination with the collective wisdom and creativity of your team, will assist you as you begin to develop the elements of your WOW Wealth Management Review.

Answer the following four questions to work toward your blue ocean strategy:

1. What are we doing in reviews that should be eliminated?
2. What are we doing in reviews that should be reduced?
3. What are we doing in reviews that should be improved?
4. What should we start doing in reviews that we have never done?

The following represents the thinking of hundreds of advisors who have done this exercise with their teams.

1. What are we doing in reviews that should be eliminated?
   - Product pitches.
   - Industry jargon.
   - Redundant reports.
   - Performance reporting at the slice level.
2. What are we doing in reviews that should be reduced?
   - Benchmark performance reporting.
   - Education on the capital markets.
   - The number of financial products.
   - Paper-based reviews.
3. What are we doing in reviews that should be improved?
   - Make financial planning more comprehensive.
   - Tie the financial plan explicitly to the client's financial vision.

- Contextualize the components of wealth management education.
- Contextualize the capital markets information.
4. What should we start doing in reviews that we have never done?
   - Advise on all aspects of wealth management.
   - Center the review on accomplishing the client's financial vision.
   - Make goals-based reporting the primary performance reporting.tool.
   - Make the Client Engagement Roadmap the primary implementation plan.

> Companies that create the future do more than satisfy customers, they constantly amaze them.
> —Gary Hamel and C. K. Prahalad, *Competing for the Future*

The first step in creating a WOW Wealth Management Review is to determine what information you will present. By replicating the client satisfaction window exercise and the blue ocean strategy exercise, you will gain insight into your client needs, develop more interesting ways of addressing those needs, and be more emboldened in creating this review.

These are some of the components you may have determined to be in the review:

- Client Financial Vision Document.
- Client Engagement Roadmap.
- Goals-based progress report.
- High-level performance reporting (optional).
- Market commentary and quarterly outlook (optional).
- One key wealth management topic per quarter.
- Education focused on next quarter's topic.

Once the components of the review have been determined, it is time to take all of the client touch points and insert at least one WOW into each point. The cumulative effect of wow-wow-wow-wow is WOW! Consider what the client sees, hears, feels, tastes, or smells as opportunities to create your service enhancements.

The following scenario of a WOW Wealth Management Review has been field-tested hundreds of times and proven to be a sound starting point. It is built around five touch points.

First Touch Point: Set the Appointment

- Confirm availability of meeting room.
- The principal calls the client to set up the review.
- Confirm availability of attendees.
- Send a handwritten note thanking the clients for the time they are going to spend with you.

What would it look like if you made the call to the Smiths, one of your best clients, to schedule the review meeting? If you reach them, it is a positive touch and will speed up the scheduling process. If you miss them, you can leave a message for them to call your administrative assistant to schedule the meeting. It is still a positive touch and pointing them to your assistant prevents phone tag. You schedule the review three or more weeks out to ensure your team has enough time to properly prepare. Immediately upon scheduling the meeting you send a handwritten note thanking the couple for the time they are going to spend with you. This is the first drop into the WOW bucket. How long do you think it would take to write this note—45 seconds?

Second Touch Point: Premeeting Package (Two Weeks Prior to Review)

- Send a letter reminding the client of the review date and time.
- Enclose an up-to-date Financial Vision Document.
- Enclose an up-to-date Client Engagement Roadmap.

Two weeks before the review, send a packet that includes a cover letter, up-to-date Financial Vision Document, and the Client Engagement Roadmap. Ask the client to review and modify their Financial Vision Document. Point them to the roadmap and the quarter that outlines the review topics. You can ask them to call your administrative assistant if there are any modifications they would like to make to the agenda. Would they be WOWed?

WOW opportunities are limited only by your imagination. Let me share a couple of examples from other advisors. Parking in downtown

San Francisco is difficult. As part of the premeeting package an advisor included a map from the client's home to the parking lot nearest the advisor's office and a parking pass. An advisor in Chicago found that the wife would be coming from the suburbs by train and would meet her husband at the advisor's office. In their premeeting package, the advisor included a train ticket and walking directions from the train station. Because the couple was discussing building a new house, the advisor also included a copy of *Architectural Digest* for her to read on the train. Do you think they were WOWed?

Third Touch Point: Greet the Client

- Tidy-up the reception area and add fresh cut flowers.
- Receptionist greets the couple by name (keep digital pictures on file if need be).
- Receptionist offers the couple their preferred drinks (track in your customer relationship management tool).
- Prep the meeting room with fresh cut flowers, ice water, and mints.
- On fine desk blotters place your client's Financial Vision Document, goals-based report, and roadmap. Print these on high-quality milled paper.
- "Welcome Mr. and Mrs. Smith" is on conference room monitor.

Make sure your office environment is professional, but comfortable and inviting. You have already modified the area to facilitate a slower, longer-term wealth management feel. *Money* magazine and the *Wall Street Journal* have been replaced with *National Geographic*, *Islands* magazine, and *Golf Digest*. When Mr. and Mrs. Smith enter, the receptionist stands and walks to greet them with "Welcome, Mr. and Mrs. Smith. Mrs. Smith, would you like a cup of Earl Grey tea? Mr. Smith, would you like a cup of black coffee? Wonderful! Have a seat over here and I will get your drinks and let (the advisor) know you are here." Would they be WOWed?

When it is time to start the meeting, you walk out and greet Mr. and Mrs. Smith and escort them to the conference room. It, too, is spick-and-span, with fresh cut flowers, mints, a glass pitcher of ice water, and fine desk blotters on the conference table. Their needs and goals are at the center of your attention and you make it clear that they are valued clients. Would they be WOWed?

Fourth Touch Point: The Review (45 to 60 Minutes in Length)

- Financial Vision Document.
- Client Engagement Roadmap.
- Goals-based progress report.
- High-level performance reporting (optional).
- Market commentary and quarterly outlook (optional).
- One key wealth management topic per quarter.
- Education focused on next quarter's topic.

After pleasantries, you display the Smiths' Financial Vision Document on the presentation monitor. A quick review confirms there is no need to make modifications—this time. You have reviewed enough of these documents with clients to know that a change in their vision is inevitable. Your primary job is to help the Smiths continue to enrich and modify their financial vision and help them realize it by implementing appropriate strategies. You also want to reinforce with the Smiths that you take this responsibility seriously. The quick review of the Smiths' Financial Vision Document took seven minutes.

You page down to the Smiths' roadmap. *Do great things for clients and make sure they know about it* is the guiding principle upon which you have built your entire service model. Now is the time to remind them of what you have done in previous quarters and reinforce the track to run on in the future. Because it is a working document and priorities frequently change, you might spend 10 minutes reviewing and modifying the wealth management topics for the next two quarters. You mention that you will send them an updated roadmap as an attachment to your meeting follow-up e-mail. This is also a good time to mention that you would be pleased to print them any of the documents that are being reviewed.

Next, bring up the Smiths' goals-based report (Figure 5.3). This is their favorite part of the review. They just want to see if they are making adequate progress. Over the past seven years, the only times they have been below the lower control limit were the fourth quarter of 2008 and the first two quarters of 2009. At that time they made the decision to move their financial independence date out two years. They also decided to move into a two-bedroom condo rather than staying in the home where they raised their kids. This topic took up the bulk of that previous meeting. These were tough but necessary decisions. Fortunately, today they have made significant progress

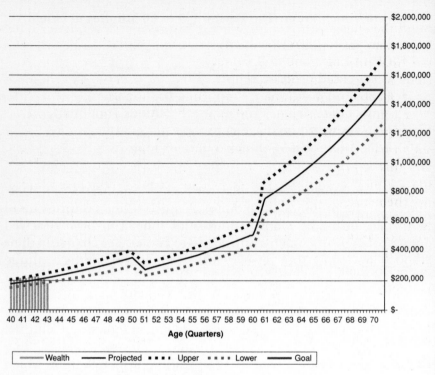

Figure 5.3   Goals-Based Reporting

toward the revised goals so the discussion doesn't take any more than five minutes.

Satisfied that they are on track, there isn't the slightest indication that they are interested in reviewing the performance of their investments, so although you have built a hyperlink from the goals-based report to performance reports, there is no need to click on it. The Smiths most likely felt the same way about market commentary and quarterly outlook, but you thought better of blowing by the quarterly outlook. The markets were still uncertain enough to spend 10 minutes explaining the contrasting data and the uncertainty of the markets, and reinforcing the diversified, long-term institutional approach you are implementing on their behalf.

Next, you move to the wealth management topic scheduled for the quarter—their spending plan. By cutting their expenses 15 percent and putting that capital to work in the marketplace you could make a profound difference in the level of confidence and peace of mind they have with regards to their financial independence date. They came prepared. Over the past three months they had read the personal finance book you gave them and, for the first time ever, came in with the details of their spending that would allow them to make fact-based decisions.

Clearly there was value in facilitating the decisions to cut expenses by 15 percent. You know that there are things that an investment solution can't fix. Sometimes there are other levers you need to pull, and this was one of them. Some pre-retirees need to be reminded that it's their savings that should be expected to do the heavy lifting, not the markets. The Smiths asked you to provide a forcing function that would help them bend to their spending plan. You have heard some of your peers refer to these requests as "babysitting," but you know that not taking action on a decision that has been made is a recipe for failure. You gladly accept the invitation of reviewing the budget with them monthly over the next three months. The Smiths are pleased to have addressed what has been a point of contention for them by confronting the issue and they are thrilled with your willingness to provide a forcing function to ensure execution. This part of the review lasted 22 minutes.

Next, you bring up their roadmap again. In this version the current quarter's topics are checked off as having been completed. You direct them to the next quarter's wealth management topic, "Modify retirement vision," and hand the couple two books: *The New Retirementality* by Mitch Anthony and *The 100 Best Volunteer Vacations to Enrich your Life* by Pam Grout. You ask them to read the two books, revisit their vision after their financial independence date, and come to the next review prepared to modify this portion of their Financial Vision Document.

Fifth Touch Point: Follow-Through

- Walk the client to the elevator or their car—listen for value-add opportunities.
- Send a timely follow-up e-mail which contains:
  - A summary of the decisions that were made.
  - Next actions for the wealth management team.
  - Next actions for the client.
  - An updated Financial Vision Document and Client Engagement Roadmap.

At the end of the meeting you offer to walk them to their car. You notice that once you leave the meeting room, their conversation changes—probably the release of tension. They begin to talk about their two children. Their daughter is in her final year at Duke, interested in alternative fuels, and wants to get her master's degree in chemical engineering. Their son, a former jock, wants to teach history and coach in high school. He is in his final quarter at Seattle University, in a program where he can simultaneously earn a master's degree and a teaching certificate.

Returning upstairs to your office, you ask your administrative assistant to go to Amazon.com and send the Smiths a copy of *Natural Capitalism* by Amory Lovins, Hunter Lovins, and Paul Hawkens, for their daughter, and Malcolm Gladwell's *Outliers* for their son. Over the next hour you sit down to write your follow-up e-mail. You review the decisions that were made and remind them of their to-dos and of the action items for you and your team. You push "Send" and enter the team's action items in your customer relationship management (CRM) software. You have another hour before your next review, giving you time to mentally rehearse and catch up on loose ends.

Six Coaching Points

1. Advisors often question the recommendation of having the principal call to set the appointment. They wonder if it is time well spent. Remember who we are doing this for—your best clients! If you reach them, it is a positive touch. How much time did it take—5 to 10 minutes tops? And if you miss them, the voice message is still a positive touch.

   With that said, this is a good time to remind you of the common sense principle. Every advisor has his unique circumstances. What works for one advisor may damage another. Should your relationship manager have a close rapport with your best clients and they are comfortable with the way reviews have been scheduled, you may not want to monkey with who calls to set up the review. But even if your relationship manager sets up the appointment, you can still send the thank you note.

2. Make your WOW Wealth Management Review your own. Your team is limited only by their imagination and your pragmatism.

3. To ensure the facility is spick-and-span, I counsel teams to conduct a fresh-eyes walk-through. Over time, it can be easy

to ignore blemishes in your office environment. You should periodically perform this walk-through, thinking about the impression your office makes. The fresh-eyes walk-through is how you overcome scotomas. A *scotoma* is an area of partial or complete loss of vision surrounded by an area of normal vision. In other words, you develop blind spots and it becomes easy to overlook things that are in plain sight. Don't let an eyesore detract from your WOW Wealth Management Review. With the entire team, start in the parking lot, walking into the facility, up the elevator, enter the reception area, and finally walk into the meeting room. By pointing out and making note of the eyesores, you can prioritize and remove them over time.

Eyesores fade when you see them every day. Be critical about the presentation of your office. When you walk through, what is the impression you get? How inviting, comforting, and confidence-inspiring is the environment you welcome clients and prospects to? I've been surprised how unappealing some advisors' offices are. One such visit highlighted a lot of typical flaws. I arrived at their building but the business wasn't displayed on the directory. They had separated from an accounting firm in the building and had not added their own listing. I guessed and took the elevator. There were two reception areas off the elevator. One was for the accounting firm that the advisors had left. I got a poor reception there because it wasn't a pleasant separation. I was pointed to the other reception area where the hallway was uninviting, lined by a good number of artificial plants. I have seen plastic plants that you have to check to see if they are real or not; I have even picked a small branch and pinched it with my thumbnail. These didn't need the thumbnail test—they were cheap, plastic, and covered with dust. As I approached the empty receptionist desk I discovered that it had become a storage area. There were old worn-out printers, excess trays, reams of paper, and more. There was no one in position to greet me. When I stepped back into their office space someone finally pointed me to the meeting room. With the exception of the eraser holder having been pulled away from the wall, the meeting room was adequate.

Don't let seemingly minor flaws get in the way of your WOW impression.

4. Take the time to review progress on individual goals. Many people respond well to visual demonstrations. Prepare illustrations that document goals in relation to dollars and time.

Goals-based reporting keeps the discussion at a strategic rather than a tactical level. The control limits exist to make certain that the client stays within a specified range as they progress toward their goals, as seen in Figure 5.3. This hypothetical example reflects a combination of personal savings (contributions) and investment earnings in relation to a goal of $1.5 million at age 63. Control limits may also need to be strategically adjusted over time in response to market conditions and investor objectives.

For example, if the client was below the lower control limit for an extended period of time you would be able to have a strategic conversation about adjustments. The adjustments you could consider would be:

- You could extend the time frame to retirement.
- You could change the vision and the amount necessary to retire.
- You may want to discuss downsizing to free up equity and get back on track.

5. Reserve a minimum of an hour after the review to write and send the follow-up e-mail like the one in Figure 5.4, summarizing the decisions that were made and highlighting the next actions for the wealth management team and the client.

6. When I reintroduce the concept of quarterly reviews in my High Speed Strategic Planning sessions, I often get push-back. After hearing my appeal about advisors' responsibility to deliver information to clients frequently enough to provide them with financial peace of mind, many advisors are still skeptical. I just ask them to trust the process long enough to see the impact the WOW Wealth Management Review has with their clients. By their next quarterly meeting, the skeptics will have become converts.

There are situations when you may need flexibility. You may come up against a client who despises fighting traffic and parking to come to your office. Or you may have one who lives in Scottsdale six months out of the year. In those

It was truly a pleasure meeting with the two of you this morning. Both of you are really wonderful people, and it is my sincere pleasure to count you among my friends and clients. I thought a quick summary and the "to-do" items from our meeting would be helpful.

Congratulations! Understanding your spending needs is easier said than done, as few people really have a good handle on what they are currently spending and even fewer have a grasp on how spending needs may change in the future. Having done this for more than two decades, I am satisfied that the decisions you made today should reduce your monthly spending by your targeted 15 percent.

Investing these savings in alignment with our current strategy will more than likely provide the cushion you want for your financial independence day target in five and a half years. My team will work with you to set up a money link to make the execution as automatic as possible, and we will get started immediately updating your financial plan to reflect this decision. I will add a review of the impact of your financial independence day plan as a topic for our next review.

Also, in preparation for your next review, if the two of you will read and discuss The New Retirementality *and* The 100 Best Volunteer Vacations to Enrich Your Life, *I know you will find them enjoyable and that they will provide ideas that will enrich your Financial Vision Document.*

Thanks again for the opportunity to help with this important planning. We love working with you!

Figure 5.4   Follow-Up E-mail

situations, you can leverage GoToMeeting.com or Microsoft Office Live Meeting as a way to provide your review. You will not be able to greet clients with their drinking preferences or have them experience a meeting room with fresh cut flowers and a pitcher of ice water, but you can do everything practical that does not require their presence. You can still call to make the appointment and follow up with a handwritten note. You can still send the premeeting package. In fact, in some ways, the online meeting is a WOW.

Remember, do great things for clients and make sure they know about it!

Most advisors came into the business as investment/insurance salespeople or as financial planners. Neither occupation will prepare an advisor to run a business. In particular, advisors migrating from investment counseling to wealth management have little experience with building systems. So building systems in support of delivering WOW Wealth Management Reviews will be a real adventure for most of you. If you will make building this system a priority and persist in its implementation, the long-term results can far exceed your expectations. I have seen hundreds of your peers experience spectacular results.

Building the WOW Review System

Begin building the system by determining the components of your WOW Wealth Management Review and then make a flowchart for each piece. By making this a team exercise, you will further clarify functional roles and determine more accurate time frames for getting the components of the review package into the premeeting and/or meeting package. See the flowchart examples in Figures 5.5 to 5.10.

Example 1 (Figure 5.5):

1. A staff member pulls the Client Financial Vision Document and the Client Engagement Roadmap from the client's file and passes it to the advisor.
2. The advisor reviews and modifies both documents as necessary.
3. A staff member cleans up and brands the documents to make it client ready.
4. A staff member places one copy in the premeeting package that is to be mailed and the other in the meeting package (paper and electronic) for the client review.

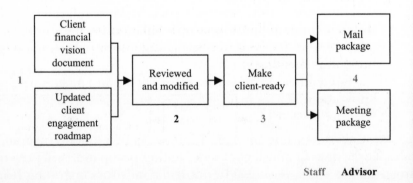

Figure 5.5   Client Financial Vision Document and Client Engagement Roadmap Process

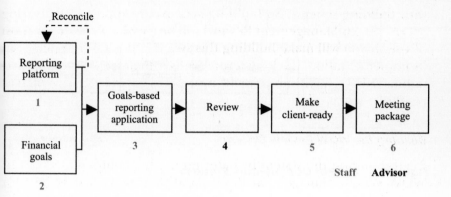

Figure 5.6   Goals-Based Reporting Process

Example 2 (Figure 5.6):

1. A staff member pulls the quarterly balances from the reporting platform, reconciles if necessary, and enters the data into the goals-based reporting application.
2. A staff member pulls the financial goals from the client file and enters the data into the goals-based reporting application.
3. A staff member runs the goals-based report and passes it to the advisor.
4. The advisor modifies or approves the goals-based report.
5. A staff member cleans up and brands the document to make it client ready.
6. A staff member places a copy in the meeting package (paper and electronic) for the client review.

Example 3 (Figure 5.7):

1. A staff member pulls the quarterly balances from the reporting platform, reconciles if necessary, and enters the data into the reporting application.

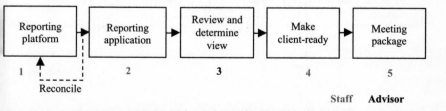

Figure 5.7   High-Level Performance Reporting Process

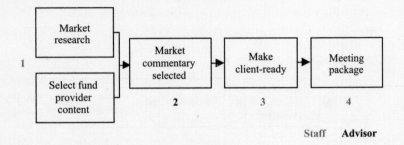

Figure 5.8   Market Commentary Process

2. The advisor reviews the performance report and selects the view to present to his client.
3. A staff member cleans up and brands the document to make it client ready.
4. A staff member places a copy in the meeting package (paper and electronic) for the client review.

Example 4 (Figure 5.8):

1. A staff member downloads market commentary options.
2. The advisor reviews the market commentary, highlights key points.
3. A staff member prepares market commentary for presentation and brands the document to make it client ready.
4. A staff member places a copy in the meeting package (paper and electronic) for the client review.

Example 5 (Figure 5.9):

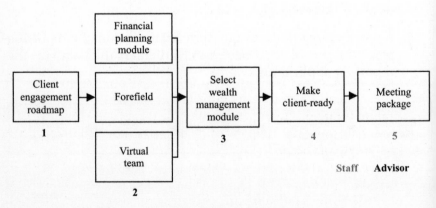

Staff   Advisor

Figure 5.9   Wealth Management Topic Process

1. The advisor pulls the Client Engagement Roadmap from the meeting file and determines this quarter's wealth management topic.
2. The advisor surveys available content from the financial planning modules, Forefield.com, or services from virtual team members/specialists.
3. The advisor selects the wealth management module.
4. A staff member scrubs and brands the module or the advisor coordinates with virtual team members to fine-tune the delivery of the wealth management module.
5. A staff member places a module and/or support material copy in the meeting package (paper and electronic) for the client review.

Example 6 (Figure 5.10):

1. The a staff member pulls the Client Engagement Roadmap from the meeting file and determines the next quarter's wealth management topic.
2. A staff member views the next quarter's wealth management topic and searches the team's educational library, Forefield .com, and select fund provider sites for appropriate educational content.
3. The advisor determines the educational content for the review.

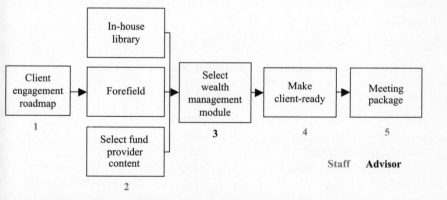

Figure 5.10   Educational Content Process

4. A staff member cleans up and brands the educational content.
5. A staff member places a copy in the meeting package (paper and electronic) for the client review.

Decisions

> Every idea you "steal" should be adapted and enhanced to fit your special circumstances . . . your goal should remain the achievement of uniqueness. Uniqueness most often comes not from a breakthrough idea, but from the accumulation of thousands of tiny enhancements.
>
> —Tom Peters, *Thriving on Chaos*

Your insight into delivering WOW Wealth Management Reviews has prepared you to make the following critical business decisions. One fun part of my job is to lay down a track for advisors to run on and then watch as these advisors begin to modify, tweak, and vary it to meet their own unique skill set and leverage the best of what they bring to clients today. In fact, I love the variety. Capturing your best ideas is the life blood necessary for me to continue to enrich this content. My only request is, if you are not sure whether you want to try a new concept or not, try it. That is the only way you will benefit from these concepts. Table 5.1 provides an example of the WOW Wealth Management Review Package.

WOW Wealth Management Review Package

What are the components of your WOW Wealth Management Review package?

Table 5.1   WOW Wealth Management Review Package

Components	Source
Client Financial Vision Document	Client file
Client Engagement Roadmap	Client file
Goals-based reporting	Client file
High-level performance reporting	PortfolioCenter, Albridge, proprietary
Market commentary	Fund and/or research firm you prefer
Wealth management topics	Virtual team of providers (see Chapter 6)
Educational content	Forefield.com

Decide the process for building the components of your WOW. Decide on the touch points and the WOW you are going to insert in each. Based on your fresh eyes walk through what changes should be made to your facility.

Actions

> Wide-ranging research on software development, airlines, the air traffic control system, oil refineries, nuclear power plants, aircraft carriers, NASA, and the automobile industry show it is impossible for even the most talented people to do competent, let alone do brilliant work, in a flawed system. Yet, a well-designed system filed with ordinary—but well trained—people can consistently achieve stunning performance levels.
>   —Jeffrey Pfeffer and Robert Sutton, *Hard Facts,*
>   *Dangerous Half-Truths & Total Nonsense*

After gaining insight and making decisions it is time to take action. The following provides a framework for you to start delivering WOW Wealth Management Reviews.

Translate the key process steps into an action plan. In the example, I have used a T-minus system and have selected the deliverables that are binary and verifiable because they allow you to manage the process. If a file has been pulled and delivered to you, it gets a checkmark. If you have phoned the client to set an appointment and it is on the team's calendar, it gets a checkmark. It is that simple—these are binary, verifiable outcomes.

Note that I have used Mondays and Fridays for preparation. That is to accommodate the best practice of reserving Tuesday, Wednesday, and Thursday for delivering WOW Wealth Management Reviews.

Select a client to use to pilot your first WOW Wealth Management Review as shown in Table 5.2. Advisors have had success with choosing one of their best clients with whom they have excellent rapport, someone who will provide unvarnished feedback. Have this client in mind as you translate the steps into an action plan. Consider using this simple paper-based system for the first three or four reviews while you fine-tune the system before migrating it to your CRM software.

> Apparent differences between people arise almost entirely from action of the system that they work in, not from the people themselves.
>   —Edwards Deming, *Out of the Crisis*

Table 5.2 WOW Wealth Management Review Action Plan

Client: Mr. and Mrs. Smith				
Day	**Milestones**	**Owner**	**Date**	**✓**
−20	Pull file and deliver it to the advisor	Staff	1/3/11	
−20	Phone client to set appointment	Advisor	1/3/11	
−20	Send hand-written thank you note/meeting reminder	Advisor	1/3/11	
−16	Create WOW Wealth Management Review action plan	Advisor	1/7/11	
−16	Action plan and assignments to team	Advisor	1/7/11	
−16	Write premeeting package letter	Advisor	1/10/11	
−15	Client-ready Financial Vision Document	Staff	1/10/11	
−15	Client-ready Client Engagement Roadmap	Staff	1/10/11	
−15	Assemble and mail premeeting package	Staff	1/10/11	
−11	Compile high-level performance report	Advisor	1/14/11	
−11	Select market commentary	Advisor	1/14/11	
−11	Select wealth management module	Advisor	1/14/11	
−11	Select educational materials	Advisor	1/14/11	
−8	Client Financial Vision Document in review file	Staff	1/17/11	
−8	Roadmap in review file	Staff	1/17/11	
−8	Goals-based report in review file	Staff	1/17/11	
−6	Market commentary in review file	Staff	1/21/11	
−6	Wealth management module in review file	Staff	1/21/11	
−6	Education content in review fie	Staff	1/21/11	
−6	Other agenda items—based on client requests	Staff	1/21/11	
−6	Insert performance report hyperlinks into goals-based report	Staff	1/21/11	
−2	Review meeting package	Advisor	1/24/11	
−2	Fresh eyes walk-through, facilities check, technology check	Staff	1/24/11	
0	WOW Wealth Management Review	Advisor	1/25/11	
0	Write meeting notes	Advisor	1/25/11	
0	Assign action items to team members or virtual team	Advisor	1/25/11	
0	Modify Financial Vision Document	Advisor	1/25/11	
0	Modify Client Engagement Roadmap	Advisor	1/25/11	
0	Follow-up e-mail to client	Advisor	1/25/11	
0	Send value add	Staff	1/25/11	
+1	Close file	Staff	1/26/11	
+1	Post Mortem of first WOW Wealth Management Review	Advisor	1/26/11	

Do great things for clients and make sure they know about it! Remember, the WOW Wealth Management Review is your show time!

Chapter Summary

Key Points

- Many advisors believe their primary value-add is their investment knowledge. To their clients, reviews feel like they are taking a statistics course in a foreign language. Even though the advisor may be aware that clients leave a review confused and sometimes embarrassed by their lack of investment acumen, the advisor cannot break the habit of delivering investment reviews.
- The discipline of delivering WOW Wealth Management Reviews breaks this ineffective habit, allowing the advisor to deliver information within the context of the client's goals and financial ecosystem.
- The WOW Wealth Management Review is your show time. Clients care very little about the amount of work you've done on their behalf; they just care about their review experience. Give them something to talk about with their friends and colleagues.
- Most of what you do is intangible—your intellectual capital and the advice you provide.
- The WOW Wealth Management Review is designed to make your business more tangible by WOWing the client's senses. It turns your intangible advisory business into a tangible business worthy of referrals.
- Quarterly engagement with your A and target market B clients provides the framework to deliver value and exceed their expectations. When you consider retention of your largest clients and their referral value, putting your effort on delivering WOW reviews will produce the greatest return on your time.
- Top firms spend significantly more time working with clients than do other firms.
- The WOW Wealth Management Review gives clients something to talk about—a prerequisite to viral marketing.
- The first step in creating a WOW Wealth Management Review is to determine what information you will present in the review.
- A client needs analysis will provide the information you need to determine the components in your WOW Wealth Management Review. Find out from your clients the things they want and get from you, the things they don't want but get from you, and the things they want but don't get from you.

This is an area of concern because the client is susceptible to leaving you if they find another advisor who will meet their needs.

- Translate that data into a decision by asking the following blue ocean strategy questions:
  - What are we doing in reviews that should be eliminated?
  - What are we doing in reviews that should be reduced?
  - What are we doing in reviews that should be improved?
  - What should we start doing in reviews that we have never done?
- Once the components of the review have been determined, it is time to take all of the client touch points and insert a WOW into each point. The cumulative effect of wow-wow-wow-wow is WOW! Consider what the client sees, hears, feels, tastes, or smells as opportunities to create your service enhancements.
- The following are examples of how you can put WOWs into the touch points:
  - After setting the appointment, you send a handwritten note thanking the clients for the time they are going to spend with you.
  - Two weeks before the review, you send a packet that includes a cover letter, up-to-date Financial Vision Document, and a Client Engagement Roadmap.
  - The receptionist stands and greets the clients by name and offers them their drink preferences.
  - There are fresh cut flowers, mints, and a glass pitcher of ice water on the conference table. On the flat screen, you review the client's Financial Vision Document, Client Engagement Roadmap, goals-based report (clients just want to see the ball move toward their goal). Handing the client Mitch Anthony's *The New Retirementality* to read will prepare the client for next quarter's wealth management topic, "Retirement Planning—Vision."
  - You walk your clients to their car, and in doing so you are reminded that the couple's daughter is in her final year at Duke and is interested in alternative fuels, while their son is in his final quarter at Seattle University, earning his master's degree and teaching certificate simultaneously.
  - Returning to your office, you ask your administrative assistant to go to Amazon.com and send the clients *Natural Capitalism* for their daughter and *Outliers* for their son.

CHAPTER 6

Stop the Rainmaker Approach and Start the Team Approach

The Sixth Ineffective Habit: The Rainmaker Approach

As an inquisitive intern, Jack paid close attention to the hierarchy in the office. Who got the corner offices, who did management listen to, who got the reward trips and dinners? They are the rainmakers. Rainmakers are the advisors who have an exceptional ability to attract new clients. They possess a rare, almost mystical quality that allows them to seed the market so that it will rain new clients—the lifeblood of a financial firm.

Acquiring new clients was so vital to the firm that a significant amount of the rainmaker's compensation was based on it. It was referred to as an "eat what you kill" environment, and the successful rainmakers were making a killing. Over time the others simply faded away. Fortunately for Jack, he developed this rainmaking ability and became one of the winners.

Face-to-face time with a prospect or client is considered to be the highest and best use of the rainmaker's time. They are coached to delegate everything else possible to administrative or service staff. Because successful rainmakers are so well compensated, their support staff isn't—and that is a problem. Profit has to come from somewhere.

An unspoken implication of the rainmaker approach is that there isn't enough money left to hire a high-quality support staff.

Jack faced constant turnover of his support staff. There were a lot of second-tier jobs around and if someone found one that was closer to home, they were gone. Others would leave after calculating the small amount they were netting after paying for child care and transportation. If he was lucky enough to find a good hire, they would soon be snapped up by someone else willing to pay more.

This revolving door severely restricted organizational learning. By the time a team member had figured out a task well enough to pass on the learning to another, they were gone. Jack thought that perhaps building systems and a training process could overcome some of the people challenges. But he didn't have a clue how to build either. Besides, it would take away from his face-to-face time with prospects and clients. He began to think that there had to be a better organizational strategy than the rainmaker approach.

The discrepancy between what rainmakers and others made created a "haves and have-nots" culture. The haves liked the attention of management, the prestige, the perks, the power, and the money. They wanted to keep it that way. The others felt resentful for not getting their fair share. The culture of the rainmaker approach fostered anything but teamwork. When assigned tasks, the have-nots procrastinated, did the very minimum, or found a way to avoid the work. Not keeping commitments created a lack of trust. In addition to not getting work done, they were often sullen. Jack had heard another rainmaker refer to his staff as psychic vampires that would suck the energy out of him any time he had to engage them.

By Jack's twelfth year in the business his service capacity was about tapped out. Ninety-five percent of his face-to-face time was now being spent servicing existing clients. No wonder his growth had slowed so dramatically. A metaphor he had heard came to mind: "A bicycle that is standing still is hard to balance, but not as difficult as a business that is standing still." With the rainmaker approach, he was beginning to feel as though he were coming to a stop with his feet trapped in the pedal clamp-ons.

How in the world would he be able to deliver wealth management advice to his best clients? Jack had made the decision that this was the year to migrate these clients to a more comprehensive service model. Many of his best clients were baby boomers nearing retirement. They needed more than just investment advice. But he didn't have the service capacity, the staff, or the time to build the competencies to bring wealth management to his clients.

Jack's dream to be a rainmaker had turned out to be a nightmare for him. The rainmaker approach wasn't good enough. Jack wanted more.

The Sixth Discipline: Start the Team Approach

The team approach is the discipline or strategy of working collaboratively as a group to achieve greater levels of client satisfaction, team rewards, and business success. Because of my coaching background, I am particularly attuned to team dynamics and effectiveness, and am excited about sharing the best practices of the team approach.

> There are many objects of great value to man which cannot be attained by unconnected individuals, but must be attained, if at all, by association.
> —Daniel Webster, speech, Pittsburgh, July 1833

Insights

Because you cannot fix a problem unless you understand what it is, the first step in breaking this habit is to gain insight into what is working and what should be improved. You should include the team in this process. Your evaluation will be more accurate, and you will therefore be more likely to determine core issues and develop more effective solutions. Additionally, the team will be more committed to improvement efforts if they are based on *our* rather than *your* insights.

Team Core Competency Audit

> A core competency is a bundle of skills and technologies that enables a company to provide a particular benefit to customers.
> —Gary Hamel and C. K. Prahalad, *Competing for the Future*

Your firm's success is largely dependent upon your team's core competencies. These are the abilities, systems, and technologies necessary to acquire and serve clients. Begin this exercise by determining the three to five core competencies most essential to building your business. Then clarify a world-class standard for each competency. Following are some examples.

- *Marketing.* Marketing is the ability to create demand for a firm's advisory services. World-class marketers have a clear strategic focus. They have identified both an exciting target market and a service focus that is explicitly designed to meet the needs of those clients. World-class advisors know the way to attract high-net-worth prospects through viral marketing (see Chapter 7). They are highly skilled at winning the hearts and minds of their existing clients and providing them with the language to refer their friends and colleagues.
- *Sales.* Consultative sales allow an advisor to understand a prospect's goals and needs by asking the right questions and listening to their answers. Through this process, the advisor can then recommend a compelling solution that will cause the prospect to become a client. Because the sales cycle occurs over time, world-class advisors have a sales process that ensures rigor and coordination between team members.
- *Wealth management advisory service.* Delivering wealth management requires a competency to help a client develop realistic financial goals, then manage strategies to achieve those goals. This requires planning, money, time, and the ongoing coordination of the client's financial ecosystem. World-class advisors have a deep knowledge of comprehensive wealth management. They utilize technologies to create systems and leverage a virtual team of experts to ensure their clients are receiving the highest-quality wealth management services. This system ensures the client's financial affairs are aligned and optimized to achieve their goals.
- *Organizational.* A team with world-class organizational competencies has well-designed systems for recruiting, training, retaining, and managing. These organizations have alignment and effective empowerment. Their collaborative environment fosters open communication and an esprit de corps that generates team synergy. They also have the ability to manage team members up, or out, if necessary.

Table 6.1   Team Core Competency Audit

Competency	Poor	Below Average	Average	Above Average	World-Class
	1	2	3	4	5
Marketing		X			
Sales			X		
Wealth management advisory service			X		
Organizational		X			

> A company must be viewed not only as a portfolio of products and services, but a portfolio of competencies as well.
> —Jim Collins and Jerry Porras, *Built to Last*

Once you have determined your competencies and a world-class standard for each, rate these on a one-to-five scale, as demonstrated in Table 6.1. Be careful not to kid yourself about how you stack up against your world-class standard. This is one area I have found where advisors have difficulty confronting the brutal facts of their current reality.

Evaluating your organizational competencies will highlight areas where you can improve. Because a core competency is a bundle of skills and technologies, improvement efforts should focus on:

- Improving current technologies or the use of them.
- Leveraging an outside resource that has a necessary competency.
- Team development plans focused on building individual competencies.
- Hiring a new team member who has a necessary competency.

Long-term team success will ultimately be predicated on the desire of the individual team member to want to improve. A team's evaluation of its ability to continually improve would be far from complete without an objective evaluation of each member's desire to improve technical skills, collaborative skills, and dependability.

Team Development Evaluation

Bruce Tuckman is a psychologist who focused much of his career work on group dynamics. He created a team development model that tracks four stages—forming, storming, norming, and performing. Figure 6.1 is an interpretation of how this cycle plays out in the advisory world.

- *Forming*: The team comes together and initially the morale is high. They feel they have assembled an exceptional team and are optimistic about their future success. As you would expect, a team in the forming phase has not had time to clarify goals, strategies, or team member roles, so their performance is understandably poor.
- *Storming*: This phase sucks. Not only does the performance continue to be poor, but team morale plummets. At its best, this team experience is a mess, largely consisting of ongoing debates about team goals, strategies, and roles. At its worst, this phase can be marked by passive-aggressive withholding, stubbornness, and negative talk behind closed doors.

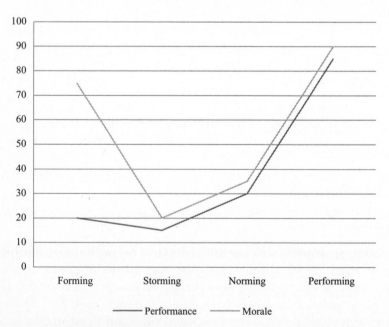

Figure 6.1   Team Development Cycle

Forming   Storming   Norming   Performing

Figure 6.2   Team Development Cycle Evaluation

- *Norming*: In this phase the team members begin to agree on their goals, strategies, and roles. Dysfunctional debates are replaced by healthier team dialog and a genuine desire for consensus. The closed-door complaining is replaced by camaraderie. As a result, both morale and performance begin to improve.
- *Performing*: In this phase, the team is kicking ass and taking names. Both performance and morale take off. Time goes by quickly. Good ideas are popping and team members engage in good-natured kidding. If a team could stay in this phase, life would be great—but it can't. The cycle will begin again if there is a major change in the marketplace, if goals change, if roles change, or if you lose or gain a key team member.

The most important thing I've learned about this team development model is that team members determine the length of this cycle. I have seen teams willing to put the cause of the team ahead of the individual; such teams move through this cycle quickly, sometimes in a month or less. I have also seen teams stay in the storming phase for years.

Use Figure 6.2 to determine where your team is on this cycle. Evaluating your team's development cycle will provide insight into how to help the team move to the next phase more quickly, thereby improving both the team's performance and morale.

Team Alignment and Empowerment Evaluation

A team is aligned when it has a compelling vision, agreed-upon strategies, supporting action plans, and clear roles for how each team member can contribute. The authority level to make decisions should be established for each role. The authority to make decisions should be based on the complexity of the decision, the competency of the team member, and the consequences for making the decision. To have role clarity, team members need to understand their authority for making decisions within their functional roles.

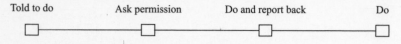

Figure 6.3   Decision-Making Continuum

> Empowerment means people have the freedom to act. It also
> means they are accountable for results.
> —Ken Blanchard, *Leading at a Higher Level*

Teams that have developed guiding principles have a head start
on empowerment, but it's not a black-and-white concept. Empowerment is not binary—it is on a continuum. (See Figure 6.3.)

There are certain things that people are told to do. There are
things, depending on the business benefits and risks, they should ask
for permission to do. There are things, depending on the business
benefits and risks, they should do and report back to the team. Finally, there will be some decisions that team members should have
complete autonomy in making. These are things that can be done
without asking or needing to report back. Team members are empowered when they feel confident to make decisions and take action.
Taking appropriate initiative is dependent upon the skills and wisdom of the team member within the context of the potential business
benefits and risks.

Where does your team rank on alignment and empowerment?
In Figure 6.4, for example, I have rated a team as a 2 on alignment

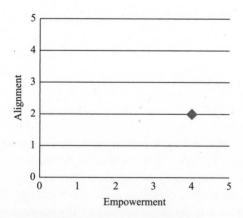

Figure 6.4   Team Alignment and Empowerment

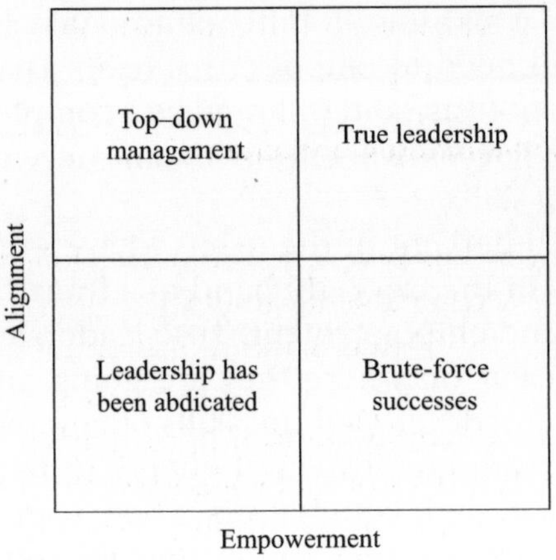

	Top–down management	True leadership
Alignment	Leadership has been abdicated	Brute-force successes

Empowerment

Figure 6.5   Management Styles

and a 4 on empowerment. The chart in Figure 6.5 explains how management styles can affect the team environment.

More than 75 percent of the advisors attending my High Speed Strategic Planning sessions start out in the bottom right-hand quadrant where they depend on brute-force successes. These teams lack alignment. The rainmaker's management style is to hire good people and get out of their way. Problems arise because their successes are not easily replicable and the price of hiring good people is typically steep. Instead, take the time to build the systems that are aligned with your goals and train and empower the team to perform within these systems. By addressing these alignment issues and building repeatable systems, teams can gain traction quickly.

Approximately 10 percent of the teams in my sessions find themselves in the bottom left-hand quadrant and lack both alignment and empowerment. Having little interest in building a high-performance team, rainmakers abdicate their leadership responsibility. This isn't surprising, because most rainmakers start out as salespeople or financial planners; neither prepares them to manage. Success will require the rainmaker to develop leadership and management skills.

About 5 percent of the teams in my sessions rate themselves as being in the top left quadrant and managed top-down. The team is aligned but lacks empowerment. This is where the people on the top do the thinking and the people below get "thunked." This culture is usually created by a dominant, smart, hands-on, micromanaging rainmaker. Change will occur only when this leader recognizes he can no longer do it all himself. If he wants to take his business to the next level, he will need to empower his team. Developing effective empowerment is not easy and will require a complete paradigm shift by the rainmaker. Success will require that he develop new leadership and management skills.

Fewer than 10 percent of the teams I have worked with initially rated themselves in the top right-hand quadrant. These teams have both alignment and empowerment. True leadership allows teams to be aligned and clear on where they are going and how they plan to get there. Having developed the skills of empowerment, they are able to unleash team creativity and energy to implement business solutions faster than their competitors. These teams tend to improve the longer they work together, as long as they continually integrate new, fresh ideas. If you want to grow your business and enjoy the journey, this is where you'll want to be.

Internal Challenges

> An essential quality of a good manager is a determination to deal with any kind of bad news head on, to seek it out rather than deny it.
>
> —Bill Gates, *Business @ the Speed of Thought*

When I was consulting at Microsoft, I accompanied two of my good friends and clients, Bill Henningsgaard and Blake Irving, on a golfing trip to Bandon Dunes on the Oregon Coast. Bill had just gotten his private pilot license and had purchased an airplane. How much fun is that?

The scenery on the flight down was marvelous—the San Juan Islands, the Washington and Oregon coasts. We had to fly under some cloud cover that made it particularly interesting. As we neared the Bandon airport, Bill turned into the wind on his approach to land. The landing was a little rough. Bill apologized over and over but Blake and I acted like it was nothing out of the ordinary. We were on the ground, safe and sound, and that's all that really mattered. We had a great day of golf on an incredible course and a less memorable flight back to Seattle.

The next week I was working with another Microsoft client, Gene Boes. I told him the story of the landing in Bandon and how Bill said he had flown the plane "into the runway." I didn't know what he meant by that. After I finished the short story, Gene told me that he flew for the Navy and had landed on aircraft carriers for nine years, having 342 *traps*, or landings. I asked him if the carrier was rocking side to side and he said, "Yes—and it is also going up and down." He told me that 156 of his landings were at night and he was often guided by a single light. He went on to explain that when the plane touches the carrier deck, you travel less than 300 feet and go from 150 miles per hour to zero in less than three seconds. Gene explained that when you land you are trying to catch your tail hook on the third of four arresting wires. After the trap, pilots go full throttle until they are signaled to cut their engines. If a wire were to break, this would enable them to take off—otherwise they would end up in the ocean. After explaining this landing procedure to me, he paused and said, "But that is not nearly as hard as managing people."

I relay this story to you because many advisors who go through an organizational evaluation beat themselves up about the situation. Don't! I make my living helping advisors go through the insight, decision, and action process and can tell you that if you are lacking significant competencies, are between storming and norming in the team development cycle, or are reliant on brute force successes in your business, you are normal. You simply need to gain insight about the issues, make decisions on how to improve, and then take action to progress. If you make this a painful experience you will not be as willing to look at the problems. And if you don't know what the problem is, you won't be able to solve it.

What are your five biggest internal challenges that, if fixed, would have the greatest impact on your business results? Do not limit your answers to the insight you gained in your competency audit, team development cycle, or alignment and empowerment evaluation. Once you have determined these challenges, decide the possible solutions to each problem. Table 6.2 is a synthesis of the challenges processed by hundreds of advisory teams.

At this point, you have processed your team competency audit, team development cycle, team alignment and empowerment evaluation, and looked at your internal challenges. You now have the context to begin the evaluation of the team approach.

The Organizational Structure of the Team Approach

Increasingly, financial products are perceived as commodities. It is becoming more and more difficult to differentiate yourself based upon product access, selection, and performance. In addition to

Table 6.2   Samples of Internal Challenges and Possible Solutions

Internal Challenges	Possible Solutions
Lack of team alignment.	Create a team business plan. Create a functional organizational chart.
Lack financial planning.	Short-term: Outsource to Garrett Financial Network. Long-term: Principals to earn CERTIFIED FINANCIAL PLANNER^{TM} designation.
Client follow-up tasks are falling through the cracks.	Create a review system and integrate task management into (CRM).
The team is too busy.	Disengage bottom 20 percent of clients.
Lack of management systems.	Create a rhythm-of-the-business plan.

making sure their services are priced competitively, advisors need to wrap their product solutions with distinguished service. Focusing your business on providing your best clients with WOW Wealth Management Reviews can have a tremendous impact on its growth.

As investment advisors migrate to delivering wealth management advice via WOW reviews, many have found the need to modify how the team is organized. The team approach is the discipline of working collaboratively as a group to achieve greater levels of client satisfaction, team rewards, and business success. By developing service teams you can position resources to deliver outstanding, scalable service that will create competitive differentiation.

By implementing service teams, you can create clear accountability, elevate client service, and effectively allocate resources to your most profitable client relationships. The organization can add additional service teams to accommodate a growing number of high-net-worth clients cost effectively. This team approach will also leverage each team member's best skills and remove day-to-day client service from senior advisors.

So what does the team approach look like? Figure 6.6 is a scalable organizational structure.

The organization is led by the senior wealth management advisor, a fully credentialed veteran with life experience in addition to technical expertise. They can deal with complex issues and relate well to high-net-worth clients seeking financial peace of mind. In most cases, the senior wealth manager retains a presence in all

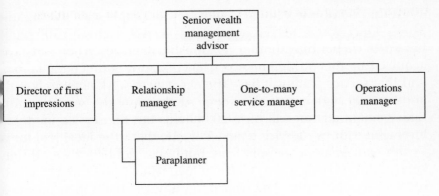

Figure 6.6   Scalable Organizational Structure

client relationships, but is removed from day-to-day tasks or meeting preparations.

The combination of a relationship manager and a paraplanner is where the day-to-day client service gets done. The relationship manager should be fully credentialed, but is likely to be younger than the senior wealth management advisor and may lack some of the executive ambiance. Most people in this role prefer to offer service and advice than to do sales.

The paraplanner supports the relationship manager. This person has sufficient financial literacy and generally enjoys the technical, clerical, and administrative client service tasks. The paraplanner should be good with financial planning and investment management tools. This is the dot-the-i's and cross-the-t's role for a detail-oriented person.

This service team consisting of the senior wealth management advisor, relationship manager, and paraplanner is capable of delivering comprehensive service to 80 to 100 high-net-worth clients. At first glance this may seem like a low number, but remember the plan is to deliver wealth management advice to clients who are paying you $7,500 or more per year. If $7,500 per year is your minimum, the average will be approximately $10,000. Let's do the math: 100 clients times $10,000 in fees equals $1,000,000. Subtract $350,000 for the cost of the service team (relationship manager and paraplanner) and you have a $650,000 margin. Once again I would like to remind you to adjust the numbers based on your payout and cost of service that we discussed in Chapter 3.

If that is not interesting enough to you, simply scale the organization. Once you've maxed out the first service team with 100 high-net-worth clients, hire another relationship manager. When you have acquired another 50 high-net-worth clients, add another paraplanner and that service team will have the capacity to work effectively with another 100 high-net-worth clients. At this time the senior wealth management advisor will have 200 clients but the service model is leveraged with two service teams. For me, that's the ideal size for a wealth management advisory firm, but it may not be for you. If not, keep adding service teams. I have helped teams build three or more of these scalable units. The typical way advisors build their business is to continue adding rainmakers, the most costly resource in the industry, at the top of the organization. Instead, you can grow your business by scaling these service teams in a very cost-effective way over time. How much time?

In my High Speed Strategic Planning sessions, I ask the attendees to count the number of mass affluent and high-net-worth clients in their business, defined by fees of $5,000 and up. Then I ask them to divide that number by the years they have been building their business. With few exceptions, the result is between one and three high-net-worth clients acquired per year—much lower than you would expect.

After applying the seven disciplines of this book, the same advisors begin to acquire 6 to 12 high-net-worth clients per year—a remarkable improvement. I point this out so that you do not get overwhelmed by the perceived enormity of building the team approach. It doesn't need to be done overnight—in fact, it won't happen overnight. If you have 50 high-net-worth clients today, it will likely take four to eight years to fill a service team. Then it will take another 8 to 16 years to fill the next. Just imagine the quality of the wealth management advisory firm you will have built over that time frame. It will be well worth your sustained efforts.

This service team structure is not only good for high-net-worth clients and more profitable to the business; it also provides a career path for your team members. A paraplanner can develop into a relationship manager. A relationship manager can develop into a senior wealth management advisor. As you develop and construct your service teams you want them to focus exclusively on delivering service to their assigned high-net-worth clients. Avoid the temptation of assigning them additional responsibilities in your office. By doing this, you allow the freedom to deliver a client experience that can differentiate you from your competition.

A good advisor friend of mine, Russ Hill, recently worked with me on a project in London. When we were through, he asked if I would like to join him for a few days at his second home in Tuscany. Just to orient you with the area, his home is situated on the property next to the one used in the film *Under the Tuscan Sun*—it is spectacular! It is surrounded by vineyards and olive trees and is within walking distance to Cortona.

Russ told me that he used to think that clients wanted great service from him. He said it hurt his feelings when he realized that they just wanted great service. But as we walked through his olive groves, under the Tuscan sun, he told me he was able to get over his hurt! Russ has built a scalable organization of service teams and his business has grown far beyond what the rainmaker approach would have allowed.

Many senior wealth management advisors wrestle with their decision to turn ongoing client service over to a relationship manager. The senior wealth management advisor often believes that the client wants great service from him. In reality, clients want great service; however, it doesn't necessarily have to flow through the advisor.

The director of first impressions is the meet-and-greet specialist responsible for the WOW impressions in your office and on your phone. There may not be a need for this person to have strong technical skills or to be credentialed, but her people skills need to be off the chart. This position can have a significant positive impact on clients. This role is so critical to your success that even if this is a shared resource within a branch or office, you should make every effort to weigh in heavily on hiring and training decisions.

The one-to-many manager is responsible for providing services to your marginally profitable clients or those you plan to disengage over time. This person is licensed and should be technically strong. Having the competency to leverage technology to service these clients is essential.

Many advisors work within a firm where operations is a part of the platform of support. If it is not, it can be easily outsourced. Once a team has grown to 100 high-net-worth clients, on its way to 200, it is time to hire an operations manager to gain the efficiencies that a competent, dedicated operations resource can provide.

Role Clarity

In the early 1980s, the Buffalo Bills emerged as a good football team. The Pittsburgh Steelers were no longer the odds-on favorite to win the Super Bowl, but they were still a very formidable opponent. I was the Bills' special teams coach at the time, and one game against the Steelers was particularly motivating for me because their head coach, Chuck Knoll, doubled as their special teams coach.

Our kicking teams had been performing well all season—all except our punt return team. It was going to be challenging for them to get on track against the Steelers. The Steelers had outstanding personnel and utilized an unusual punt formation. The situation demanded a modification of our punt return strategy. Instead of using fairly sophisticated blocking schemes, we simplified. We decided to establish crystal clear roles by putting a player in front of each Steeler and playing "smash-mouth" football. Players were asked to do whatever they could to choke out their opponent. Our plan was to hold every Steelers player at the line of scrimmage for as long as possible. Once he freed himself and released downfield, we wanted to attack him again and again until the play was over. Simple and physical, but would it be effective?

In the special teams meeting on Wednesday, I announced the changes we were going to make. I explained the scheme, the techniques to be used, and the effort that was expected. I let them know that the entire team would be evaluating the performance of each player on the punt return team.

Rather than limit the opportunity to those who had been on the punt return team, I opened it up for the entire squad. I posted the Pittsburgh Steelers' punt formation and personnel on the bulletin board and invited our players to sign up across from the Steelers player they wanted to beat the crap out of. The players literally ran to the bulletin board, pushing one another aside for a chance to sign up.

That day, after practice, Isiah Robertson, a former Pro Bowl linebacker who had not been a special teams player for years, came into my office demanding the opportunity to go against Mike Webster, the Pro Bowl center for the Pittsburgh Steelers. I looked at the sign-up list and saw that Isiah had been the third player to claim Webster. I told him that he obviously didn't have enough passion for the job; otherwise he would have found a way to sign up sooner. He walked closer, glared into my eyes and said, "Steve, I want him." Isiah was a pretty big guy with a real mean streak. I opted to let him have his choice of assignments. The other assignments were decided upon in a similar fashion. I wanted to make sure that each assigned player had the passion and competency to get the job done.

What were the results? Ordinarily a punt returner has 5 to 10 yards of space between himself and the punt coverage when he catches the ball. Often, the punt coverage is so close that the returner is forced to signal for a fair catch to afford an opportunity to catch the punt without being immediately hit, risking a fumble. When our punt returner, Michael Holt, caught the ball, the closest Steeler to him was an unbelievable 35 yards away. The confrontation looked more like a street brawl than a punt return. Tremendous power was created when each team member knew his role and was fiercely committed to it.

The functional assignments for football players are much like the positions in any business. And yet, on most business teams, job descriptions are a joke. Often, they are created to satisfy a human resource requirement and then filed away and referenced only during annual performance reviews. This is not the case on effective teams. The coordinated effort and task interdependency of teamwork requires team members to have a crystal clear understanding of their roles, a fierce commitment to those roles, and the ability to act on them. Team members must know how their roles relate to other team members and how they each contribute to achieving the vision. The level of role clarity will have a tremendous impact on the performance of your team.

Functional Responsibilities   There should be no gaps in functional responsibilities. Critical team functions must be identified, and the team members who are accountable for each function must be clear about their role. After deciding the strategies to implement, teams must identify the key functional or tactical activities that must occur for that strategy.

Teams should work to reduce the overlap of their functional responsibilities. On nearly every advisory team, there is a tremendous opportunity to free up resources and increase execution by recognizing and reducing the amount of overlap between team members.

Effective team members must also have the ability to cover for another in a time of need. This mutual accountability is one way to distinguish an effective team from a group of people working together. If a team member's function begins to slide, others, knowing the relative importance of that function, must pitch in to bring the functional level back up to par. Perhaps this is why Peter Drucker suggests that "team members must be able to cover for one another when necessary."

Create a Functional Organizational Chart   Creating a functional organizational chart is an effective way to ensure role clarity and that there are neither gaps nor overlaps in functional responsibility. A critical function that falls through a gap can have dire consequences, and there is simply nothing that can upset a team member more than if someone else is performing a task that they believe belongs to them.

Begin developing your functional organizational chart by listing all of the critical tasks that need to be done for your business to be successful. Then, in a team meeting, ask each team member to write down his own critical functions on 3×5 cards. As each team member shares his list, you can fill in the gaps and resolve the overlaps. The result of this exercise is increased role clarity and the necessary accountability to ensure operational efficiency. This is not a one-time exercise. Anytime you discover a gap or overlap, you will want to work with your team to update your functional organizational chart. Table 6.3 is an example of a functional organizational chart.

As you organize and put team members in positions to be successful, they may need some time to process new responsibilities or roles. Whenever I talk about personnel changes, I'm reminded of my time as a coach with the Buffalo Bills. We picked up Conrad Dobler very late in his colorful career. He had been a great offensive lineman for the St. Louis Cardinals but by his second season with us, he was so beat up from injuries it was apparent that he was near the end of his playing career.

Midway through that season, we were playing the Dallas Cowboys and he was matched up against John Dutton, their star defensive tackle. Conrad could no longer hold up against the much younger pass rusher. Conrad's pride and competitiveness kicked in and he resorted to some special techniques he had perfected over the years. After his third leg-whipping penalty our head coach, Chuck Knox, was forced to replace him with a younger player and pulled him from the game. The following Monday, Chuck brought Conrad in and told him he was going to have to move him to a backup position. He had brought great pride, energy, and leadership to the offensive line, and still could, but he wasn't going to be in the starting lineup anymore. Chuck asked him to go home and think about that. If he could handle it, we would keep him. If not, we'd waive him. Conrad

Table 6.3   Functional Organizational Chart

Wealth Management Advisor
1. Prequalify new opportunities.
2. Conduct initial client meetings/fact finding.
3. Create high-level planning and investment strategies.
4. Deliver quarterly reviews.
5. Cultivate centers of influence.
6. Manage community visibility.

Relationship Manager
1. Prepare Client Engagement Roadmap.
2. Prepare agenda and materials for meeting.
3. Handle day-to-day client contact.
4. Conduct quarterly reviews.
5. Create proposals.
6. Handle investment policy/allocation.
7. Produce and oversee plan.

Paraplanner
1. Perform data entry for planning tool.
2. Handle account paperwork.
3. Do performance reporting.
4. Perform data retrieval/documentation.
5. Handle incoming client requests.
6. Prepare quarterly review package.
7. Vendor management.

One-to-Many Service Manager
1. Coordinate/manage one-to-many service delivery.
2. Handle e-mail drip to one-to-many clients.
3. Do performance reporting.
4. Plan/organize group meetings.
5. Act as primary contact for one-to-many clients.

Operations Manager
1. Oversee new accounts/asset transfers.
2. Manage trades.
3. Conduct quarterly rebalancing.
4. Handle operational issues.
5. Conduct asset/revenue tracking.
6. Manage cost basis.

Director of First Impressions
1. Perform WOW service touches.
2. Handle reception/phone.
3. Perform filing, paperless office tasks, scanning.
4. Plan and schedule events.

came back in on Tuesday to see Chuck and said, "Pride is hard to swallow, but it will go down."

Managing the Team Approach

> The teams we investigated that accomplished truly remarkable things—or that functioned unusually well in more routine activities—were always characterized by genuine dedication to the goal and a willingness to expend extraordinary amounts of energy to achieve it.
>
> —Carl Larson and Frank LaFasto, *TeamWork: What Must Go Right/What Can Go Wrong*

A team's goal consists of its five-year mission, fiscal-year unifying goals, and supporting strategic objectives. These strategic objectives are translated into functional responsibilities for team members. Team members should understand that the achievement of the team's strategic objectives is dependent upon executing their functional responsibilities.

It is common practice in the business world for individuals to have their own personal goals. This practice is not appropriate for advisory firms implementing the *team approach*. Advisory teams are usually smaller and require much tighter coordination between team members. Shared strategic objectives are more appropriate because team members gain synergy by aligning their efforts to achieve these joint strategic objectives.

For functional roles to be clear, team members must also understand their interdependencies. They do not perform in a vacuum. The effects of each action on the team are interrelated. Understanding these connections and dependencies is another distinction demonstrated by high-performing advisory teams. In this regard, a team develops in a way that is similar to the brain.

As the brain develops, many researchers believe cells grow to an optimal number. As this brain engages in rich learning experiences, the connections between the cells become stronger and a higher quality of thought is produced. Likewise, a team that develops an understanding of the connections between team members is better able to utilize the collective intelligence and skills of the group and produce more coordinated actions.

The parameters for team member roles should also identify the things that each team member should avoid. By tapping the collective intelligence of team members, failure paths can be identified. All members should be armed with this knowledge as they develop the tactical aspects of their functional roles.

Rhythm of the Business

> We believe that the truly committed team is the most productive performance unit management has at its disposal—provided there are specific results for which the team is collectively responsible, and provided the performance ethic of the company demands those results.
>
> —J. R. Katzenbach and Douglas Smith, *The Wisdom of Teams*

Keeping the team on track will keep the business on track—it's one and the same. The challenge is that the environment doesn't stay the same. With a *rhythm-of-the-business* plan you will be able to keep a finger on the pulse of your clients, competitors, and the execution of your strategies. It will give you the insight to make the subtle but necessary adjustments to your strategies. Your rhythm-of-the-business plan will require planning and probably more staff meetings, but once you have orchestrated a flow to this process, expectations and standards will be set for how your business is run.

A few years ago, my family leased a boat out of Anacortes, Washington and we toured the San Juan Islands. Before each leg of the journey, we made sure the boat was seaworthy by going through the checklist provided by the charter company (Figure 6.7). By taking the time to examine these items, we were reasonably certain that the vessel was ready to get us where we wanted to go.

Navigating the San Juan Islands is a unique experience. If it were not for five essential navigational tools, this novice yachtsman might still be touring the islands. Fortunately, our vessel, the *Kittiwake*, was equipped with a compass, a depth finder, a map, a global positioning system (GPS), and a CB radio.

We used the map to establish our destination and chart our course. We had to take into consideration tide tables, travel time, and hazards. We also considered sightseeing and recreational opportunities.

The compass showed us our general direction, information I found particularly useful at the start of our journey. The depth finder saved us from running aground when pulling into a cove for a closer look at bald eagles perched in the trees, or while following a pod of whales.

The navigational tool I found most useful was the global positioning system. The GPS provided ongoing feedback about our latitude and longitude. By continually evaluating the discrepancy between our destination and our current position, I was able to make the course adjustments necessary to arrive at our intended destinations.

We also needed to be aware of small shifts in the weather. Storms can build very quickly in the Strait of Juan de Fuca, posing a tremendous threat to boaters. A fog bank can overtake you in minutes. If your crew is not alert to environmental changes, you can get into serious trouble. By monitoring the Coast Guard reports, we were able to avoid these dangers.

1. Visual
   A. Check outside: Dock lines, Loose gear
   B. Check inside: Engine room
      Check fluids: oil, water, transmission
      Check sea strainer & valves
      Check bilges
      Check fuel, filters, valve & fuel level
      Check batteries, cable & condition
      Check generator
      Check passengers & gear
      Check charts & navigational gear
2. Prestart
   A. Review Gray Manual Start Procedures
   B. Disconnect shore power, switch off 1st switch to DC power in yacht
      Check battery switch position
      Check breaker switches
      Check electronics and CH-16 (leave on)
3. Engine Start Up
   A. 1st check position of engine controls
      Black in neutral   Single control button
      Red in idle   Out & neutral
   B. If required – preheat engine. Key on
      Oil pressure alarm must sound
   C. Start engine(s)
      Check exhaust water *now*
   D. Quick test – forward & reverse while still tied
4. Getting Under Way
   A. Yachts tend to drift forward at idle (neutral)
   B. Have fenders well placed and have a roving fender
   C. Preplan your exit & your return:
      Check wind, current, weather channel
      Check maneuvering room
   D. Always maintain clear communication with crew

Figure 6.7   Anacortes Yacht Charters Underway Checklist

In similar ways, the rhythm-of-the-business process requires you to monitor the external and internal environments to more accurately navigate your business. On an ongoing basis you must be able to gain insight and adjust your course accordingly. The rhythm-of-the-business process helps teams sustain motivation, fine-tune their strategies, and improve performance.

First, awareness of the current situation is an essential component for maintaining team motivation. Motivation is elevated when the team establishes business goals. Establishing goals produces a discrepancy—between the way things are and the way the team would like them to be. But if the team loses sight of the current situation, the discrepancy will disappear and so will the team's increased motivation.

Second, with the rhythm-of-the-business plan, your team members will continually improve their ability to understand the interconnectedness between the components of your business. This is not dissimilar from the way you manage a client's financial ecosystem. The benefits are as profound. Team members need to be aware of current and future client needs; team competencies; technological advances; competitor strengths and weaknesses; and threats and opportunities in the team's regulatory, social, economic, business, and competitive environments. As team members understand their impact, the whole business system will improve.

> Dividing an elephant in half does not produce two small elephants. . . . To understand the most challenging managerial issues requires seeing the whole system that generates the issues.
> —Peter Senge, *The Fifth Discipline*

Third, the rhythm-of-the-business plan provides insight into the current situation and is essential for fine-tuning your business disciplines and strategies. Roles to execute these strategies need to be fine-tuned accordingly. Only then will team members have the insight to design improvements and adjust their roles.

There is a tendency for entrepreneurial leaders to dilute their team's efforts with too many good ideas. In *TeamWork,* Larson and LaFasto write, "one of the biggest blind spots leaders have is how they 'dilute' the team's efforts with too many priorities." As you drive your rhythm-of-the-business plan you must be ever vigilant and rigorous about prioritization.

Your rhythm-of-the-business plan should include:

- Annual planning.
- Quarterly fine-tuning.
- Team monthly status reporting.
- Monthly one-on-one meetings.

- Weekly WOW review prep meetings.
- Weekly sales meetings.

Annual Planning An annual two-day team planning retreat will provide you the opportunity to reaffirm your vision. This strategic planning session is designed to get agreement on fiscal-year goals, supporting strategic objectives, strategies, and team member functional roles. Because this meeting is comprehensive, it will require preplanning and the gathering of data necessary for the team to make fact-based decisions.

Agenda for First Day—Situation Analysis

- Status of goals.
- Client needs analysis.
- Client base analysis.
- Competitive analysis.
- Industry trend analysis.
- Evaluate execution of core strategies.
- Team evaluation.

Agenda for Second Day—Strategic Plan

- Reaffirm and/or modify vision—mission, guiding principles.
- Establish fiscal-year unifying goals and supporting strategic objectives.
- Reaffirm strategic focus.
- Fine-tune current strategies.
- Determine new core strategies.
- Determine disengagement strategies.
- Fine-tune organizational structure and functional organizational chart.

Quarterly Fine-tuning This quarterly one-day team planning session focuses on evaluating and fine-tuning the execution of your current strategies. Team members will need to bring the data necessary to evaluate the systems of your business.

Agenda

- Status of strategic objectives.
- Highlights and lowlights of each core strategy.

September Status Report			YTD Plan	YTD Actual
Recurring revenue		$450,000	$300,000	$300,000
Recurring revenue per client		$3,600	$3,500	$3,500
Strategic Objectives			**YTD Plan**	**YTD Actual**
Disengage	125	D clients	125	125
Engage	32	A clients	25	22
WOW	32	A clients	25	20
Add	10	Clients > $5,000	5	8
Red Flags: Serious problems or threats to your goals.				
Platform change is creating havoc and late hours.				
Director of first Impressions is leaving to take a part time job and focus on family.				
Yellow Flags: Potential problems that might become red flags.				
We lack the process to manage multiple WOW reviews in the same month.				
Our biggest client has rescheduled his quarterly review for the second time.				
Green Flags: Extraordinary successes.				
One-to-many meeting was very well received.				
Both recurring revenue and recurring revenue per client goals are on track.				
The eight new clients have all been call-in client referrals.				

Figure 6.8   Monthly Status Report

- Fine-tune strategy implementation plans.
- Fine-tune functional roles.

Team Monthly Status Reporting   This should be a 30-minute monthly team meeting designed to provide the feedback necessary to benefit from effective goals, celebrate extraordinary successes, and address problems or threats. The monthly status report shown in Figure 6.8 provides your team with a framework to for this meeting.

Monthly One-on-One Meetings   These monthly 30-minute meetings are held between the senior wealth management advisor and each team member. The individual status report (see Figure 6.9) will be modified for each team member and reflects their shared strategic objectives. Problems tend to be either hard to see and easy to fix, or easy to see and hard to fix. "It is better to know the truth early, when situations can be remedied, than later when it may be too late to do much," write Pfeffer and Sutton in *Hard Facts, Dangerous*

September Status Report: One-to-Many Manager				
Strategic Objectives			**YTD Plan**	**YTD Actual**
Disengage	125	D clients	125	125
Migrate	55	Clients to one-to-many service model	30	40
Red Flags: Serious problems or threats to our goals. We are behind in disengaging unprofitable clients by 20 percent. The 20 percent that remain are very time consuming.				
Yellow Flags: Potential problems that might become red flags. Venue for the first one-to-many meeting is not determined. Migrated only 30 of the 55 to one-to-many investment solutions.				
Green Flags: Extraordinary successes. The 30 clients migrated to the investment solution seem very pleased. Clients we talked to about one-to-many meeting are excited and feel they are getting more service under this model.				

Figure 6.9   Status Report of One-to-Many Manager

Half-Truths & Total Nonsense. The yellow and red flags are designed to catch problems while they are still easy to fix. This meeting also allows an opportunity for the senior advisor to coach each team member. The senior advisor will take the input from all the one-on-ones, synthesize the information, and use this data as input to create the team's monthly status report.

Advisors have found public praise and private correction to be most effective. The correction should be positively stated. Saying "You are off 40 percent" should instead be phrased "You are 60 percent of the way there." Once you have pointed out what needs to be corrected, always leave them with the way you would like it to be. Instead of saying, "Don't fumble," you should say, "Hold on to the ball like this."

Weekly WOW Review Prep Meetings   This is a 30-minute weekly meeting designed to check and coordinate the tasks necessary to prepare the upcoming WOW Wealth Management Reviews. Once the WOW system is operating, wealth management advisors should be able to deliver nine reviews per week—three reviews, three days a week. This means a large number of reviews are being prepared at any given time. The purpose of this meeting is to manage and coordinate the necessary tasks. For the WOW wealth management process to be institutionalized you will need to integrate it into your customer relationship management (CRM) tool.

Weekly Sales Meeting   This weekly meeting is designed to check the status and coordinate the tasks necessary to reengage existing clients or move prospects through the sales pipeline. It should be limited to 10 minutes and the focus needs to be kept solely on sales advances. If you extend this meeting, creative avoidance causes it to be morphed into a service or operational issues meeting. Managing the sales process is covered in more detail in Chapter 7.

The following coaching point should be helpful as you begin formulating your rhythm-of-the-business plan. You may have team members who have excellent ideas but are not the best at getting those thoughts across to the group.

I coached for the Buffalo Bills from 1978 to 1983. In 1982 I was a very young special teams coach. During the draft that year we selected a place kicker out of Syracuse University in the seventh round. He was spectacular in training camp. The Bills already had a veteran kicker, and during the preseason games this rookie didn't have enough opportunity to demonstrate what he could do.

Coaches have heated debates throughout the preseason as to who will remain on the squad. Just before the season started, the decision was made to start our veteran kicker. The debate over whether we kept the rookie kicker on the reserve squad became a hot topic. One of the veteran coaches wanted to keep a backup linebacker rather than my rookie. Because I was the junior coach, my input didn't have enough weight to sway the other coaches. For me, the decision to keep the rookie kicker instead of the linebacker was a no-brainer, but I lost this battle. This linebacker never added any value to our squad and was soon out of the league.

After we cut this rookie place kicker, he was immediately picked up by the Pittsburgh Steelers. He played for the Steelers for 12 seasons and was in the Pro Bowl four times. In the 1998 season he became the first NFL kicker to have a perfect regular season, making every field goal and every point after touchdown. My rookie is always on the short list when people debate over who was the greatest kicker in the history of the NFL. The rookie we cut was Gary Anderson.

Losing this heated debate was an eye-opening experience for me and it showed me how important it is to listen to all points of view. The following is a very useful brainstorming exercise which will bridge the gap during team meetings to ensure that every team member has a chance to have their voice heard. This process can be used to answer most questions that come up during the rhythm-of-the-business meetings.

Begin this exercise by posing a question that needs to be answered to solve a strategic or tactical challenge facing your team. Using silent brainstorming, each team member spends 45 seconds listing their answers in the form of bullet statements. After 45 seconds, they pass their sheet of paper to their neighbor on the right. After reading the brainstormed list, this team member spends another 45 seconds piggy-backing off those ideas and adding to the lists. This process continues until every team member has added their input to each list. The process stops when the last person receives the list, adds their input, evaluates the answers, and then records the three best ideas on post-its. These ideas are relayed to the group as they are randomly posted on a flip chart.

The next step requires the team to vote on the brainstormed ideas. Each team member writes a 3 next to the idea they think is best, a 2 on the next best, and finally a 1 on their third choice. After all team members have voted, the scores are added together and ranked. Most often there will be a consensus as to what is the best solution and it will be implemented. If there is not a consensus the principal will make a unilateral decision as to which ideas will be implemented.

Coaching the Team

Great advisory teams are built on the desire of the individual team members to want to improve. Knowledge is your team's most important asset, and is easy to gain from outside resources. By sharing best practices, benchmarking, studying competitors' strengths, and distilling the knowledge from consultants, strategic partners, and suppliers, your team can assimilate knowledge that will improve the team's capacity to satisfy client needs.

Advisory teams are so busy that you will need to prioritize the areas where you want to acquire this outside knowledge. First, determine where you have knowledge gaps and then identify sources for this information. Once you have targeted a learning project you will need to set clear learning objectives for that project. After the knowledge has been obtained, the final step in this process is to apply the learning through strategy implementation.

The implementation challenges that you and your team will face are significant but doable. Building an optimistic team culture and one where team members believe they have the ability or can develop the ability to implement the disciplines is a particularly important leadership role.

Learned Optimism: Expecting a Positive Outcome   In *Learned Optimism*, Martin Seligman provides information that has tremendous implications for teams that want to develop the persistence to achieve their business goals.

Optimistic team members believe they will be successful and believe they are responsible for their success. Pessimistic team members do not believe they will be successful and believe that nothing they do will improve their results. For these reasons, optimistic team members are resilient and will persist when things get tough, while pessimistic team members give up.

Seligman led a research team that demonstrated that optimism and helplessness are learned. His work suggests that when team members decide that nothing they do matters, they feel helpless and will do little to improve their situation. The good news that came from discovering that helplessness can be learned is the revelation that optimism can also be learned. Of particular importance is how team members explain setbacks to themselves.

Optimistic team members explain setbacks as temporary, specific, and, where appropriate, externally caused. They do not view the event as long-lasting or permanent. They believe that the event is a temporary setback that can be corrected and refuse to consider it a catastrophe. For them, it is a single event with a specific negative impact. Finally, they only own the result if they should. Optimistic team members don't own the negative returns if the market goes down.

Pessimistic team members are on the other end of the continuum. They explain setbacks as permanent, pervasive, and personal. They believe the negative setback is long-lasting. They globalize the setback and believe "all hell is breaking loose." Pessimistic team members also believe that they are responsible for the setback even when they are not. To make matters worse, pessimistic team members tend to play the setback over and over again in their minds. Because we tend to move toward those things we think about, this ruminating can lead to a self-fulfilling prophecy.

Teams reflect the attitudes of the individual team members. If team members explain setbacks as temporary, specific, and (where appropriate) externally caused, the team will be optimistic about their future success and will continue to persist. However, if as a group a team tends to explain setbacks as permanent, pervasive, and caused by the team members, the team will develop a pessimistic explanatory style and will quit, giving up on their goals.

What seems to be of lesser importance in developing team persistence is how teams and their members explain successes to themselves. It is interesting that explanatory styles are completely turned around when they experience success. Optimistic teams explain the success as permanent, pervasive, and personally caused. Pessimistic teams explain successes as temporary, specific, and externally caused.

> Man is not fully conditioned and determined, but rather determines himself whether he gives in to conditions or stands up to them. Man does not simply exist but always decides what his existence will be, what he will become in the next moment.
> —Viktor Frankl, *Man's Search for Meaning*

Victor Frankl is credited with the discovery that we can control our thoughts. Seligman's work on explanatory style demonstrated that we can decide how we think. Coaching a team takes on new meaning once these concepts are understood.

Explanatory style is composed of team members' automatic thoughts. They must understand that they can change the way they think about their setbacks and successes. Pessimistic teams can change their habitual explanatory style by first becoming aware of these automatic thoughts.

The following scenario will help explain this principle. An advisory team begins to roll out WOW Wealth Management Reviews to their top clients. The team works to schedule their first five reviews, and four cancel at the last minute. This is a major setback for the team.

The pessimistic explanation would be something like this:

- Our clients don't really want reviews. (Permanent)
- We are at real risk with these clients. If this trend continues we could be out of business. (Pervasive)
- Nothing we do seems to have an impact. We must not be good enough to deliver reviews that attract high-net-worth clients. (Personal and pervasive)

The optimistic explanation would be something like this:

- The advisor will call the clients, determine the reason for the cancellation, and we will design a tactic to overcome the challenge. (Temporary)
- We know our WOW Wealth Management Review is strong and we need to persist to get these clients in to experience it. (Specific)
- We know these four clients are very busy. (External)

A coaching technique you can use when a team experiences a setback is to ask optimistic questions. An optimistic question is any question that causes the team to think about the things they want to have happen.

The mind is a problem-solving machine. When presented with a problem, it goes to work to solve it. Asking, "How can we engage our top clients in WOW Wealth Management Reviews?" forces the team members to interpret the setback as temporary, specific, and external, and one they can fix. The natural optimists on the team should take a leadership role by recognizing setbacks and asking optimistic questions. In time, asking these questions will become part of the team's culture. By developing the team's optimism, they will learn to persist until the disciplines and strategies are implemented and their goals are achieved.

Self-Efficacy: Your Belief in Your Ability to Cause or Make Things Happen   Team efficacy is the collective belief of the team's ability to execute specific tasks. Albert Bandura, the father of self-efficacy theory, will tell you that we are limited more by our beliefs than by our abilities. In that regard, Bandura is aligned with Henry Ford, who said, "Whether you think that you can or that you can't, you are usually right."

Part of our job when we coach a team is to continue to build the team's self-efficacy. When implementing the disciplines in this book, it will be necessary for the team to grow bigger than the implementation challenges they face. As their coach, you can help improve your team's self-efficacy through mastery experience, peer and mastery modeling, and social persuasion.

Mastery Experience.   The number one way to improve self-efficacy is through mastery experience—saying you are going to do something and then actually doing it. Nothing breeds success like success. The unfortunate part is, the number one way to erode self-efficacy is to say you are going to do something and then not do it. As their coach, you should give your team members tasks that they can actually do. It is important to provide a safety net so that the consequence of failed attempts is minimal. Experiencing success is the most significant way team members improve their self-efficacy.

Peer and Mastery Modeling.   Valerie Bertinelli, spokesperson for Jenny Craig, appears in many commercials where she proclaims, "If I can do it, you can do it!" If she can lose weight by using the Jenny Craig program, then the audience can lose weight as well. While viewing the before and after pictures of Valerie, a portion of the audience begins to think, "Perhaps she is right. If she can do it, I can do it." With the goal to lose weight in mind, they become motivated to get off the couch and join Jenny Craig. Valerie modeled her success, and people changed their belief in their ability to lose weight as a result.

There are two types of models that can help team members improve their belief in their ability to be successful: peer models and mastery models. Peer models demonstrate continual improvement. At first, their performance is flawed, but over time they improve on the sequential steps, the strategies for overcoming obstacles, and the thought processes necessary for success. They convey how persistence can lead to success. Peer models can help team members improve their beliefs and execution of any number of specific tasks, from financial planning to delivering a WOW Wealth Management Review. Because models convey what the team member can expect, it is critical that they demonstrate how persistence can lead to success.

The most impactful peer models are those who are similar to the team member. Gender, race, competency level, learning style, personality type, educational background, and other experiences are areas in which a team member can find commonality. The more similar the model, the greater the expectation of comparable results.

Mastery models demonstrate successful execution of a specific task. They demonstrate the proper sequential steps, the strategies for overcoming obstacles, and the thought processes necessary for success. We don't have to look any further than 12-year-olds learning to play quarterback to see the impact that mastery models like Peyton Manning have on improving the self-efficacy of these future stars. Mastery models can lift team members to new levels of belief and performance.

Comparing ourselves unfairly with someone else is a way we can weaken our self-efficacy. My friend made several positive comments about another man's ability to speak five languages. It was clear that he believed speaking five languages distinguished this individual as a man of superior intelligence, and that my friend felt *less than* in comparison. I explained to my friend that the man was the son of an American diplomat, had a French mother, and was raised in a South American home with Spanish- and Portuguese-speaking maids. The adults in this young man's life regularly conversed with the children in their native tongues. This man learned four of his languages as easily as my friend learned English, and he learned his fifth language, Russian, as part of a military assignment. An inappropriate model can cause team members to develop limiting beliefs.

Social Persuasion   This is another way to build team members' self efficacy. They continually receive judging comments and body language from authority figures, peers, and others whom they respect. If their negative judgments are wrong, or if they believe that ability is more inherited than acquired, their beliefs about their ability to perform specific tasks can be weakened. As their coach, you have the obligation to manage social persuasion in a way that builds your team's self-efficacy.

Peer Coaching   Advisors often believe they are the best judges of performance. This opinion is not supported by research. Peer evaluation, done well, is valid and can serve to reinforce roles and interdependencies, and can play an important role in assisting team members to improve their competencies.

The peer evaluation should cover technical competencies, interpersonal skills, and, above all, dependability. The evaluation should relate directly to the team member's contribution to the team's strategic objectives and will need to rely on team members' opinions, which are quite reliable: Team members know better than you do how their peers are performing.

In addition to a formal evaluation process, teams can benefit greatly from peer coaching. The sole purpose of peer coaching is to help a team member improve on competencies that they choose to improve. Team members can work together to target specific areas of individual improvement and provide unbiased, nonjudgmental, confidential feedback to one another. This is a particularly effective method of receiving feedback and improving upon complex and difficult-to-measure areas, such as meeting behaviors or group problem-solving skills.

Peer coaching is a five-step process. First, the team members need to meet and decide what improvements they want to address—the more specific the better. Second, the peer coach observes the team member in a real setting and begins the process of collecting information. Third, the peer coach organizes this information in an understandable, useful format. Fourth, the peer coach and team member meet to discuss the coach's observations. And fifth, the team member critiques the feedback and develops improvement strategies where necessary.

Peer coaching can reinforce roles and interdependencies and provide the necessary feedback for sustained competency improvement. Goal research indicates that team members experience the benefit of goals when the mission and fiscal-year unifying goals are first translated into strategic objectives and then into functional responsibilities for team members. Peer evaluation and peer coaching support this process precisely.

Team members should understand the consequences of achieving or not executing their functional roles. In many instances, these will be natural consequences. An example is the story of the Bills' punt return team. Team members knew that if they did not do their individual jobs, the punt return team would not perform well, and the natural consequence could be losing the game. Of course, for that team there was the added incentive of peer recognition. Many professional athletes crave recognition for doing a good job. In the time I have spent with advisors, I have found that professional athletes are not the only ones craving recognition for a job well done.

Peer coaching is an effective way for team members to improve their competencies. Another way to improve is to obtain as much useful knowledge as possible from outside learning opportunities. In *Thriving on Chaos*, Tom Peters writes, "Become a 'learning organization.' Shuck your arrogance—'if it isn't our idea, it can't be that good'—and become a determined copycat/adapter/enhancer."

The Acquisition of Talent

> Of all the decisions an executive makes, none are as important as the decisions about people because they determine the performance capacity of the organization.
> —Peter Drucker, *The Frontiers of Management*

Acquiring the right people for your advisory firm can be challenging. To grow and improve your business you need to hire the right talent. Start by revisiting your functional organizational chart to determine what functional roles you need filled. Next, identify the five most important competencies necessary to perform those functions. Design an interview loop consisting of people who have the ability to judge whether candidates possess those competencies. If your firm is small you may need to go outside for help. Consider asking your virtual team, business associates, or even clients to help you with this interview process. It may surprise you that you may not be the best person to make these judgments.

After initial screening, set up 45-minute interviews for candidates with a minimum of three interviewers. After the first interview, have the candidate wait in the reception area while that interviewer puts his thoughts together and pings the second interviewer about areas that might need more investigation. After the second interview, repeat the process prior to the third interview. Areas to probe include whether the candidate has the competencies to execute the job function and whether the candidate is team oriented. Find out if they have had the opportunity to collaborate in the past and, if so, whether they put the team ahead of themselves.

Interviewers will need to get together after the interviews and compare notes. You will need to take time with the process and find the right person to fit each functional role. The worst thing is to feel pressured to fill the job and hire someone who is not right for the position. If it is not a clear yes, it is a no—move on and keep looking. They are out there. Warren Bennis writes in *Organizing Genius*, "Recruiting the most talented people possible is the first task of anyone who hopes to create a Great Group."

The Quickest Way to Improve

> The most severe complaint about team leadership from team members involves leaders who are unwilling to confront and resolve issues associated with inadequate performance by team members.
> —Carl Larson and Frank LaFasto, *TeamWork: What Must Go Right/What Can Go Wrong*

A coach's job is to field the best team possible. Players are classified as "win because of," "win with," and "win in spite of." At the end of each season our quest was to replace "win in spite of" players with "win because of" players.

My first coaching job in the National Football League was in 1978 with the Bills. I was the youngest coach in the league and acted as the gofer coach—go for this, go for that. I did the majority of the film breakdown. I was the advance scout (scouting our next opponent). I helped our offensive line coach with the blocking combinations between the tackles and the tight ends. I helped our running back and special teams coach, Elijah Pitts, with special teams. Eli had been an outstanding running back on the great Green Bay Packers teams under Vince Lombardi, and he was a good mentor for me.

The part of my job I hated the most was informing players that they had been cut from the squad during training camp. I was complaining about it to Eli when he stopped me and said, "Better him than me." I asked Eli to explain and he said, "I like it here. I want to stay here for a long time! I know some coaches who have moved so many times that they could pull a moving van up in front of their house, whistle, and the furniture would load itself. I don't want that! If we don't make good personnel decisions we are the ones who will be moving on. Better him than me."

As I began my career change I did a lot of reading and found that the best business leaders have the same philosophy. It's their job to field the best team. There will be times that you will not want to replace a "win in spite of" team member, but you must because ultimately it's "better him than me."

In crafting your team approach, be mindful that your job is to create a winning wealth management advisory business. In some cases, this will entail letting someone on your team go and replacing them with someone who is better suited for the functional role. Jim Collins in *Good to Great* advises, "When you know you need to make a people change, act." It is a dreaded task. Every time I ask an advisor how he felt when he finally pulled the trigger, his response is inevitably, "We should have done it a long time ago." No one likes to fire people. But remember, your success is dependent on fielding the best possible team.

Team Incentive Compensation

When I was a coach for the Seattle Seahawks we regularly played the Denver Broncos. The old Denver stadium had no elevator to take the coaches to the press box. We had to walk up a long, spiral ramp with the Denver fans.

During one game we were about halfway up the ramp when some Denver fans decided to pick a fight with us Seahawks coaches. Security intervened and we were escorted to the press box. The Denver fans sit directly in front of the press box and can literally beat on the press box window. As the game progressed, they yelled at us, shouted obscenities, and made obscene gestures. We lost the game, and I vowed I would never have that experience again.

The next time we played in Denver, three security guards were waiting to take us up to the press box. After getting settled, I stepped out and introduced myself to the Denver fans sitting in front of the press box. I called over the beer guy and told him I wanted to run a tab for these fans.

The first time the Seahawks made a good play, the Denver fans turned to our window and cheered our success. They continued cheering for the Seahawks throughout the entire game. This experience showed me you could win hearts and minds with the right incentive compensation.

The rainmaker compensation model is based solely on sales. If sales go up, the rainmaker makes more money. If sales go down, compensation goes down accordingly. I believe this "eat what you kill" model was created because firms did not want to be at risk of market volatility. They did not want to, nor did they know how to, manage a sales force. They simply put the financial carrots where they wanted their sales force to go, and if salespeople got enough carrots they would survive. If they didn't, they would be gone! By its very nature the rainmaker compensation model attracts individual gunslingers. They tend to possess the attributes that are the antithesis of those necessary for effective teaming. Individual incentive compensation puts the cause of the individual ahead of the team and promotes withholding, obstruction, rivalry, and internal competition.

In the NFL, the players get paid a sixteenth of their salary every Monday after the game. Supply and demand dictates that the highly skilled players get a bigger check—until the playoffs. Then every team member gets paid the same. If the team wins, each player gets so much. If they lose, they get half as much. It doesn't matter if a player catches the winning touchdown or doesn't get into the game. They all get paid the same. I have never seen a motivational problem with players during the playoffs.

I am not advocating you pay each of your team members the same, but I am suggesting you incent them on the same outcomes. Consider targeting the single most important process goal and building your team incentive compensation to support it. For example, if you think that delivering WOW Wealth Management Reviews to all your A and target B clients is the single most important discipline to implement over the next year, you could create a 20 percent team bonus for hitting that goal.

This is how it could play out. Say you previously paid a team member $100,000. With this new model you would pay the same team member a base salary of $90,000. If the team hits its joint process goal for a certain number of WOW reviews, that person would be eligible for a 20 percent bonus. Instead of making $100,000 he would make $108,000 with this system in place. As with any process goal, it should be connected to things that are within the team's control—incentive compensation is within their control in a shared kind of way.

Team incentive compensation not only creates team motivation, it creates an atmosphere for collaboration and synergy. *Synergy* is an energy that is more than the sum of the parts, and you only experience it when the team is pulling together. Team incentive compensation causes team members to encourage and correct each other when performance is not sufficient to win.

Create a Best-of-Kind Team of Experts and Suppliers

> Ask yourself: How effectively are we using suppliers as a source
> of innovation? Do we regard them as integral to our business
> model?
>
> —Gary Hamel, *Leading the Revolution*

Fifteen years ago my wife, Carol, and I moved into a nice, smaller home. Our adult children had moved out of the house long before, and this new home fit our changing needs as we began the next phase of our lives. Then our grandson, Zach, started spending more time with us. As he grew older, and as more of his friends came over, we found the house too small. We hired a contractor to build an addition that would meet these changing needs. Our building contractor had a comprehensive list of subcontractors—a best-of-kind team. He had a ranked order he would leverage throughout the project—excavation, foundation, framing, plumbing, electrical, heating, insulation, drywall, finish carpenters, roofers, and so on. The wealth management advisors I work with seldom have such a list of best-of-kind team of suppliers. Though their job is much more complex, they do not have their ranked list.

To deliver comprehensive wealth management advice, you will need to leverage external resources. Whenever external expertise provides scale and/or increases client satisfaction, you should consider outsourcing. Many suppliers have core competencies that allow them to deliver a service faster, less expensively, and of higher quality than your team can produce on its own. You have natural connections to potential best-of-kind team members. You can begin by asking your clients about their accountant, attorney, and other professional advisors.

It is important to do your research. Find out what your clients like and don't like about other professionals they work with. Ask about a professional's strengths and weaknesses. Find out if your client would recommend this professional to one of their family members. Base your evaluation on their competence, character, and, above all, their dependability.

Suppliers supplement your team's work by providing services that fall outside your team's core competencies. Your team should evaluate suppliers in terms of ability to deliver the quantity and quality needed, in the time frame required, for the right price. Look at the supplier's financial and managerial practices to ensure that you will be able to count on them in the future.

After gaining validations from your clients and doing your due diligence, you should have a dialogue with these professionals. Make sure you are compatible and make sure they will care for your clients' needs as well as you do. One of your jobs is to bring your clients the best resources available.

When you coordinate the various best-of-kind team members and introduce them to your clients, it is best if you control the environment and further define yourself as their wealth management advisor. Invite them to your office for an introductory meeting and arrange the seating so that you sit on the same side of the table as your client. You can help facilitate the meeting by asking appropriate questions to help your client learn about the other professional's expertise. You may also want to prep your client with questions they should ask.

When the introductory meeting is over, let your client know that you can attest to the professional's character and competency. Tell your client that what you can't do for them is make a judgment about compatibility. Ask them if they would be comfortable working with the professional. If yes, provide them the contact information and, if necessary, help them set up the next appointment.

It may also be beneficial for your firm to outsource some of your day-to-day business functions. You may be more productive if other professionals handle your accounting, marketing, financial planning, or event planning. You should give these outsourcing opportunities consideration and make decisions how to best handle these functions.

Decisions

Your insight into the team approach better prepares you to make the following critical business decisions:

- What competencies need to be improved? How do you plan to improve them?
- How should your team be organized?
- What positions do you need to upgrade or add over the next year?

- What critical team functions need to be done for your business to be successful?
- What is your rhythm-of-the-business plan?
- How will you evaluate team performance?
- What modifications should be made to your team compensation model?
- What client service functions should be outsourced?
- What other (non–client service) functions should be outsourced?
- How do you plan to find a best-of-kind team of suppliers?
- Who is on your best-of-kind team of suppliers?

Figure 6.10 provides you an example of a best-of-kind team of suppliers list for both client service functions and non–client service functions.

Actions

What actually provides competitive success and what is difficult to copy is not so much knowing what to do—deciding on the right strategy—but instead having the ability to do it.

—Jeffrey Pfeffer and Robert Sutton, *Hard Facts, Dangerous Half-Truths & Total Nonsense*

Client Service Function	Frist Choice	Second Choice
Tax attorney		
Accountant		
Insurance agent		
Estate attorney		
Private banker		
Money manager selection		
Performance reporting		
Non–Client Service Function	**Name**	
Event management		
Accounting		
Compliance		
Billing		
Event Management		

Figure 6.10   Best-of-Kind Team of Suppliers

After gaining insight and making decisions, it is time to take action. The first thing you should do is schedule your rhythm-of-the-business activities on your calendar. Then use the action plans in Figures 6.11, 6.12, and 6.13, which provide a framework for you to begin to start using the team approach.

Milestones	Owner	Date	√
1. Determine business goals and critical strategies.			
2. Create organizational chart in support of strategies.			
3. Create a checklist of critical functions.			
4. Hold functional organizational chart meeting.			
5. Post functional organizational chart.			
6. Schedule quarterly review of organizational chart.			

Figure 6.11   Create an Organizational Chart and Supporting Functional Organizational Chart

Milestones	Owner	Date	√
1. Create a list of client service functions to outsource.			
2. Determine due diligence process.			
3. Complete due diligence.			
4. Set expectations/working relationship with suppliers.			
5. Create list of best-of-kind team of suppliers (client service).			

Figure 6.12   Create a Best-of-Kind Team of Suppliers to Support Your Client Service

Milestones	Owner	Date	√
1. Create a list of other functions to outsource.			
2. Determine due diligence process.			
3. Complete due diligence.			
4. Set expectations/working relationship with suppliers.			
5. Create list of best-of-kind-team of suppliers (non–client service).			

Figure 6.13   Create a Best-of-Kind Team of Suppliers for Non–Client Service Functions

Chapter Summary

Key Points

- The rainmaker approach does not scale and it creates resentment and passive-aggressive behavior in a group.
- The team approach is the discipline of organizing to deliver wealth management services as a team and working collaboratively to achieve greater levels of client satisfaction, team rewards, and business success.
- Service teams are much more scalable than the rainmaker approach. Your first service team can manage 100 high-net-worth clients. You can hire excellent service team members for much less than you can add a high-caliber rainmaker.
- Because you cannot fix a problem unless you know what it is, the first step in moving from the rainmaker approach to the team approach is to gain insight into what is working and what should be improved.
- Creating a functional organizational chart is an effective way to ensure role clarity and that there are neither gaps nor overlaps in functional responsibility.
- Shared strategic objectives are more appropriate than individual goals because team members gain synergy by aligning their efforts.
- Team members should understand that the achievement of the team's strategic objectives is dependent upon executing their functional responsibilities.
- Awareness of the current situation is an essential component for maintaining team motivation.
- With the rhythm-of-the-business plan, your team members will continually improve their ability to understand the interconnectedness between the components of your business.
- As team members understand their impact, the whole business system will improve.
- Your rhythm-of-the-business plan should include:
  - Annual planning.
  - Quarterly fine-tuning.
  - Team monthly status reporting.
  - Monthly one-on-one meetings.
  - Weekly WOW review prep meetings.
  - Weekly sales meetings.
- There is a tendency for entrepreneurial leaders to dilute their team's efforts with too many good ideas. As you drive your rhythm-of-the-business plan you must be rigorous about prioritization.

- Great advisory teams are built on the desire of the individual team members to improve. The purpose of evaluations is to find the right areas to improve.
- Optimism can be learned.
- Optimists persist and are therefore more successful.
- Optimists explain setbacks as temporary, specific, and externally caused.
- A coaching technique you can use when a team experiences a setback is to ask optimistic questions that cause the team to think about the things they want to have happen.
- Self-efficacy is your belief in your ability to cause or make things happen.
- We are limited more by our beliefs than by our abilities.
- The number one way to improve self-efficacy is through mastery experience—saying you are going to do something and then actually doing it.
- Peer evaluation, done well, is valid and can serve to reinforce roles and interdependencies. It can play an important part in assisting team members to improve their competencies.
- Peer coaching is a five-step process.
    1. Meet and decide what improvements need to be addressed.
    2. Peer coach observes and collects information.
    3. Peer coach organizes this information.
    4. Peer coach and team member meet to discuss the coach's observations.
    5. Team member critiques the feedback and develops improvement strategies.
- Team members should understand the consequences of achieving or not executing their functional roles.
- The acquisition of talent starts with the following steps:
    - Fine-tune the functional organizational chart.
    - Identify the five most important competencies necessary to perform those functions.
    - Design an interview loop.
- A coach's job is to field the best team possible. Players are classified as "win because of," "win with," and "win in spite of." At the end of each season our quest was to replace "win in spite of" players with "win because of" players.
- Team incentive compensation: Consider targeting the single most important process goal and building your team incentive compensation to support it.

- Team incentive compensation not only creates team motivation, it creates an atmosphere for collaboration and synergy. Synergy is an energy that is more than the sum of the parts, and you only experience it when the team is pulling together. Team incentive compensation causes team members to encourage and correct each other when performance is not sufficient to win.
- To deliver comprehensive wealth management advice, you will need to leverage external resources. Whenever external expertise provides scale and/or increases client satisfaction, you should consider outsourcing.
- Your team should evaluate suppliers in terms of ability to deliver the quantity and quality needed, in the time frame required, for the right price.

CHAPTER 7

Stop Selling to Prospects and Start Selling through Clients

When Jack's expanded network began to dry up, his manager gave him a Dun & Bradstreet sales lead list of business executives from the largest companies in town. Jack assumed correctly that this wasn't the first time this list had been handed out. After a short coaching session, Jack headed to the phone to begin *selling to* this cold-call list.

Though he approached this strategy with vigor and put three months of significant effort into it, he was unable to get past the executives' gatekeepers. This smile-and-dial effort to sell to business executives didn't even produce a return phone call. For the first time Jack began to doubt his ability to attract clients.

Midway through his second year, Jack began to pick up accounts orphaned by other young advisors who had moved on. *Selling to* these inherited clients produced more small-commission transactions and two high-net-worth clients—enough to keep him in the game.

With new life, Jack decided to make another attempt at *selling to* a new targeted list. This time he was going to scale down his aspirations and sell education funding solutions to couples with kids in elementary and junior high school. The marketing department helped him create an e-mail campaign with a compelling value proposition and an interesting enough call to action that produced 27 prospects. *Selling to* the 27 prospects produced six clients and more chump change.

Next, Jack tried *selling to* 50- to 60-year-old, semiaffluent prospects by delivering a seminar on retirement. Marketing provided a list of 2,500 people to invite and an e-mail template with a compelling value proposition and an online seminar registration process. The preparation was substantial and the out-of-pocket expenses for the room, equipment, and refreshments were more of an investment than Jack had anticipated. Eleven people attended and three checked the box on the session evaluation indicating they would like additional information. Unfortunately, two of these he could not pin down to schedule a meeting, and the third had his money tied up. Selling to prospects using a seminar was a bust.

For 15 years Jack jumped from one sell-to-prospects strategy to the next. As part of his December planning ritual he decided to count the number of mass-affluent and high-net-worth clients he had acquired over 15 years. He counted 35 mass-affluent clients—those with $100,000 to $1 million of investable assets. He had just five high-net-worth clients—those with over $1 million in investable assets.

His sell-to strategy had produced just over two mass-affluent or high-net-worth clients per year. Not good enough! Jack wanted more.

The Seventh Discipline: Start Selling through Clients

Selling through clients is done by viral marketing. This is the social network phenomenon where your clients tell their friends and colleagues of the value you deliver, and the word spreads. Selling through clients via viral marketing is far and away the most effective method an advisor has to acquire high-net-worth clients.

Insights

In my planning sessions I ask the participants if anyone has had a surgery they wouldn't mind sharing with the group. I select one of the volunteers and ask them about their surgery. The operations range from a repair of a torn meniscus to a total knee replacement; from a surgery to eliminate atrial fibrillation to heart valve replacement; or from cataract surgery to cornea implants.

I ask the volunteer whether their family doctor or a specialist performed their surgery. It is always a specialist. Then I ask if they found the specialist through the yellow pages, a newspaper advertisement, a seminar, or if the specialist called them in the evening with a special offer. After the chuckles in the room die down, I ask how they found their surgeon.

Unless it was an emergency surgery, they always say that their family doctor or a friend, who had a similar procedure, recommended the surgeon. They went to someone they trusted and asked for a recommendation. That is how specialists are selected. When people make big decisions about their health they ask someone they trust. The same is true when they deal with large sums of money. They ask someone they trust for a recommendation.

This sell-through-client strategy is so powerful that many elite advisors depend solely on viral marketing for their lead generation engine. Advisors create engaged clients. As those engaged clients go about their day-to-day lives, they have opportunities to tell friends and colleagues about the value their wealth management advisor provides. As outlined in Figure 7.1, this prospect (who likely comes from the same target market) calls the advisor—a call-in lead.

The first step is for the advisor to create engaged clients. Vanguard sponsored the 2008 Advisor Impact study. The study segmented 40,000 clients into four groups. Thirty-three percent were classified as *engaged* clients, defined as having "a higher degree of

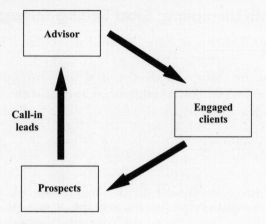

Figure 7.1   Viral Marketing

contact and a deeper personal relationship" with their advisor. One hundred percent of the engaged clients provided referrals, as can be seen in Figure 7.2. On average, each provided 2.3 referrals to their advisor.

You create engaged clients by a sustained effort to provide wealth management advice and deliver WOW Wealth Management Reviews. In an article called "The Only Number You Need to Grow," Frederick Reichheld writes, "When customers act as references, they do more than indicate that they've received good economic value from a company; they put their reputation on the line." Before your clients will put their reputation on the line, they need to trust that you will

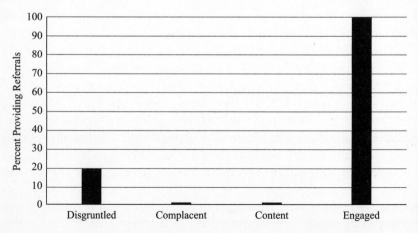

Figure 7.2   Percentage of Client Type Who Provided Referrals

deliver outstanding service to someone they refer. This trust is built over time by consistently delivering exceptional service. It could take two, three, or more quarterly WOW reviews before this level of trust is built. This is why I emphasize that it will take your sustained effort providing wealth management advice and delivering WOW reviews to derive the benefits from this powerful sell-through-clients strategy.

In Chapter 2, I recommended considering the viral marketing opportunity of market segments as part of determining your target market. A virus will spread more rapidly in a concentrated community. The same is true with viral marketing. The more concentrated the community, the more powerfully this social network phenomenon works.

> Word-of-mouth epidemics are the work of Connectors.
> —Malcolm Gladwell, *The Tipping Point*

You should consider engaging target market clients first. Getting client referrals is not like coming into a room, turning on a light switch, and seeing the room light up. There is a significant lag time between the time you engage clients and when the referrals begin to flow. The sooner you get started, the sooner you will experience the benefits of this sell-through-clients strategy.

The second step in creating viral marketing is to make it easy for your engaged clients to spread the virus—to talk about you in a compelling way to their friends and colleagues when the occasion arises. As shown in Table 7.1, a 2008 study by Advisor Impact sheds light on how these conversations occur. The engaged clients were asked, "What were the circumstances of providing the last referral?" This table shows the results.

Table 7.1   Reasons for Referring

What Were the Circumstances of Providing the Last Referral?	
My advisor told me he was interested in referrals and I provided a name at that time.	6%
A friend/colleague asked me if I knew about a good financial advisor and I made the introduction.	45%
A friend/colleague told me about a financial challenge they were having and I suggested my advisor might be able to help.	54%

Source: 2008 Advisor Impact Study.

Notice that the vast majority of the leads accrued in an impromptu situation, as part of the regular and ongoing interactions within their network. How do you equip clients to recommend you in those types of situations? You give them the only sales tool they need—an irresistible sound bite.

In *The Tipping Point*, Gladwell writes, "There is a simple way to package information that, under the right circumstances, can make it irresistible." Your task is to create this sound bite and drip it on your engaged clients enough times that when the occasion arises to recommend you, it just spills out of them.

Let me provide an example of how equipping your clients with an irresistible sound bite can help them generate leads for you. One of my consulting projects was with the Microsoft's Xbox leadership team. At the end of a planning session, one of the executives responsible for building the Xbox device asked if I would have lunch with him the following day to tie down the next actions resulting from the planning session.

At the end of our lunch meeting, I stood to leave, and he asked where I was headed. He had assumed that I was going to another meeting on the Microsoft campus. I told him I was headed down to Russell Investment Group in Tacoma, Washington. He asked what I did for Russell and I told him that I worked with some of their high-net-worth advisors. He then said, "I need one of those." And I replied, "Of the top 25 wealth managers in the United States, there is only one located in Seattle and they are friends of mine." He asked if I could connect them, and I did that evening via e-mail.

This irresistible sound bite was the only sales tool I needed: "Of the top 25 wealth managers in the United States, there is only one located in Seattle." Who gave it to me? The advisor! It wasn't my job to create the sound bite. It was the advisor's job. How did he give it to me? He simply kneaded it into every conversation we had, dripping it over and over again, and when the situation called for me to use it, it just flowed out.

An irresistible sound bite is a concise statement that articulates one of the following:

- Your value proposition.
- Your unique position in the marketplace that implies your value proposition.
- A proof point that implies your value proposition.

In practice, a sound bite based on a proof point that implies the value you bring to your clients has been the most effective for advisors. The example I used with the Microsoft executive is a sound bite based on a proof point. As the result of a credible survey in an industry publication, this team had been recognized as one of the top 25 wealth management firms in the United States—and there were no other Seattle firms listed. "Of the top 25 wealth managers in the United States, there is only one located in Seattle" was indeed a fact.

Proof points are based on third-party recognition, but they are hard to come by. Proof points are usually dependent upon surveys where you may fall outside the scope. With that said, I know several advisors who determined the proof point they wanted to create and worked with the sponsor of the survey to ensure they were included. You might imagine working with a local newspaper to create a proof point similar to this next example.

One of my High Speed Strategic Planning graduates was acknowledged as "the most recognized retirement specialist in New Orleans." She and her team began to weave it into every client interaction. During a review, if a client thanked her for a referral to an attorney she had recommended, she would say, "Thank you very much. For us to retain our position as the most recognized retirement specialist in New Orleans we must have relationships with the leading specialists in town." A little later in the review, if a client comments on the consistent performance of the investment solution, she says, "For us to retain our position as the most recognized retirement specialist in New Orleans, we had to find a consistently performing investment solution." Drip, drip, drip, and it isn't long before that client is out playing bridge with a friend or having lunch with a colleague who mentions a financial challenge they are having, and out it comes: "Oh! You should be working with my advisor. She is the most recognized retirement specialist in New Orleans."

If you are fortunate enough to be recognized as number one in any area, follow the lead of network and cable television stations. If they get a number one rating, they claim it quickly and hold on to it for dear life. You might see an advertisement, "The number one drama on prime-time television." After the next rating period you might see the same show advertised as "The number one drama on Thursday night." After the next rating period you might see the same show advertised as, "The number one drama on Thursday night after

10 P.M." They just keep cutting the scope to retain the number one rating as long as possible.

> Strategic positioning attempts to achieve sustainable competitive advantage by preserving what is distinctive about the company. It means performing different activities than rivals, or performing similar activities in different ways.
> —Michael Porter, *On Competition*

You can use the same approach, creating a sound bite based on your unique position in the marketplace. For example, if an advisory team has been in business for 20 years, they may want to claim, "The most experienced *investment advisory team* in Chicago." Because there are 22 more experienced investment advisory teams in Chicago, they could move to a field with fewer players. Because there are fewer wealth management teams, they could say, "The most experienced *wealth management team* in Chicago." If they can't claim that statement because there are still 12 more experienced wealth management teams in Chicago, simply tighten the scope to, "The most experienced wealth management team in the *Chicago Loop*." Or tighten the scope even further with, "The most experienced wealth management team in the *central business district*."

Claiming to be the most certified or most comprehensive are two other unique positions that advisors have used successfully in creating their sound bites.

A sound bite can be built based on your value proposition—the value you bring to your clients. Consider the framework shown in Table 7.2. Moving left to right, select your role, add your client focus, decide the action you intend to help your clients take, and add an outcome word or phrase.

Don't limit yourself to the words in this framework. They are merely examples and designed to jump-start your creativity. An irresistible sound bite will give your engaged clients the only sales tool they need to recommend you to their friends and colleagues.

I have helped a number of advisors who were at one time insurance specialists evolve into investment counselors and then on to become excellent wealth management advisors. In their insurance salesmen years, "10-3-1" had been pounded into them so hard and so frequently, it was difficult for them to comprehend any other way

Table 7.2   Framework for Building Your Sound Bite

Your Role	Target Market	Action	Outcome
Help	Electrical engineers	Pursue	Financial security
Guide	**Physicians**	Work toward	Financial peace of mind
Support	Corporate executives	Create	Retirement goals
Develop	Microsoftees	**Develop**	Financial goal
Improve	Accenture partners	Preserve	Multigenerational wealth
Assist	Business owners	Improve	**Wealth management strategies**
Coach	Suddenly single women	Track towards	Desired future
Council	Orthodontists	Achieve	Financial affairs are in order
Advise	Oil and gas executives	Attain	Financial aim
Lead	Green energy entrepreneurs	Build	Financial objectives
Direct	Building contractors	Protect	Financial targets

of growing their businesses. Ten leads would produce three appointments, and those appointments would result in one sale.

I like 10-10-9 better than 10-3-1. Ten prospects call you, you answer the phone 10 times, and 9 become clients! And, if you have engaged the right clients, the wealth management opportunity will be significantly better. You will be able to build an elite wealth management firm by acquiring 6 to 12 high-net-worth clients per year with this sell-through-clients strategy. Creating an irresistible sound bite and kneading it into engaged clients, so they can refer you when the impromptu situation arises, is the single most effective way to acquire new high-net-worth clients. This sell-through-clients strategy produces call-in leads. You will be happy with your close rates on call-in leads.

Client Introductory Event

A client introductory event is another effective way to sell through your existing clients. Though this strategy is a distant second to tapping into the viral marketing of your engaged clients, it still is significantly more efficient than selling to prospects.

The objective is to make it easy for your engaged clients to intro-duce their friends and associates to you. Knowing that, in many cases, people's friends and colleagues are similar to them, the "bring-a-friend" invitation creates an opportunity to cultivate your target mar-ket. The following have all been successful client introductory events. As I present these, be thinking through the common attributes.

I worked with an advisor from Boise, Idaho. He would invite an engaged client and "a friend" to go fly fishing. A drift boat holds three people. The engaged client fishes off the back of the boat. The client's friend fishes off the front. And the advisor turned fishing guide rows from the middle. Every Saturday morning he has a four-hour client appreciation event and an introduction to a prospect.

An advisor in Chicago loves golf—in fact he is a scratch golfer. Ev-ery Friday afternoon he invites an engaged client golfing and suggests they bring two friends along, giving him a five-hour introduction to two prospects.

One of my High Speed Strategic Planning graduates went through college on a music scholarship and still loves to play the piano. His wife is a gourmet cook. On a regular basis, they invite two of their client couples to their home for dinner and suggest they each invite a couple to join them. They have a wonderful meal and then after dinner, he entertains their guests at his piano. He has an entire evening to get to know two more prospective clients.

I've worked with several advisors who focus on business owners. They put on small, informal business forums. These forums can be as simple as inviting three to five business owner clients and suggest that each bring a fellow business owner to engage in a discussion of issues affecting businesses in their community. On a regular basis, these advisors are introduced to prospects within their target market.

An advisor in Long Beach, California, hosts a simple wine and cheese reception on the last Thursday of each month. His office building has a wonderful patio that overlooks the Pacific Ocean. He simply invites a manageable number of clients and suggests that each invite a friend. The clients feel appreciated and the event makes it easy for them to introduce their friends.

So what are the common attributes to the client introductory event?

- They are all bring-a-friend events. The primary purpose is not client appreciation. It is to make it easy for your engaged clients to introduce their friends to you.

- The advisor enjoys the activity. This will not be a sustainable strategy unless it is enjoyable.
- The events are not investment related. If clients get the slightest indication that it is a sales event, they will not invite a friend.
- They are small and intimate venues. You have to assume that your client has already vouched for your character and competence. Otherwise, they would not have taken you up on the opportunity to introduce their friends. The venue should allow for enough interaction so that the client's friend can decide whether you are compatible with them.

The follow-up to the event is a good opportunity to make a WOW impression. A wonderful example of two soft follow-ups comes from an advisor located in New Orleans. She is a licensed tour guide of the French Quarter and has made these tours her client appreciation bring-a-friend event. During the tour, she takes pictures of her clients and their guests enjoying the experience. When she gets back to her office she asks one of her team members to put the photos into Microsoft's Movie Maker and then immediately e-mails them out. Two weeks later, she sends a post card from the French Quarter and writes a short note letting the prospect know how much she enjoyed meeting them. They are reminded of the good time they had and once again receive her contact information. If the prospect wants to reach out to you, they will. If they don't, don't waste one more calorie thinking about it.

In *Competing for the Future*, Gary Hamel writes, "Sooner or later, in every industry, the battle revolves around the capacity to leverage resources rather than the capacity to outspend rivals." You have the opportunity to leverage clients who can become a powerful sales force for you.

Center-of-Influence Marketing

Done properly, this strategy is a hybrid of selling through clients and selling through centers of influence. Though ranking a very distant third in lead-generation effectiveness, it is still a credible strategy and warrants consideration. In particular, advisors in organizations such as banks that require leads to be appropriately passed will find the following tactics very useful.

Creating engaged clients is a prerequisite to this strategy because you will need your clients to provide an endorsement to their centers of influence. It is a common mistake for advisors to focus on the center of influence before they have created engaged clients within their target market.

First list the clients who are within your target market. Then determine the two categories of professionals who are most likely to be working with this market. In Table 7.3 I have selected accountants and estate attorneys. Then data-mine your client folders and use the framework to identify the centers of influence who work with these clients. I am always surprised how few advisors have this information. If you buy into delivering wealth management advice, you will assuredly begin to collect this information as part of the re-fact process described in Chapter 4. Identify centers of influence who are working with two or more of your clients. The reason for prioritizing these professionals will become apparent. I have identified Head, Kors, and Armstrong as meeting these criteria.

Next, call these professionals to introduce yourself and share thoughts informally. You might say, "Hello, I'm with ABC Wealth Management Advisors. As you probably know, we are both working with several mutual clients. I was hoping we could get together to learn more about each other's business so that we can better serve these clients. Could I bring box lunches to your office for a meeting?"

Table 7.3   Identifying Center-of-Influence Opportunities

Target Market Clients	Accountants	Estate Attorney
Archer	**Head**	Warren
Broadhead	Whitmore	Brown
Curtis	**Kors**	Swan
Chandler	Adams	**Armstrong**
Hoff	Hudson	Jackson
Kasper	**Head**	Craig
Keegan	Wood	**Armstrong**
Marshall	**Kors**	Warner
Martin	Stark	Greene
Metcalf	Gibbons	Peterson
Peters	Whitmore	Bishopp
Quigley	Wooden	Brown
Smith	**Kors**	Williams
Thompson	Kerr	Walsh
Wilson	**Head**	Largent

In the meeting, simply listen and ask questions to understand their business model and the scope of their service. This meeting is a wonderful due diligence opportunity should you choose to use them as part of your best-of-kind team of suppliers.

After they have completed the overview of their business, present them your one-page overview. The one-pager is a marketing piece designed specifically to present your business and service models to potential centers of influence. The front side contains your sound-bite value proposition, your most compelling proof points, the differentiating aspect of your service model, and your target market. Informing the prospective center of influence about your target market will do two things. First it will cause you to stand out. For example, if your target market is medical specialists on Pill Hill, then the accountant will be reminded of you the next time he is working with a medical specialist from Pill Hill. Second, it will prequalify leads for you.

An example of a one-pager is shown in Figure 7.3.

Next, present your process to the center of influence, showing how you develop solutions to meet your clients' needs. Explain how this includes helping your clients develop their vision document and roadmap. Include an example roadmap (Figure 7.4) on the back of the handout.

ABC Wealth Management Advisors

We help medical specialists create, protect and preserve multi-generational wealth.

- The only top 25 wealth manager located in the Seattle area.
- We have 45 years of successful professional relationships.
- We have two CERTIFIED FINANCIAL PLANNER™ practitioners on the team.

We get results by:

- Providing a vision document that clarifies financial goals.
- Providing a Client Engagement Roadmap that crystallizes expectations.
- Providing comprehensive wealth management solutions.
- Delivering services as a team.
- Leveraging a sophisticated investment process to optimize risk/return balance.

We have become specialists by focusing on the complex needs of medical specialists working on Pill Hill.

Figure 7.3   ABC Wealth Management One-Pager

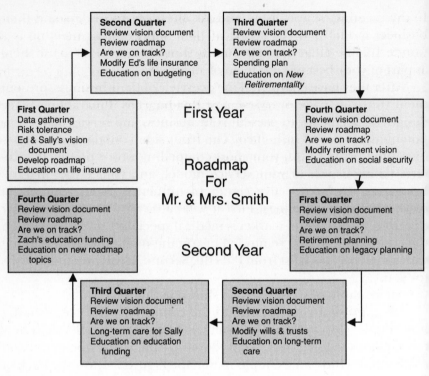

Figure 7.4   Client Engagement Roadmap

What happens next is a very interesting study of the power of third-party endorsements. The next time the mutual client meets with the accountant to get their taxes done, the accountant will ask for the mutual client's endorsement of your work. He will say something like, "I had lunch with your advisor, Valerie, the other day. What kind of a job does she do for you?" If the mutual client says, "Oh, she's okay," you will not get, nor should you get, a referral from that accountant. Clients are the accountant's lifeblood, and she should not put her business at risk based on such a flimsy endorsement.

However, if the mutual client endorses your work, you have a reasonable chance of getting a referral from that accountant. This is why I stress that the client must be fully engaged with your wealth management service model prior to embarking on an effort to develop your centers of influence.

Your center-of-influence strategy will require attention to remain effective. Invite them to lunch, a client appreciation bring-a-friend event, or visit their office. If you are never visible you may soon be forgotten—out of site, out of mind. (This isn't a misspelling—I mean to use *site*: You have to be present in their sight and at their site.) Just as you use the Client Engagement Roadmap to illustrate the good work you're doing for your clients, keep influencers informed about your progress with referrals they deliver to you. Let them know you appreciate their support, and notify them when you have information that might help their business.

Managing the Sales Pipeline

Whether a call-in lead is generated from viral marketing, a bring-a-friend event, or from a center of influence, it must still be managed to maximize the opportunity. Many advisors have found it effective to break down their sales pipeline into clear stages, allowing for communication and coordination among team members. This also provides the accountability that is often necessary to advance the prospect through the sales process. The best practice shown in Figure 7.5 is based on yes-or-no, verifiable outcomes.

Qualify a Call-In Lead

Even though selling through clients produces call-in leads, they must still be qualified. Many advisors spend way too much time

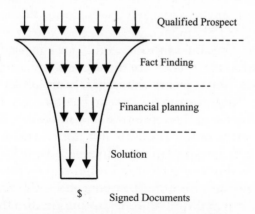

Figure 7.5 Pipeline Funnel—From Prospect to Client

scheduling appointments and then wasting precious face-to-face fact-finding time with nonqualified prospects. Having invested their time, advisors tend to take these clients on even when they shouldn't. These problems go away by having the qualifying criteria defined and having a 15-minute phone conversation with the prospect.

The qualifying criteria can be as simple as:

- *Establishing a minimum.* Example: $7,500 or more recurring revenue opportunity.
- *Establishing a value-add opportunity.* Example: Can your wealth management firm satisfy the client's expectations?

During the 15-minute qualifying phone call, you first need to determine whether the prospect has a need you can satisfy. You can determine this by asking, "Why did (referring client) think I might be able to help you?" From this conversation the client's needs should surface, and more than likely the size of the opportunity will become clear. If it doesn't, simply ask, "How much and where are your assets today?" If the opportunity does not meet your minimum, you will need to explain that you deliver comprehensive wealth management advice and you have a $7,500 annual fee. Let them know it doesn't sound like they require wealth management advice at this time and direct them to an advisor who can help them.

Fact Finding, Planning, Solutions

These steps are the same as those used to reengage existing clients, as covered in Chapter 4. They are binary, verifiable steps in the sales pipeline process. *Binary* means that the steps are either completed or not—yes or no. *Verifiable* means they can be observed. The qualifying checklist is in the file and is either done or not done. The fact finder is in the file and is either done or not done. The same principle applies for the financial plan, the financial vision document, and the roadmap. In the final step, the transfer papers are signed and in the client file or they are not. Managing this sales pipeline process should be rigorous and verifiable. To institutionalize the process you will want to integrate it into your customer relationship management (CRM) workflow.

Decisions

> Is the success you observe by the benchmarking target because of the practice you seek to emulate? Why is a particular practice linked to performance improvement—what is the logic? What are the downsides and disadvantages to implementing the practice, even if it is a good idea?
>
> —Jeffrey Pfeffer and Robert Sutton, *Hard Facts, Dangerous Half-Truths & Total Nonsense*

Your insight into sell-through-client strategies better prepares you to make the following critical business decisions:

- What is your irresistible sound bite?
- What is your client introductory event?
- What two categories of advisors are most likely to be working with your target market?
- What are the three to five proof points to your value proposition?
- What are the three to five differentiating aspects of your service model?
- What are your qualifying criteria?
- What questions do you plan to ask to determine whether a prospect meets your qualifying criteria?
- To whom do you refer unqualified prospects?
- What are the steps of your sales pipeline?

Actions

> No strategy delivers results unless it's converted into specific actions.
>
> —Larry Bossidy and Ram Charan, *Execution*

To help you and your staff learn the sound bite and begin to incorporate it into your daily communication with clients, prospects, and influencers, encourage your staff to say the sound bite out loud five times a day for 30 days. It doesn't matter if it is to each other, a client, or a center of influence. The repetition will cement its use and make it flow in your conversations.

Your irresistible sound bite!		
1. ~~||||~~	11. ~~||||~~	21. ~~||||~~
2. ~~||||~~	12. ~~||||~~	22. ~~||||~~
3. ~~||||~~	13. ~~||||~~	23. ~~||||~~
4. ~~||||~~	14. ~~||||~~	24. ~~||||~~
5. ~~||||~~	15. ~~||||~~	25. ~~||||~~
6. ~~||||~~	16. ~~||||~~	26. ~~||||~~
7. ~~||||~~	17. ~~||||~~	27. ~~||||~~
8. ~~||||~~	18. ~~||||~~	28. ~~||||~~
9. ~~||||~~	19. ~~||||~~	29. ~~||||~~
10. ~~||||~~	20. ~~||||~~	30. ~~||||~~

Figure 7.6   Repeat Your Sound Bite

Many people respond well to feedback or some kind of tracking as shown in Figure 7.6. Consider making a simple 3×5 card with numbers 1 through 30 on it. Have your staff members carry it in their pocket and tally the number of times they've used the sound bite.

Additionally, you can use a compliance-approved copy in your e-mail signature, as a tagline on your web site, or in other prominent places. Whatever it takes to make this a part of your regular communication will pay off when others start to use it in their conversations.

Figures 7.7, 7.8, and 7.9 provide action plans to begin selling through clients. You will start by designing your irresistible sound-bite, then developing your client introductory event and finally work on your center-of-influence marketing plan.

Milestones	Owner	Date	√
1. Team meeting to determine sound bite.			
2. Distribute 3x5 sound bite cards.			
3. First week—check usage count and confirm or refine.			
4. Second week—usage count.			
5. Third week—usage count.			
6. Fourth week—usage count.			
7. Fifth week—usage count.			
8. Sixth week—usage count.			

Figure 7.7   Developing an Irresistible Sound-Bite Action Plan

Milestones	Owner	Date	✓
1. Identify the golfers in your top 32 clients.			
2. Determine golfing dates.			
3. Determine clients per golf date.			
4. Call to invite—handwritten follow-up note.			
5. Golf—take digital pictures.			
6. Send pictures to client and guests (day after).			
7. Send golf course postcard (one week after).			
8. Postmortem of event—refine the process.			
9. Integrate the process into CRM workflow.			

Figure 7.8   Client Introductory Event Action Plan

Milestones	Owner	Date	✓
1. Create one-pager.			
2. Data-mine existing target clients for pockets of COIs.			
3. Identify first center-of-influence prospect.			
4. Phone to invite—follow up with handwritten note.			
5. Brown-bag lunch and present one-pager.			
6. Follow-up handwritten note.			
7. Repeat.			

Figure 7.9   Center-of-Influence Marketing Action Plan

Chapter Summary

Key Points

- Traditional direct sales methods net just one to three affluent or high-net-worth clients per year. Though these initiatives produce little more than chump change, advisors continue the ineffective habit of selling to prospects via seminars, advertising, cold calls, and unendorsed leads.
- Selling through clients is done by viral marketing. This is the social network phenomenon where your clients tell their friends and colleagues of the value you deliver, and the word spreads. Selling through clients via viral marketing can produce 6 to 12 or even more affluent or high-net-worth clients per year.
- To locate a specialist to help them make important financial decisions regarding significant amounts of money, people ask or listen to someone they trust for a recommendation.

- Advisors create engaged clients. As those engaged clients go about their day-to-day lives, they have opportunities to tell friends and colleagues about the value their wealth management advisor provides.
- The first step to selling through clients is to create engaged clients. Before your clients will endorse you, they need to trust that you will deliver outstanding service to someone they refer. This trust is built over time by consistently delivering exceptional service. There is a lag time between the time you engage clients and when the referrals begin to flow.
- The second step in creating viral marketing is to make it easy for your engaged clients to spread the virus—to talk in a compelling way to their friends and colleagues about you when the occasion arises.
- The more concentrated the community, the more powerfully this social network phenomenon works.
- In *The Tipping Point*, Malcolm Gladwell writes, "There is a simple way to package information that, under the right circumstances, can make it irresistible." Your task is to create a sound bite and drip it on your engaged clients enough times that when the occasion arises to recommend you, it just spills out of them.
- An irresistible sound bite is a concise statement that articulates one of the following:
  - Your value proposition.
  - Your unique position in the marketplace that implies your value proposition.
  - A proof point that implies your value proposition.
- To help you and your staff learn the sound bite and begin to incorporate it into your daily communication with clients, prospects, and influencers, encourage your staff to say the sound bite out loud five times a day for 30 work days.
- With a client introductory event, the objective is to make it easy for your engaged clients to introduce their friends and associates to you.
  - This will not be a sustainable strategy unless the activity is enjoyable to you.
  - The event should not be investment related.
  - It should be a small and intimate venue so that the prospect can decide whether you are compatible with them.
- Have two soft follow-ups to client introductory events.
- Center-of-influence marketing is a very distant third in lead generation. Creating engaged clients is a prerequisite to this strategy because you will need your clients to provide an endorsement to their centers of influence. It is a common mistake for advisors to focus on the center of influence before they have created engaged clients within their target market.

- Identify centers of influence who are working with two or more of your target market clients. Seek first to understand their business and then present them your one-page overview.
- The next time the mutual client meets with the potential center of influence, the center of influence will ask for the client's endorsement of you. If the mutual client endorses your work, you have a reasonable chance of getting a referral.
- Timing is important. If you have not yet reengaged your clients, it is unlikely they will provide a compelling endorsement of your work. First reengage, then launch your center-of-influence marketing campaign.
- Whether a call-in lead is generated from viral marketing, a bring-a-friend event, or from a center of influence, it must still be managed to maximize the opportunity.
- A formalized sales pipeline that has binary, verifiable outcomes will allow you to manage the sales process.
- Even though selling through clients produces call-in leads, they must still be qualified. Develop your qualifying criteria and utilize a 15-minute phone conversation to ensure the prospect is qualified before spending any face-to-face time.
- To institutionalize your sales process you will want to integrate it into your CRM tool.

CHAPTER 8

Jack's Awakening: An Elite Wealth Management Company

For 15 years Jack was held captive by ineffective habits. Breaking these habits by developing the seven disciplines was harder, sloppier, and took longer than Jack and his team anticipated. What made the process even more challenging was that the short-term results they hoped for just weren't there. In the early going, the team was paralyzed with self-doubt. Jack felt he was about to lose them and needed to do something about it. One Friday afternoon he called an impromptu staff meeting. When the team assembled he turned on the flat screen and showed *Lorenzo's Oil*, staring Susan Sarandon and Nick Nolte.

> Life has meaning only in the struggle. Triumph or defeat is in
> the hands of God. . . . So let us celebrate the struggle!
>
> —Swahili warrior song

Lorenzo Odone was diagnosed at age six with adrenoleukodystrophy (ALD), a rare, inherited disease. ALD is a metabolic disorder that causes the myelin covering the cells of the brain to disintegrate. The usual progression of this disease is to slowly lose eyesight, hearing, speech, and bodily functions. Death usually occurs about two years after being diagnosed with ALD.

This is a story of courage and persistence. Lorenzo's parents were not willing to let their son's disease follow the normal progression and began their courageous struggle to save their son. Lorenzo's parents' research found different therapies but none worked for their son and he continued to decline. Each time they found a new therapy Lorenzo's doctors feared that it would be too much for Lorenzo to tolerate. The Odones felt blocked at every turn. Their son lay dying and they couldn't do anything about it.

After endless hours of research the Odones came across a finding that was helping some boys afflicted with ALD. This therapy came from the oil of rapeseed (uric acid) which is widely used for cooking in India and China. Doctors said it was too dangerous to try and there were too many possible side effects. But it was Lorenzo's only hope. The treatment saved his life and his metabolism began to improve almost immediately. Slowly he began to regain some of his bodily functions. Today hundreds of ALD boys now receive Lorenzo's Oil therapy.

This inspiring story showed Jack's team the unwavering persistence of people who refused to give up. It also showed the team that success is not always easy. The movie drove home the point that if they persisted they could find the solutions—their own Lorenzo's Oil.

The transformation of Jack's team started five years ago when he finally said:

- I have had enough and I'm not going to take this anymore.
- For 15 years I have been living their dream rather than my dream.
- I have been focused on quantity of clients rather than quality of clients.
- I have been making scarcity decisions to hoard unprofitable clients rather than disengaging from unprofitable clients.
- I have been providing only investment advice rather than wealth management advice.
- I have been delivering investment reviews rather than WOW Wealth Management Reviews.
- I have been working as a rainmaker rather than using the team approach.
- I have been selling to prospects rather than selling through clients.
- This isn't good enough! I want more!

Images of desired future events tend to foster the behavior most likely to bring about their realization.
—Albert Bandura, *Social Foundations of Thoughts and Action*

Once Jack made the decision to change his business and help his team understand the benefits of this new way of doing business, the team held planning sessions to determine what their new firm would look like. The team knew they wanted more and they knew the type of business they wanted to build. They persisted through tough market conditions, technology breakdowns, cash flow challenges, implementation mistakes, and management pressure not to disrupt the status quo.

Jack told the team that they were going to envision their own dream. The process began by creating a compelling vision that provided them the opportunity to design their future. Their purpose stated that they wanted to "provide financial peace of mind for their clients." Five years ago they set their mission to drive $2 million in recurring revenue and $12,500 in recurring revenue per client. They supported this mission with fiscal-year goals that they exceeded. They set strategy goals of reengaging their high-net-worth clients, delivering WOW Wealth Management Reviews, disengaging from unprofitable clients, and acquiring 10 new quality clients per year. Focusing on these strategy goals was particularly valuable when things were tough.

Their two guiding principles also served them well. The first was "do great things for clients and make sure they know about it." Jack and his team recognized that too often you can do good things for clients and a week later they have forgotten it. This guiding principle created a standard of service and follow-up that was sure to be remembered. The other guiding principle was to "make win-win-win decisions." Win-win-win decisions meant the client needed to win, the team needed to win, and the business needed to win. These guiding principles served as cornerstones of empowerment for Jack's team.

Creating your dream starts by deciding what you truly desire rather than accepting someone else's dream. Jack and his team found that you determine your future by the vision you create, the decisions you make, and the actions you take.

One of the critical decisions the team made was to focus on the quality of their clients. Quality clients are those who have complex

financial needs and an asset base to generate superior revenue results. The team created a strategic focus consisting of their target
market and service focus. Their target market became physicians
over 50 years of age. Their service focus was to deliver wealth management advice to these physicians affiliated with the University of
Chicago Medical Center. Over the five-year period they realized that
by creating this strategic focus they built a high-quality client base
and experienced the financial and intrinsic rewards as clients referred their friends and colleagues to them.

Early in their strategy discussions, Jack and his team discovered
that the bottom 50 percent of their client base represented less than
5 percent of their revenue. The discipline of disengaging unprofitable clients helped them see that the scarcest resource they had was
their time and once it was spent it could never be gotten back. Over
the past five years Jack's team has been able to disengage all of these
unprofitable clients. By bending to this discipline they were able to
spend their time where the payback was best—the top 20 percent of
their client base.

As the planning process continued, Jack's team began to understand that their target market wanted more than only investment
advice. They wanted an advisor who would help them achieve their
financial goals—those that require planning, money, time, and the
ongoing coordination of their financial ecosystem; they want wealth
management advice. Reengaging with these clients at a deep enough
level to deliver wealth management advice required a lot of competency building. This was challenging, but in the end was incredibly
rewarding for the team.

Jack and his team determined that their cornerstone service
model was going to be delivering quarterly WOW Wealth Management Reviews to their target market and others in the top 20 percent
of their current client base. These reviews were made relevant by providing information that was within the context of the client's goals
and financial ecosystem. These WOW Wealth Management Reviews
also turned their intangible advisory business into a tangible business
worthy of referrals.

The success that Jack and his team experienced over the past five
years would not have been possible if they had not implemented the
team approach. This approach enabled them to deliver wealth management services while working collaboratively to achieve greater

levels of client satisfaction, team rewards, and business success. By developing service teams they were able to position resources to deliver outstanding, scalable service to 200 quality clients and create competitive differentiation.

The WOW Wealth Management Review was the prerequisite to leveraging a viral marketing campaign. Jack's team armed their clients with the sound bite "the premier wealth management firm serving U of C physicians" to make it easy to refer their colleagues and friends. Over the past year the team received 10 call-in leads that became clients.

Having implemented the seven disciplines, the long-term business results for Jack's team have been spectacular. Over the past five years the team has more than doubled revenue, going from $433,000 to over $1.2 million while increasing revenue per client dramatically. They just received the news that they were one of the top 25 wealth management teams in the United States and the only one in Chicago. More importantly, their client satisfaction scores have continually improved.

Though the long-term business results have been spectacular, they pale in comparison to the benefits Jack and his team have personally experienced. They have a deep sense of doing worthwhile work by helping their clients, mainly physicians, get to a spot where working for income is discretionary. They are often awestruck by the worthwhile accomplishments of their clients after retirement.

In addition to these intrinsic rewards, team members have benefited financially. It is not just a theory that working with high-net-worth clients produces more cash flow. Team members' compensation has paralleled the steady increase in revenue per client. A salary survey put Jack's team in the top quartile of similar wealth management advisory firms.

The new abundance of time and profit margin has afforded significant competency building. It is a self-perpetuating cycle, and as team members grow they are able to bring more to their clients. The more value they deliver, the more high-net-worth referrals these clients generate.

Implementing the disciplines will be less than perfect. At times it will be downright sloppy. There will be times this transformation is going to be more difficult than you imagined. Because the short-term business results are likely to be less than what you hope, your belief and perseverance are going to be challenged. But if you will keep your vision alive, stay focused on your strategy objectives, and stay optimistic, you will succeed. If you do, the business success will be far greater than you can imagine and more satisfying than you thought possible.

Please stay steadfast on this journey!

Bibliography

Albrecht, Karl. *The Only Thing That Matters.* New York: Harper Collins, 1992.

Allen, David. *Getting Things Done.* New York: Viking Penguin, 2001.

Anthony, Mitch. *The New Retirementality.* Chicago: Kaplan Publishing, 2006.

Bandura, Albert. "Organizational Applications of Social Cognitive Theory." Presented to the Australian Graduate School of Management in the University of New South Wales, August 1988. *Australian Journal of Management* 12, no. 2 (December 1988).

———. "Perceived Self-efficacy in the Exercise of Personal Agency." Coleman Griffith Memorial Lecturer at the British Psychological Society, St. Andrews, Scotland, April 1989. Printed in *Applied Sport Psychology* 2 (1990): 128–163.

———. *Self-Efficacy: The Exercise of Control.* New York: Worth Publishers, 1997.

———. *Social Foundations of Thought and Action.* Englewood Cliffs, NJ: Prentice-Hall, 1986.

Bandura, Albert, and David Cervone. "Self-Evaluative and Self-Efficacy Mechanisms Governing the Motivational Effects of Goal Systems." *Journal of Personality and Social Psychology* 45, no. 5 (1983): 1017–1028.

Bandura, Albert, and Dale H. Schunk. "Cultivating Competence, Self-efficacy, and Intrinsic Interest through Proximal Self-motivation." *Journal of Personality and Social Psychology* 41, no. 3 (1981).

Bennis, Warren. *On Becoming a Leader.* New York: Addison-Wesley, 1989.

———. *Organizing Genius.* New York: Addison-Wesley, 1997.

Blanchard, Ken. *Leading at a Higher Level.* Englewood Cliffs, NJ: Prentice Hall, 2007.

Blanchard, Ken, and Sheldon Bowles. *Raving Fans.* New York: William Morrow, 1993.

Booker, P. J., G. C. Frewer, and G. K. C. Pardoe. *Project Apollo: The Way to the Moon.* New York: American Elsevier Publishing Company, Inc., 1969.

Bossidy, Larry, and Ram Charan. *Execution.* New York: Crown Publishing, 2002.

Collins, Jim, *Good to Great.* New York: HarperCollins, 2001.

Collins, James C., and Jerry I. Porras. *Built to Last.* New York: HarperCollins, 1994.

———. "Organizational Vision and Visionary Organizations." *California Management Review Reprint Series* 34, no. 1 (Fall 1991).

Covey, Stephen R., *Principle-Centered Leadership.* New York: Summit Books, 1990.

———. *The 7 Habits of Highly Effective People.* New York: Simon and Schuster, 1989.

Darwin, Charles. *Origin of the Species.* London: John Murray Publishing, 1859.

Deming, W. Edwards. *Out of the Crisis.* Cambridge, MA: MIT Press, 1986.

Drucker, Peter F. *The Frontiers of Management.* New York: Harper & Row, 1982.

———. *Managing for the Future.* New York: Penguin Books, 1992.

———. *On the Profession of Management.* Boston: Harvard Business Review, 1998.

———. *Post-Capitalist Society.* New York: Harper Business, 1993.

Dychtwald, Ken, and Daniel J. Kadlec. *The Power Years.* Hoboken, NJ: John Wiley & Sons, 2005.

Foot, David K. *Boom Bust & Echo: Profiting from the Demographic Shift in the 21st Century.* New York: Stoddart Publishing, 2000.

Frankl, Victor. *Man's Search for Meaning.* Boston: Beacon Press, 2006.

Gates, Bill, *Business @ the Speed of Thought.* New York: Warner Books, 1999.

———. *The Road Ahead.* New York: Penguin Books, 1995.

Gladwell, Malcolm. *The Tipping Point.* New York: Time Warner, 2002.

Glasser, William, *The Quality School.* New York: Harper & Row, 1990.

Goldratt, Eliyahu M. *The Goal.* Great Barrington, MA: North River Press, 1992.

Hamel, Gary. "Breaking the Frame: Strategy as Stretch and Leverage." Unpublished: London Business School, 1991.

———. *Leading the Revolution.* Boston: Harvard Business School, 2000.

Hamel, Gary, and C. K. Prahalad. *Competing for the Future.* Boston: Harvard Business School, 1994.

Harvard Business Review, *Leaders on Leadership: Interviews with Top Executives.* Boston: Harvard Business School, 1992.

Juran, J. M. *Juran on Leadership for Quality.* New York: Free Press, 1989.

Katzenbach, Jon R., and Douglas K. Smith. *The Wisdom of Teams.* Boston: Harvard Business School Press, 1993.

Kim, W. Chan, and Renee Mauborgne. *Blue Ocean Strategy.* Boston: Harvard Business School, 2005.

Larson, Carl E., and Frank M. J. LaFasto. *TeamWork: What Must Go Right/What Can Go Wrong.* Thousand Oaks, CA: Sage Publications, 1989.

Locke, Edwin A., and Gary P. Latham. *A Theory of Goal Setting and Task Performance.* Englewood Cliffs, NJ: Prentice-Hall, 1990.

Maslow, A. H. *Motivation and Personality.* New York: Harper and Row, 1954.

Miller, Lawrence M., and Jennifer Howard. *Managing Quality Through Teams.* Atlanta: Miller Consulting Group, 1991.

Mintzberg, Henry, Bruce Ahlstrand, and Joseph Lampel. *Strategy Safari.* New York: Simon & Schuster, 1998.

Nanus, Burt. *Visionary Leadership.* San Francisco, CA: Jossey-Bass Publishers, 1992.

Parker, Glenn M. *Cross-Functional Teams.* San Francisco, CA: Jossey-Bass Publishers, 1994.

———. *Team Players and Teamwork.* San Francisco, CA: Jossey-Bass Publishers, 1990.

Peters, Tom. *Liberation Management.* New York: Alfred A. Knopf, 1992.

———. *Thriving on Chaos.* New York: Harper & Row, 1987.

Pfeffer, Jeffrey, and Robert I. Sutton. *Hard Facts, Dangerous Half-Truths & Total Nonsense.* Boston: Harvard Business School Press, 2006.

William Pfeiffer, Leonard Goodstein, & Timothy Nolan, *Shaping Strategic Planning,* 1989.

Porter, Michael E. *Competitive Strategy.* New York: Free Press, 1980.

Reichheld, Frederick. "The Only Number You Need to Grow." *Harvard Business Review,* December 2003.

Ries, Al. *Focus.* New York: Harper Business, 1996.

Robbins, Harvey, and Michael Finley. *Why Teams Don't Work.* Princeton, NJ: Peterson's/Pacesetter Books, 1995.

Seligman, Martin E. P. *Learned Optimism.* New York: Alfred A. Knopf, Inc., 1991.

Senge, Peter M. *The Fifth Discipline.* New York: Bantam Doubleday Dell Publishing Group, 1990.

Shonk, James H. *Team-Based Organization.* Homewood, IL: Business One Irwin, 1992.

Surowiecki, James. *The Wisdom of Crowds.* New York: Doubleday, 2004.

Wall, Bob, Robert S. Solum, and Mark R. Sobol. *The Visionary Leader.* Rocklin, CA: Prima Publishing, 1992.

Welch, Jack. *Winning.* New York: HarperCollins, 2005.

Welch, Jack, and John A. Byrne. *Jack: Straight from the Gut.* New York: Warner Books, 2001.

About the Authors

Steve Moore

Steve is a specialist in the field of strategic planning and business management. He is a *resultant* with unique perspective. His uncommon insight is the result of:

- Hands-on consulting and coaching of more than 750 wealth management teams, helping them achieve their goals with his proprietary High Speed Strategic Planning program.
- Twelve years of game planning as a coach with the Buffalo Bills, Seattle Seahawks, and Los Angeles Rams.
- Ten years of helping Microsoft teams develop their product and go-to-market strategies.
- Directing an international consulting/training company.
- Three years as director of practice management for Russell Investment Group.
- Continual study of leading-edge business practices and optimal performance psychology.

Steve is a leading management consultant, mentor, and coach. He has exceptional experience and business knowledge. Through his inspiring and entertaining stories he makes the information relevant to advisors, allowing them to address their challenges and opportunities. He helps advisors think more effectively about their competitive position and develop a strategic focus that drives exceptional business results—quickly.

After stepping away from the NFL in 1989, Steve earned a master's degree at Seattle University and became a managing director and later chief operating officer of the Pacific Institute, an international corporation specializing in performance improvement, professional growth, change management, and leadership development.

In 1993, he founded Moore Solutions. This led to a decade of consulting on key initiatives at Microsoft, including long-term strategic planning with senior executives. Steve developed High Speed Strategic Planning as a product of Moore Solutions. He later accepted an offer to direct the practice management capability of Russell Investment Group, a global investment management firm. During this time, Russell's practice management expertise earned a number one industry ranking among value-added outside wholesaler programs based on the Horsesmouth/FRC Wholesaler Effectiveness Survey, February 2007.

In 2008, Steve returned full-time to Moore Solutions, continuing to deliver High Speed Strategic Planning to advisors in the United States, Canada, and the United Kingdom.

Gary Brooks

Gary Brooks is a CERTIFIED FINANCIAL PLANNER in Tacoma, Washington. He is the president of Brooks, Hughes & Jones, a registered investment advisor.

Gary previously worked with Steve Moore, assisting his practice management program at Russell Investments. He began his career as a newspaper reporter and currently writes a monthly financial planning column for *The News Tribune* in Tacoma.

Index